THE RIVALS

THE RIVALS

Chris Evert vs. Martina Navratilova:
Their Epic Duels and Extraordinary Friendship

Johnette Howard

YELLOW JERSEY PRESS
LONDON

Published by Yellow Jersey Press 2005

2 4 6 8 10 9 7 5 3 1

Copyright © Johnette Howard 2005

Johnette Howard has asserted her right under the Copyright, Designs
and Patents Act 1988 to be identified as the author of this work

First published in Great Britain in 2005 by
Yellow Jersey Press

Yellow Jersey Press
Random House, 20 Vauxhall Bridge Road,
London SW1V 2SA

Random House Australia (Pty) Limited
20 Alfred Street, Milsons Point, Sydney,
New South Wales 2061, Australia

Random House New Zealand Limited
18 Poland Road, Glenfield,
Auckland 10, New Zealand

Random House South Africa (Pty) Limited
Endulini, 5A Jubilee Road, Parktown 2193,
South Africa

The Random House Group Limited Reg. No. 954009
www.randomhouse.co.uk

A CIP catalogue record for this book
is available from the British Library

Hardback ISBN 0 224 07505 5
Trade Paperback ISBN 0 224 07766 X

Papers used by Random House are natural, recyclable products made from wood
grown in sustainable forests. The manufacturing processes conform to the
environmental regulations of the country of origin

Printed and bound in Great Britain by
Clays Ltd, St Ives plc

CONTENTS

THE RIVALS

REMEMBER
MY NAME

She used to sit on the tram to Prague on the way to her tennis lesson as a child, notice the other passengers watching her as she clutched her racket, and think to herself, *One day you'll know my name.* But by the time Martina Navratilova earned her first trip from Czechoslovakia to America in early 1973, she was still an anonymous player on these shores. The iron curtain was still drawn. But she knew who Chris Evert was.

A poster of Evert, just eighteen but already a star, hung on the wall of Navratilova's tennis club in Revnice, a village just outside Prague. Evert was celebrated in the tennis magazines that Navratilova's cousin Martin mailed back to Czechoslovakia after he defected to Canada. Evert was the favorite player of Martina's grandmother, Andela Subertova. "You're *the* Chris Evert?" an awestruck Subertova cooed when she met Evert for the first time, as if Evert were some mythic figure and not her granddaughter's friend or flesh-and-blood tennis peer.

Navratilova was just sixteen when she left Prague on a bleak winter day, connected through Frankfurt and New York, and stepped off the plane in sun-drenched Miami. It was her first trip to the United States, and she felt exhilarated. One of the first things she did was pick a coconut off a palm tree near the Fort Lauderdale Tennis Club, where she played her first tournament. She ate her first-ever hamburger there, as well—the first of too many hamburgers, as it turned out. She gained twenty pounds before her six-week American tour was through.

As Navratilova walked across the tournament grounds in Fort Lauderdale one day, her heart leaped. There sat Evert, playing backgammon with the tournament referee. To Navratilova's astonishment—even if she *was* gawking—Evert saw her and nodded. A few days later, Navratilova passed Evert again and—lo and behold—Evert smiled and said hello.

"I was excited, I was mesmerized," Navratilova said. "Chris was like a perfect blond goddess who was challenging Billie Jean King and Virginia Wade. Before I even met her, she stood for everything I admired about this country: poise, ability, sportsmanship, money, style."

"I remember Martina was really aggressive, real emotional, and she screamed at herself on the court all the time," Evert said with a laugh.

Evert and Navratilova played the first of their eighty career matches in Akron, Ohio, three weeks later, to no fanfare. It was March 22, 1973, and Navratilova—who was merely hoping to make Evert remember her name—lost the first-round encounter 7–6, 6–3 before a few hundred people. It wasn't until two years later in their sixth match, a 1975 quarterfinal in Washington, D.C., that Navratilova beat Evert for the first time. Navratilova was so thrilled, she didn't sleep at all that night. It wasn't until 1976 and their seventeenth meeting—after Navratilova had dropped weight and improved her game—that Evert, by now Navratilova's friend and sometime doubles partner, publicly betrayed her first scintilla of concern. Navratilova had just beaten her in Houston for the first time ever in a final.

"If she keeps this up," Evert said afterward, "she could be . . ."

Yes?

"Pretty good," Evert allowed.

E ven for Chris Evert, an inscrutable athlete given to understatement, choosing the words "pretty good" to describe Navratilova
seems comical now, given their eventual fixation on each other and
the way their showdowns evolved into the greatest and longest-
running individual rivalry in sports history—a captivating, seesawing eighty-match set piece that unfolded over sixteen years, included
sixty finals, and is approached in individual sports annals only by
Joe Frazier's fabled fights with Muhammad Ali.

"But how many times did Ali and Frazier fight?" Navratilova
once asked, knowing the answer: just three.

For nearly two decades, Evert and Navratilova drove each other
through storybook realms of pain and glory, epic duels and high-
stakes drama. They defined an era. Evert and Navratilova came of
age just as women's tennis was rising from backwater to big time,
thanks to the whip cracking and cajoling of Billie Jean King. The tennis they played wasn't the polite pitty-pat game of the country club
set. They played tough, grimacing, pressure-laden matches. Their
lockstep career march, which began in the early 1970s, played out
against the backdrop of contentious change: the women's movement;
the gay rights movement; the 1989 fall of the iron curtain; and the
fight for Title IX, the landmark 1972 federal law that led to the
women's sports boom in America and beyond.

The performance standards and personal convictions that Evert
and Navratilova evinced influenced female athletes for years to
come. For twelve consecutive years, from 1975 through 1986, either
Evert or Navratilova finished the season ranked number one in the
world.

To Evert and Navratilova, tennis was more than just a game: it
was serious work, a self-defining push to see where their personal
limits might lie. They were among the new breed of fiercely independent, unapologetically ambitious women whose partners, boyfriends,

or husbands were often a peripheral presence in their public lives. At those junctures when their love lives clashed with their careers, Evert's and Navratilova's careers almost always won.

Evert foreshadowed the emerging new career woman who could do it all. Years before Anna Kournikova or Serena Williams arrived, Evert was women's sports first crossover star. *People* magazine covered her romances. Andy Warhol asked her to sit for a portrait. *Saturday Night Live* invited her to be the first female athlete to host the show. She broadened conventional ideas about what so-called feminine women were capable of.

"I wanted to be tough and I wanted to be a woman—I wanted both," Evert says.

Navratilova revolutionized the way in which women athletes train and perform. She presaged what life would be like for people who dared to be openly gay. She defected from the former Czechoslovakia in 1975 and rose to prominence before the cold war ended. Along the way, she made us countenance the idea that being an American is not just a birthright but also a state of mind.

To this day, a trace of Czech remains in Navratilova's accent, her syncopated cadence, but she has always believed she was meant to land in America. "I felt it in my blood, even before I had reason to," she said. "I have always had this outrage at being told what to do, how to act, whom to love."

Over the years, people who followed the Evert-Navratilova rivalry came to refer to the players on a first-name basis: Chrissie and Martina. It wasn't athletic greatness alone that drew fans to them. People fell in love with their stories. Evert and Navratilova were a study in contrasts, a collision of styles and politics and looks. Fans felt so attached to each player, many declared themselves either "Chrissie fans" or "Martina fans," as if that was some defining choice, something akin to identifying oneself as a Democrat or a Republican, a liberal or a conservative, a Hatfield or a McCoy.

But often the pat portrayals of Evert and Navratilova were too simplistic or misguided. They were reduced to broad caricatures: Evert the so-called Ice Maiden versus the shrieking, head-clutching, blunt-to-the-bone Navratilova, or "Navrat the Brat." Chrissie the girl next door vs. Martina the lesbian outsider. Chris America vs. Navratilova the Communist defector, the iron curtain Amazon whose forearm veins stood out in bas-relief.

The truth, of course, was more complicated. Both Evert and Navratilova made fascinating personal migrations during their careers. Evert, the strictly raised Catholic girl, admits that she spent a significant portion of her twenties "making up for lost time." She dated actors and rock stars, television personalities, and even a president's son. She was once engaged to Jimmy Connors, tennis's king of the vulgar gesture. Some of her postretirement interviews had a confessional tone.

Three years into her retirement, Evert admitted a career-long discomfort with her squeaky-clean image because she knew she was "no angel." What didn't people know about her? "Without getting into it, just that I'm not as goody two-shoes as people think," Evert explained. "I'm a normal woman. I've dated a lot of guys, I've had a few drinks . . . I've cursed, I've been rude to my parents. There's nothing in my life, no skeletons in my closet, that people should be so shocked about. But I've lived a normal life."

People tended to pigeonhole Evert anyway, dwelling on her good looks, propping her up as some dainty feminine ideal, rarely giving her enough credit for being the ruthlessly competitive jock that she was. Evert was adept at mind games. One reporter said she had a smile that could "chill wine." She sometimes dug comments into rivals like velvet shivs. "She's had one good year, I've had seven," Evert said when asked about Navratilova's all-out campaigning for the 1982 year-end number one ranking, which was still voted on by a panel. "One year doesn't get you immortality."

Evert caused a stir in the early 1990s by saying she was pro-choice, and that she had tried marijuana. "I didn't like it," Evert says. "It made me feel brain-dead." Few people beyond the tennis world knew that Evert was also considered the women's tour leader when it came to dirty jokes.

Asked once by an interviewer if she could tell a clean joke, Evert thought about it, then finally cracked, "There are no clean jokes that are funny."

By the time anyone beyond tour had even the slightest inkling of that side of her, Evert's eyelet-and-lace image had its own unshakeable inertia. She was Our Chrissie. The Ice Princess. The Baseline Machine. "Just wind her up," Evert drolly said of herself, "and she plays."

Though Evert could do no wrong in the public's eye, Navratilova's career-long fight for acceptance got easier, but it remained a struggle. Navratilova was routinely marginalized as the lesbian with the outrageous entourage in tow. For eight years her partner was a divorced Texas beauty queen and mother of two. One of her coaches was a six-foot-two transsexual ophthalmologist, Renee Richards. Once Navratilova began to reverse her lopsided early career history against Evert—improving from a 5–20 won-lost record after their first twenty-five meetings to a 30–30 deadlock by her 1984 Wimbledon win—she was increasingly cast as a villain. She was transmogrified during her unbeatable years into a fearsome, sneering colossus. But the truth is that she has always had a heart that dents like a pillow. She is quick to cry.

Navratilova never stopped doing or saying what she believed as she went on to dominate women's tennis, even though endorsements never came. People made wisecracks about her sexuality and the physicality she brought to women's sports, failing to acknowledge that the sort of training regimen and support team she first embraced is now commonplace for athletes.

Navratilova had many well-chronicled bouts of excess—too much junk food, too much shopping, too much overboard largesse. But at age twenty-five she hunkered down, determined to find out how good she could be. And the results were astonishing.

Navratilova's stunning reinvention of her body and game—combined with her refusal to tolerate Communist oppression and her unwavering insistence on being treated with basic human decency—was not unlike the young Cassius Clay converting to Islam and changing his name to Muhammad Ali. It ranks as one of the most daring and influential acts of self-creation in our time.

But the price for her freedom was steep. At age eighteen, Navratilova left behind her parents, a younger sister, and her dear grandmother when she defected in New York during the 1975 U.S. Open. She was immediately declared a nonperson back home. Remembering the two-year jail sentence she was threatened with if she returned, she never took flights over Communist countries until she received her U.S. citizenship in 1981, just in case the plane had to make an emergency landing and she was detained.

Navratilova's career didn't take off until 1981, her eighth season, but her statistics are nonetheless amazing. From 1982 through 1986, Navratilova had shimmering annual won-lost records of 90–3, 86–1, 78–2, 84–5, and 89–3. She was ranked number one for 331 weeks in her career, second only to Steffi Graf. She once won 74 straight singles matches and 109 consecutive doubles contests with partner Pam Shriver, both professional records. She amassed an unmatched 167 career singles crowns and 173 doubles titles by the start of 2005.

Evert had impressive runs of dominance too. She won 125 consecutive matches on clay early in her career and posted a 103–7 mark in 1974, still a one-season record for most singles wins. Though Navratilova's sheer athleticism shone brighter, Evert's unique, spectacular consistency strains credulity. Her career winning percentage of .900 (1,309–146) is the best in tennis history. Over the eighteen years Evert competed from 1971 to 1989, she advanced to at least the semifinals in the first thirty-four major (or "Grand Slam") tournaments she played, and fifty-two of her fifty-six majors overall. Her 157 singles titles rank second only to Navratilova's total.

Evert and Navratilova's sixteen-year rivalry unfolded in three fairly distinct phases. Evert dominated the early years, winning twenty of the first twenty-five matches she and Navratilova played, from 1973 in Akron to Navratilova's first major title at Wimbledon in 1978. The middle stage of the rivalry continues from that 1978 Wimbledon and runs through Navratilova's 1981 Australian Open win over Evert, a period in which both Evert and Navratilova also grappled with fame and success and falling in love. Martina showed rumblings of her dominant years to come in this period, winning ten of her nineteen encounters with Chris, and three of their four Grand Slam tournament meetings. The third stage was Navratilova's near-invincible years from 1982 through Evert's retirement in 1989, or five years before Navratilova stopped playing full-time singles.

Evert and Navratilova each finished their careers with eighteen Grand Slam singles titles, including a monopoly on eighteen of the twenty contested between 1982 and 1986. The two of them exchanged the number one ranking seventeen times. Evert's seven French Open singles titles are a professional record. Navratilova won an unprecedented nine singles titles and twenty titles overall at Wimbledon—the last of them, remarkably enough, in 2003 in the mixed doubles competition at Wimbledon, at the age of forty-six.

For excellence and longevity, import and drama, no other great individual sports rivalry approaches Evert and Navratilova—not Sampras against Agassi, Borg against McEnroe, Palmer against Nicklaus, Chamberlain against Russell.

Yet, surprisingly, neither woman looks back with complete pride or fondness on her untouchable years. "I was aware of all my [negative] qualities as a player," Evert once told *Sports Illustrated*. "I recognized them and justified them. In my mind I thought, 'Well, while I'm playing, the people around me who are close to me have to understand that I'm going to be moody, that I'm going to have a short temper at times, that I don't have a lot of patience.' You just get so involved. And everything revolves around you. I was aware of it, and the last three years, I didn't like it."

Navratilova has said, "I'm a much better person now, and a much better human being."

Evert and Navratilova's ability to forge and maintain a friendship during sixteen years of often cutthroat competition has always provoked admiration and curiosity. At the start of their respective careers, both of them set out to be the best. But what each of them independently found was that the closer they got to their goal, the more they began to question what it took to get there, and to stay there.

Therein lies one of the abiding mysteries about Navratilova and Evert: How could two such supremely determined athletes indulge in niceties such as sharing bagels an hour before taking the court to compete for one of tennis's biggest titles? And then, the match over, how could they return to the locker room together with the winner often consoling the heartbroken loser?

The answer is at the core of understanding Evert and Navratilova's remarkable story: They were two people who fervently wanted the same thing, found the other blocking the way, and ultimately forgave each other for it. They were bound by their athletic superiority. They were operating so far above everyone else on tour, needing to fear only each other, and they realized that they were the only two people who really, truly understood what the other was going through.

There was the hellish pressure. The unforgiving expectations. The stark way their self-images admittedly hinged on one question: "Did I win or did I lose?" There was the pinhole focus. The isolating "me, me, me attitude"—Chris's words—that it took to be a champion. There were their overlapping personal dramas and the strain of living very public lives. And then, after all that, there were the unparalleled feelings that still came from somehow managing to win, dominate, succeed.

Evert and Navratilova often confided in each other. They supported each other. Their relationship extended to off the court as well.

It was Navratilova who coaxed Evert to Aspen for the 1986 Christmas holidays when Evert was dejected about her nearly complete divorce from British tennis star John Lloyd. At a New Year's Eve party, Navratilova introduced Evert to her current husband, Andy Mill. Six months earlier, it was Evert who ignored a knee injury so she could play for the 1986 U.S. Federation Cup team and accompany Navratilova on her emotional first return to Czechoslovakia since Navratilova's defection eleven years earlier.

The iron curtain was still intact. On the first day of play, when the band in the sold-out arena in Prague began to play the Czech national anthem—ironically titled "Where Is My Home?"—Evert reached over to a choked-up Navratilova and sweetly rubbed the back of her neck. Days later, when Navratilova stood on the same court and bade goodbye again to her countrymen after the U.S. team won, she and Evert both wept as the stadium shook with waves of deafening cheers.

Like those of most transfixing sports rivals, Navratilova's and Evert's games were a classic contrast in styles—the swashbuckling serve-and-volleyer versus the methodical baseliner. That image of the two of them—Navratilova rushing forward, always bravely, and Evert determinedly answering every charge—is among the mental pictures that endure.

Evert, a self-described shy girl who "craved something I could be good at," and Navratilova, a woman so long without a country or visible constituency to call her own, are proof that all serious daring starts from within. They did more than challenge each other during their careers. They revealed each other.

The circumstances that conspired to funnel them inexorably toward each other started nearly five decades ago on two clay courts half a world apart, one of them in Fort Lauderdale, Florida, and the other in a sleepy Czechoslovakian village called Revnice.

As usual with Evert and Navratilova, the particulars were as different as they could be.

CHAPTER ONE

THE MAKING OF
THE ICE PRINCESS

In the beginning, it wasn't Chris Evert's idea to play tennis. She was a small, slight girl with a distaste for adventure and an acute shyness around strangers. She was born smack in the middle of the serene and ordered 1950s, came from the most loving and traditional of families, and liked to while away time with her younger sister, painting her nails and brushing each other's hair. The foment and tensions of the 1960s never reached her. She was so sheltered that she recalls her main worries were the boy sitting next to her in class, getting her first serve in, and deciding when she should start wearing a bra. Had her exacting father been an accountant rather than a public parks tennis teaching pro, Evert might have willed herself to become the best CPA of the twentieth century and not a tennis champion. She began her climb on a clay court in Fort Lauderdale, Florida, at the age of five, hitting each ball that her father lobbed at her from a supermarket cart brimming with hundreds more.

An uncanny number of legendary athletes speak of having some monumental epiphany as a child, some unforgettable, crystalline moment at which they knew, absolutely knew, that they would go on to do remarkable things and, quite often, they just had to tell somebody about it. Evert's great tennis rival, Martina Navratilova of Czechoslovakia, was already dreaming sugar-plum visions of grandeur by age ten as the drab green commuter trains she rode went hurtling through suburban Prague towns of Dorbrichovice and Zsenory, Mokropsy and Radotin, whisking her toward her lessons with her dashing first coach, George Parma. Tennis star Billie Jean King, Evert's friend and frequent sounding board in the pros, vividly recalls "this burning, tingling, literally white-hot feeling" that came over her one day at five years old, when she was washing dishes with her mother: "All of a sudden I turned to my mother and I said, 'Mom, I am going to do something great one day! I know it! You just watch.' "

Chris Evert never evinced such certainty as a young girl. Neither did her disciplinarian father, Jimmy, the man who molded her. Jimmy Evert was a two-time U.S. age-group champion who won a tennis scholarship to the University of Notre Dame and notched the best finish of his short-lived postcollege career in 1942, winning the Canadian national championship. In many ways, Jimmy Evert was a character sprung straight from a Frank Capra movie, a man who advocated virtues such as clean living and humility, a doting tennis father who deftly walked the tightrope of having ambitions for his five children without ever making them the casualties of those dreams.

Jimmy Evert was a staunchly Catholic, conservative man who grew up in Chicago during the Great Depression, endured deprivations like canned food rations as a boy, and never seemed to abandon the rigorous self-discipline that the two enduring influences in his life—his faith and his austere upbringing—demanded. He saw his own father switch from farming to the banking business only to lose nearly everything in the stock market crash of 1929. Though Jimmy and his family lived across the street from the Chicago Town and Tennis Club, the Everts were never members. Jimmy earned his way onto the courts there (and later at the Chicago Armory, one of two indoor facilities in the city) by working as a ball boy for five cents an hour. From the start, tennis enthralled him. He often spent ten hours a day at the courts, sometimes stopping only to rush home for a quick dinner before hurrying back again, with his mother calling after him that he hadn't eaten enough.

By 1952, the same year he married Colette Thompson, a vivacious woman to whom he was introduced at a friend's wedding, Jimmy was working as the teaching pro at Holiday Park, a twenty-one-court municipal tennis facility in Fort Lauderdale. The features of Chicago and Jimmy's youth—the gunboat gray skies, biting winds, and shoulders hunched against the cold—were a distant memory. Jimmy's daily existence now featured bone-warming sun, swaying palms, and the white sand beaches of the Atlantic Ocean just a few miles away. Yet one of Jimmy's Holiday Park coworkers quickly nicknamed him "Lash" because of his no-nonsense habits. He routinely worked seven days a week, often twelve hours a day. His adult life settled into a contented orbit of work, church, and family, and the same was true for Colette and their five children: Drew, Chris, Jeanne, John, and Clare. Theirs was a quintessentially American, blue-collar existence. "Growing up, we were the most important thing in the world to my parents," Chris said. "What I remember most is the time, the love they gave us."

Jimmy Evert went to Mass daily, and so did Chris and her four siblings once they began Catholic school. Colette, who is as outgoing as Jimmy is introverted, worked in the school cafeteria and made Chris's tennis dresses. All the Evert children became state champions and age-group national finalists, and all of them eventually made careers in tennis, same as their dad. Chris, who was born on December 21, 1954, shared a childhood bedroom with her sister Jeanne, who is two years younger. The two girls were so close that they would reach across the space between their twin beds and hold hands when a noise frightened them in the middle of the night.

Jimmy thought it was important to take each of his children onto the courts at Holiday Park as soon as they were able to swing a racket. "There are a lot of great people associated with tennis," he always explained. "And besides, kids need goals. Kids without goals come home from school and just wander. It's not healthy. . . ." He continued, "Maybe I'm old-fashioned, but I like to have time to take my kids to the tennis courts and knock balls to them. Why, if a man can feed, clothe, and shelter his family, plus have good health and a lot of fun with his kids, what else does he need?

"Tennis opened some great doors for me. I thought maybe it would do the same for our kids."

Though Chris collected state and national age-group titles from ages eight to sixteen, any convictions about her future as a professional were slow to take hold. She was amassing junior titles, but often only narrowly, her mother says, pulling out finals victories on sheer determination.

The game that Chris's father taught her was a patient, no-frills baseline style that emphasized limiting errors more than going for flashy winners. Laurie Fleming, a childhood friend and tennis rival, says that for a long time there wasn't one shot in young Chris's arsenal that made anyone say, "Wow." Even Evert's signature two-handed backhand—her most lethal stroke throughout her career—developed by necessity, not as part of some grand design. Jimmy Evert says Chris was too small and weak to hold a racket with one hand when she first started to play. As she got older, Jimmy made several attempts to get her to adopt a one-handed backhand, but, seeing her revert to two hands once she was playing with friends, he finally said, "Forget it."

If Jimmy had any private, quietly percolating dreams that his daughter might someday mature into someone capable of playing the women's tour, they slowed when Margaret Court, the great Australian champion, came to Holiday Park in 1969 to practice for a nearby women's tournament. Chris was fourteen and still waiting for her first adolescent growth spurt. When Jimmy strolled over to one of the Holiday Park hard courts to watch Court hit with Judy Dalton, another established pro, he thought, "Why, Chrissie can't stay with them at all. They hit the ball so hard! And she's so darn small."

That was still Jimmy's opinion when Chris won another title—this one the national sixteen-and-under championship—and a sharp-eyed promoter named Clifford Brown telephoned him in September of 1970. Brown was looking to fill out the tournament field in the Carolinas International, his eight-player clay court tournament in Charlotte. He offered to send a Learjet to pick up Chrissie and her friend Laurie Fleming, another top junior player at Holiday Park. To Jimmy, the offer looked to be one of those opening doors that he had always spoken about, a way for his daughter to meet some great people in tennis. Thinking it would be a flattering, unexpected reward for Chris's hard work as well, Jimmy told Brown sure, his daughter could make the trip.

Knowing that Court, Nancy Richey, and Françoise Durr of France, all world-ranked players, would also be in the field, Colette sent Chrissie off to Charlotte with just one change of clothes.

"I figured she'd be home the next day," Colette says.

When Chris and Laurie Fleming arrived at the private family housing in Charlotte that the tournament had arranged for them, their hosts showed them to their room, and the two girls stayed up well past midnight, talking and laughing and watching television. Their parents had stayed in Fort Lauderdale, telling the girls to be sure to call when their matches were over.

When Colette answered the telephone the next afternoon, Chris excitedly told her she had beaten Françoise Durr, 6–1, 6–0. "You *did?*" Colette said. She promptly called Jimmy at Holiday Park. "Are you *sure?*" he asked.

Durr was the second-best clay court player in the world.

Chris's next opponent was Margaret Court, the queen of tennis the previous few months because of her just-completed calendar-year sweep of tennis's four major (or "Grand Slam") titles: the Australian Open, French Open, Wimbledon, and U.S. Open. Court was twenty-eight years old, she stood nearly six feet tall, and she was famously strong and fit. Her nickname on tour was "The Arm," given to her by five-foot-two Rosie Casals because of her seemingly post-to-post reach at the net. (Casals didn't have a florid imagination. When university researchers in England measured Court for a physiological study on athletes, they found Court's arms were indeed three inches longer than the average for a woman her size, and Court's grip strength was about the same as those of the male college athletes the researchers tested.)

Evert, who still stood only five feet two and was a shade over ninety pounds, shocked Court 7–6, 7–6, seizing both sets in tiebreakers. The slow clay court negated some of Court's power advantage, and Evert outrallied her from the baseline. She snapped off passing shots that left the champion flummoxed and standing at the net, disconsolately watching the ball blur by.

"*No!*" Colette exclaimed when Chris called home again.

"Let me get up off the floor!" Jimmy said when Chris told him the news. He and Colette caught a plane that night to Charlotte.

Evert lost the final in straight sets to Nancy Richey. But her performance didn't go unnoticed. The following summer, the United States Lawn Tennis Association invited Evert, now sixteen, to play in the 1971 Wightman Cup, an annual competition between the United States and Britain. Evert, the youngest player ever to appear in the competition, again showed a startling imperviousness to pressure. Evert led an American team playing without its two best players, Billie Jean King and Rosie Casals, to an unexpected 4–3 victory with wins in both of her singles matches. Evert dispatched Winnie Shaw, a six-time Cup veteran, 6–0, 6–4, and clinched the Cup by drubbing Virginia Wade, Britain's number one player, 6–1, 6–1, in just thirty-eight minutes.

American veteran Julie Heldman, a perennial top ten player, was sitting next to Evert on the sidelines during one particularly tense part of the competition. She remembers Evert turning to her and remarking, "Huh. My hands are sweating more than usual." Then, crinkling up her teenage face as if nerves were a completely new sensation, Evert added, "I must be reacting to the atmosphere."

Heldman just stared at her in disbelief.

When Evert also won the national eighteen-and-under junior title that summer, she landed her most prestigious invitation yet: a spot in the 1971 U.S. Open at the West Side Tennis Club in Forest Hills, New York. It would be her first Grand Slam tournament, and what happened there was so outrageous, it left her life and the sport of tennis irrevocably changed.

Only a few American teenagers had achieved renown in tennis before Evert, most notably Maureen "Little Mo" Connolly, a Californian who won the 1953 Grand Slam at eighteen but suffered a calamitous horseback riding accident less than a year later that forced her to retire by age twenty-one. But Evert was the first tennis phenom to come along after the 1968 start of tennis's Open era, a time when tournaments began offering aboveboard prize money and allowing amateurs to compete alongside pros for the first time.

In so many ways, the timing of Evert's arrival was impeccable.

The Virginia Slims circuit, the first pro tour for women, had just been founded one year earlier, in 1970, and its prize money and media coverage were all growing, thanks to the unstinting work of its brightest star, Billie Jean King. Unlike Connolly or even King, Evert enjoyed another inestimable advantage: her entire career, starting with her thunderclap debut at the 1971 U.S. Open, unfolded in the television age of sports.

During her scintillating debut at the U.S. Open that September, Evert went from a virtual unknown to an overnight sensation, a coast-to-coast curiosity. Spectators were stunned by her unfathomable calm under pressure, her expressionless game face, the surprising sting on her two-handed backhand for such a small player.

Everything about Evert was arresting, right down to the way she delicately splayed the fingers on her left hand as she lashed back forehand shots with her right.

The crowds packed the stadium court to see her as she tore to the semifinals, and newspaper and magazine editors ordered their writers to find out more. Who was this ponytailed high school junior with the hoop earrings, hair ribbons, and frilly white dresses of ruffles and lace? Where did she come from? How was she pulling off these implausible wins?

From the Everts' tidy three-bedroom ranch house on Northeast Seventh Place in Fort Lauderdale, Chris would make the five-block walk down the road and then over a well-worn path to Holiday Park, the city-owned complex where Jimmy Evert worked giving lessons, stringing rackets in a room off his tiny office, and presiding over one of the most distinguished tennis hotbeds in Florida.

"I can still see Jimmy working with Chrissie on Court Ten—that was his private teaching court—and I can still remember laughing and thinking to myself, 'Jimmy Evert has to be the most monotone instructor in the history of tennis,' " says Harold Solomon, one of seven Holiday Park regulars who went on to play the men's or women's pro tours. "Even after it was obvious how good Chrissie was, it was always interesting to watch Jimmy out there with her, never raising his voice, never changing the intonation, just always talking in that same flat monotone: 'Okay, good, Chris. Bend your knees. Great. Follow through. Yes . . . now do it like this.' He stressed endless repetition. Everything about him was calm and quiet. But once you were on the court, you knew there was no fooling around. To him the court was like the office. He had this presence that you just felt, even though he wasn't physically imposing."

Jimmy Evert was a slender man of five feet, nine inches, with a pigeon-toed gait and a habit of walking with his head down and his hands stuffed in his pockets. He had a lifelong aversion to large crowds and a stubborn case of high blood pressure that made watching Chris's matches intolerable for him. While his wife, Colette, traveled the world with Chris during her first few years on tour, Jimmy preferred to stay home, tending to his duties at Holiday Park and looking after their other four children. Even a decade into her pro career, Chris would hustle to find a courtside telephone to call her father immediately after her matches to let him know how she had fared.

"In the beginning, especially, I played for my father," Evert admits.

But Jimmy was a shy man who expressed himself in so few words, even to his family, that Chris was often left yearning to hear him prattle on to her about how proud she made him feel. "That just wasn't his personality," says Dennis Ralston, who helped coach Evert during the last half of her pro career. "I remember different times where she said, 'I just wish my dad would have called to say, "Nice going, Chrissie." ' I think all daughters want their father to think well of them. And he absolutely did. He just wasn't real comfortable expressing it."

No, Jimmy Evert was a serious man who worked hard to make ends meet, never bought anything on credit, and never, ever allowed himself or his children to presume that success was guaranteed, not even when they were visited by great amounts of success—or in Chris's case, rapidly accumulating snowdrifts of success and money and fame. Many of the traits Evert would become famous for during her career—her dislike of pretense, her laserlike focus and brutally honest self-assessments, her inability to allow herself to savor her successes—started with her father back at Holiday Park.

Praise seemed to genuinely embarrass Jimmy. He had no use for hyperbole. Brian Gottfried, another Holiday Park player who enjoyed success on the men's pro tour, says, "That first year Chrissie played U.S. Open, I can remember standing around Holiday Park one night when Jimmy got a phone call. Somebody wanted to plan a welcome home event for Chrissie—I think a parade down Main Street or something. All Jimmy said was 'No. She didn't win the event.' Then he hung up.

"But that was Jimmy," Gottfried says with a chuckle. "He kept things in perspective. His take was 'Yeah, getting to semifinals of the Open is a pretty good effort at her age. At any age. But there's more to do. Better stay grounded.' "

Even at the height of Chris's career, Jimmy Evert charged just ten dollars for a lesson at Holiday Park, grudgingly raising his rate from six dollars at Chris's urging. He carefully managed her playing schedule and endorsements after she turned pro at eighteen, once vetoing a pre-Wimbledon Converse ad in which she was photographed wearing a crown because he feared it could be construed as disrespectful to the queen of England. He kept his pro job at Holiday Park for forty-nine years, shunning numerous offers to start his own private tennis academy or write an instructional book. "Nobody will read it," Jimmy Evert told sportswriter Jim Martz—this though Chris's splashdown at the 1971 U.S. Open soon sparked a boom of ponytailed little girls honing their copycat backhands on tennis courts across America.

"But the one thing no one could copy was Chris's mind," said British tennis star Virginia Wade. "Her mind is what made her great."

Ask any Holiday Park regular what it was like to play Chris Evert when she was a teenager, let alone a battle-hardened pro, and what often follows is a knowing laugh . . . a wince . . . then perhaps a groan. The trait everyone invariably mentions first is Evert's unshakeable, remorseless will.

Junior opponents told stories of walking by Evert at the net and having her toss off a comment like "I see you've been working on your backhand. Hmm . . ." After that, Evert's self-conscious opponent might not be able to hit a backhand the rest of the day.

Laurie Fleming, a frequent victim of Evert's merciless drubbings throughout high school, laughs and says, "You almost cringed even if you did beat Chris at something." Fleming remembers defeating Evert in a Ping-Pong game once. Without speaking, Evert calmly put down her paddle, silently walked back to Holiday Park with Fleming, and didn't say another word to her the rest of the day.

"We used to joke that even if you were Chrissie's best friend, all she'd give you is ice in the wintertime," Harold Solomon says, laugh-

ing. "That attitude was from Jimmy too. There was no giving anything away. Nothing. That's how Jimmy taught her. When you're out
there on the court it's your job. You go out there and destroy the
other person if you can."

Even as a teenager Evert already had "The Look"—that squinting,
stern-looking mask of concentration that Navratilova, even during her
invincible years, would see across the net and then think, *Oh no.*

Evert didn't reserve The Look for matches. It could surface during workouts too, if, say, Evert felt her practice partner was too scattershot. Then—oh no, all right—here it came: the withering glare,
and perhaps an incinerating one- or two-word remark. It wasn't unheard of for Evert's sister Jeanne or younger brother John to storm
off the practice court, yelling over their shoulder, "Just look at yourself, Chris . . . You are HORRIBLE!"

Billie Jean King says, "Oh my God, she was hysterical. After
Chris joined the women's tour, people were petrified to practice with
her. I'd say, 'Chris.' She'd say, 'What, Billie?' I would tell her, 'Chris,
I will practice with you, but the minute you give me that look, I am
gone. Understand?' Because I knew. Sometimes she would get so
mad at me, I would find myself yelling at her: 'CHRIS, I AM *TRY-
ING* MY BEST, OKAY? BUT MY GROUND STROKES ARE JUST
NOT AS GOOD AS YOURS, OKAY? I DO NOT GET EVERY
BALL RIGHT BACK WHERE YOU WANT IT.' "

Evert would look back impassively and await the next ball.

Chris Evert was initially unhappy when her father told her it was
time for her tennis education to begin. "I was still in kinder-
garten," she says, "and just getting used to these wonderful pool
parties at my friend Cara Bennett's house." But it wasn't long before
her attitude began to change. Evert and Laurie Fleming, Harold
Solomon, and Brian Gottfried all describe Holiday Park as an idyl-
lic, bustling place where they would happily while away entire days.
Demand for playing time on the twenty-one courts was so great
that Jimmy and his staff installed a buzzer that could be heard across

the grounds to signal when one group's forty-five-minute session was up and the next group could begin. When Chris and the other kids were shooed off the courts, they'd often go across the street and play football or tag until they could get back to tennis again.

"It was a great way to grow up," Chris says. "Everything was always boys and girls together, and everything was competitive. This was my life. And it was great because I got to spend time with my dad. I was sort of fearful of my dad. He was the authority figure at home and at the courts."

Evert always described herself as a plain and introverted girl. "I was the last one along the wall at the school dance." Even at the height of her celebrity in her late twenties, when asked by a reporter if she considered herself pretty, Evert smiled poignantly and said, "Just missed."

But Evert was secretly delighted when she overheard her classmates whispering, "There goes Chris Evert" as she walked the school hallways after her latest tennis success. "As soon as you win that first trophy, the work is all worth it," she says. "You feel great about yourself." After she started winning titles at age eight and nine, the spectators who paused to watch her Holiday Park practices thrilled her too. Evert often said that she was raised to work hard and keep her mouth shut, but tennis became a condoned means to vent whatever ambition or emotion or ego she kept tamped down inside. "It was *really* good for my ego," she admits with a laugh. She began to feel that tennis gave her an identity, a foothold that made her feel special. And the better she did, the more she came to love the game.

"I know Chris says she was shy," says her friend Laurie Fleming. "But I think she was 'shy' like a lot of actors and actresses say they were shy, and so they honed their craft to express themselves, you know? You look at them later and it's like, 'You? Shy? Gimme a break.' I think 'reserved' is a better word for Chrissie. She was more reserved and held in—like, don't show how you feel, not just in tennis, but all things."

There were occasions when Evert's devotion to tennis wavered, especially as she moved into high school and contemplated trying out for cheerleading or joining an after-school club. She sometimes wished it would rain so she could get a reprieve from her daily tennis practices, which typically ran two hours on school days and twice a day on weekends. Once she began playing junior tournaments, she was rarely permitted to sleep over at friends' houses anymore, though friends could sometimes stay at the Everts' home. "I think Jimmy thought if she was up all night talking and goofing around at my house, it would ruin the next day of tennis," Fleming says.

Parties became out of the question too, especially during tournament season. "My dad was totally against it, so my mom would actually sneak me to them," Evert says with a smile. "It was my mom who tried to make sure I had as normal a life as I could."

Sometimes Colette would cup her hand over her mouth and whisper to Chris, "You go ahead to the party and I'll pick you up at ten-thirty." When Jimmy returned home from Holiday Park he would invariably say, "Hey, where's Chrissie?" And Colette would sit up with a start and say, "Ah! I forgot to tell you. She's at a party. But I'll go pick her up."

Colette liked to joke that an artfully won compromise with Jimmy often felt like a victory to her and Chris.

If Evert at times resisted her daily tennis regime, there was no denying the beneficial effect her sessions with her father had on her game. Chris was always a nerveless, pinpoint shot maker, a skill she honed as a girl by slamming hundreds of ground strokes in a row at the little orange cones her father set up as targets. Jimmy emphasized the sort of fundamental skills preached in all the tennis instructional booklets until they were second nature to Chris—things like racket preparation, or maintaining the proper footwork to hit a winner whether from a standstill or on the run.

During Evert's headline-grabbing run at the 1971 U.S. Open, one fact often overlooked was that though she was young, she was not an inexperienced player. By age sixteen, she had already put in eleven years of work with her father on the courts at Holiday Park. She had no illusions about her game or what she had to do to win a match.

Unlike for a serve-and-volley player, who tries to end points quickly, committing to the life of a baseliner demands surrendering to a long list of grueling realities. That was especially true for Evert and her fellow Holiday Park players, who grew up performing in searing heat on slow clay.

Being a baseliner also first demands that you be exceptionally fit. Your ground strokes must be unerring and precise. More than merely patient, a baseliner must be obstinate, uncompromising, unyielding. Helen Wills Moody, the legendary American champion of the 1920s and '30s, used to propel herself after every ball while silently repeating, *Every point, every point, every point . . .*

A great baseliner also must have unwavering powers of concentration to win long rallies. The best of them have a diamond cutter's nerve too—a jaw-dropping ability to ignore pressure and execute an exquisitely placed passing shot or a clean winner when a sliver of daylight or hard-earned patch of open court is finally won.

To say it's a punishing way to play is an understatement. Evert took the baseliner's credo to the extreme. In addition to the Ice Maiden label that Evert picked up during her first Wimbledon in 1972, another of her early nicknames was "Little Miss Metronome." Some of her matches had the feel of a hypnotically swinging watch. During one of her late-1970s wars against Tracy Austin, her younger mirror image, a reporter wrote that Evert and Austin *averaged* an exhausting twenty-eight strokes per point during their match. Whether the man's math was off or not, the more salient point is that it could have been true. As Julie Heldman, Evert's frequent opponent after their Wightman Cup days, joked, "Chris played points like a siege war during the Middle Ages."

Nearly all the top Holiday Park players had a conceit about their toughness, especially once they began traveling the country to play tournaments. Nearly all of them were the same kind of never-say-die baseline player as Evert. And still, says Laurie Fleming, Chris's tenacity stood out.

"You know how you're driving on the turnpike and maybe five minutes later you haven't noticed a thing?" Fleming asks. "You can't remember where you've just been, and you think, 'Wait a minute. I don't even know how I got here'? As a baseliner, you sort of do that on the court. You just hit it back, hit it back, hit it back—you almost let your mind blank out—and then, all of a sudden, you pop back in. It's like you get in a zone or some rhythm that's beyond fatigue, and hitting the ball back becomes almost automatic.

"But even if you were used to playing that way," Fleming continues, "playing Chris would still discourage you. Because you knew she would stay out there for fifteen minutes and put her head through the wall for a single point. *One point*. Beforehand, you'd sometimes think, Ugh. Am I really up for this today?"

Evert always was. That constancy is partly what made her a marvel. Her career winning percentage of .900—1,309 wins against, remarkably, just 146 losses—is the highest in professional tennis history. Whereas a player like Navratilova joked about having to "concentrate on concentrating," Evert explains, "Concentrating was just something I always had. On every point. And it always seemed to come easier for me than it did for other players."

At times Evert was almost apologetic about her style, maintaining that her matches weren't much fun to watch. But that wasn't true, especially to a trained tennis eye. Evert had a great feel for the nuances of the game. She knew how to hit shots at wicked angles that opened up the court, and when to suddenly change the pace of her shots during a rally, causing the ball to go ticking off her surprised opponent's racket frame in a mistimed swing.

Sports commentator Mary Carillo, who played three injury-shortened years on the pro tour, winning a 1977 French Open mixed doubles title with her childhood friend John McEnroe, says she used to love watching Evert's practices with her father just to hear what was being said. Carillo noticed that Chris would often do tiny, imperceptible things right after Jimmy quietly told her something—maybe some minor hip adjustment, maybe something you couldn't really even see.

"And it wouldn't necessarily mean that Chrissie was just looking for extra power," Carillo says. "It could just mean she was looking for disguise. Because that's another thing that made her so tough. Her strokes were so clean, everything looked the same."

Because the way Evert took back her racket never changed, opponents usually couldn't read what shot Evert was about to hit, especially on her backhand side. They didn't know if Evert was preparing to hit a drop shot or a lob, slam the ball crosscourt, or rifle a passing shot down the line.

"The funny thing was, people always thought, 'God, she's just doing the same thing over and over again,' when she *wasn't* doing the same thing over and over again," Carillo says. "Chrissie would hit one shot down the line. Then she'd hit another shot down the line, but this time it was hit a little bit harder, or a little bit deeper, or with a little bit more spin. It was all very intentional, and her opponents often weren't noticing, say, that their contact point, where they hit the ball, was shifting imperceptibly. So they'd lose a little length on their reply. Maybe she'd have moved them a little bit farther off the court, a little bit farther off the court, and then"—here Carillo smiles in admiration—"she had 'em."

Evert's comprehension of such details from a young age, combined with her ferocious will to win, explains how she mowed down a career-long succession of rivals who were supposedly more physically gifted than she, including Margaret Court and Billie Jean King and Navratilova.

In tennis, the term of art is called "constructing a point." Shockingly enough, many successful pros, even major tournament winners, never really learn how to do it.

Diana Nyad, the long-distance swimmer who also hails from Fort Lauderdale, is four years older than Chris Evert. She remembers going to Holiday Park in the early 1980s to take a few tennis lessons from Jimmy Evert before she was to compete in *Superstars,* a multi-sport made-for-TV challenge among top athletes of the day. To Nyad's surprise, Jimmy Evert began by interviewing her.

"He'd say, 'I'm just wondering, Diana, when you swim in those oceans, when there's a shark sighting or you've been in that water for fifty hours and you want to give up, what do you do?' He was curious about the mental approach. What is it? He wanted to know if I said to myself, 'My God—I'm tired, I'm seasick, I'm cold. What the hell am I doing this for? I mean, I *wanted* to do it about forty hours ago, but how do I remind myself of that now and go on?' Then Jimmy tried to translate it to tennis for me because, he said, 'That's what it's about: Who are you? How hard will you fight?'

"He said, 'You're going to come out there and look at that big green rectangle and *decide.*' "

Nyad came away from their encounter with more than improved tennis strokes. She left feeling that she and Jimmy Evert shared a purist's love for what they did. And Nyad felt that Chris had the same love and pride. "In the beginning, Jimmy wasn't grooming Chrissie to make a lot of money," Nyad says. "I don't think anybody in those days was shooting for that, or anticipating what the women's tennis tour became. It was more just 'How are you going to put your values as a human being into the game?' "

Evert's ability to transfer that rock-ribbed ethic onto the court defined her during her career as much as her renowned ground strokes. By the time she turned pro on her eighteenth birthday, the planks of her personality and game were already in place.

From her sweet-natured mother, Colette, Chris learned her sense of graciousness, her first ideas about femininity, and a diplomatic habit of not saying anything publicly if she couldn't say something nice. "To be honest," Colette admits, "you don't always want to be sportsmanlike or clap for the other person when you lose." Then, brightening, she adds, "But you just feel so darn much better about yourself when you do!" Rather than ask Chris if she was nervous before a big match, Colette would nudge her and say, "Oh, Chrissie, isn't this exciting!"

From Jimmy, Chris got earfuls of axioms and tennis insights, not just a quiver full of shots. Anything less than maximum effort was not an option. Unforced errors were galling. Making excuses? Out of the question. "I was taught that good behavior was just as important as good strokes," Chris says. Her natural stoicism was encouraged, not discouraged. "When I look at that grim little fixed expression, I know that's not me," Evert said. "My father instilled it in me at a young age. I remember him telling me, 'Don't show any emotion on the court. It will be to your advantage because your opponent will be frustrated.' "

As Chris grew older, she did more than play for her father and parrot her parents' convictions. Her mind-set became a fierce point of personal pride to her as well. It was the root of her champion's arrogance and the foundation from which her victories sprang. Over the years, it was telling that citing her superior mental makeup was the one boast Evert repeatedly allowed herself to make.

Grueling as her style was, Evert could never have played with such spectacular consistency if she hadn't taken some perverse personal enjoyment from the exquisite torture she put her opponents through. It hardly mattered that doing so required a similar or even greater expenditure of energy from her.

That's another trait of the best baseliners: they're pitiless toward themselves too. They ignore their own physical distress or self-doubt as they hungrily pan each match for that telltale moment when their opponent's resistance begins to creak and snap.

"And oh yeah, you can feel it, all right," Evert's contemporary Harold Solomon says. "I had the same experience as Chris because I played baseline too. You're out there and you just know. You look over to the other side and you think, 'This match is over because that other person is just *gone*.' It was actually quite egotistical. It was a great feeling to just look over and think, 'I have totally worked it out so that that other person is just physically and mentally kaput, and I had something to do with it—I *made* it happen.' With Chris it was like, 'Okay, I have methodically destroyed that person on the other side of the court.'

"That's pretty cool," Solomon says.

He bursts into laughter.

"It's pretty sadistic too."

As much as Evert and her father drilled and endlessly rehearsed the parts of her game that could be taught, there was still the matter of what sixteen-year-old Chris brought to the stage. During Evert's debut at the U.S. Open in September of 1971, Billie Jean King walked across the tournament grounds at Forest Hills to get a look at the new kid. King was as curious as anyone.

King's decision to watch Evert's second-round match against Mary Ann Eisel was partly self-interest. King knew she could play the winner of the match in the semifinals. The other impetus was that King was already deep into her rabble-rousing efforts to build the Virginia Slims pro tour, which was less than a year old. Evert, a potential recruit, was still playing as an amateur.

King, though just twenty-seven years old, already called herself the "Old Lady," a wry nod to her length of service and stature in the sport. She had been ranked number one in the world and she had already won five of her twelve Grand Slam singles titles. Her knees were laced with centipede-like scars from several serious knee surgeries. But King remained a lithe and eager champion capable of great things.

That's why it was so startling a few days later when, following her warm-up for her semifinal match against Evert, it was King—not young Evert—who slipped off to a shower stall in the women's locker room, turned the water on as high as it would go, and began sobbing uncontrollably, shaking with fright.

CHAPTER TWO

MADAME SUPERSTAR

As King made her way to the stadium court at Forest Hills to see Evert play her second-round match against Mary Ann Eisel, Bud Collins, the respected *Boston Globe* sportswriter and broadcaster, was already at work in the CBS television booth. Collins was announcing the match with Jack Kramer, the retired American tennis star who had become a tournament promoter. Evert narrowly lost the first set to Eisel, 6–4, and slid behind 6–5 in the second set. As Eisel, a capable pro, prepared to serve at 40–love, triple match point, Collins and Kramer were attempting to give Evert a nice send-off.

"I remember we were being very gentle, almost patronizing," Collins says. "Chrissie was so young and she had already won one match in the tournament over Edda Budding of Germany, so we were trying to be very upbeat and saying, 'Why, this kid is just an amateur. This is good experience for her. She's hit some pretty darn good shots today. You just keep this name in mind—Chris Evert. She'll be back, don't you worry.' And then, almost as an aside, we said, 'Oh, look. She saved a match point. Why, good for her.' Then she saved another one—and another one—and she kept saving them and kept saving them, and by the sixth match point it became, 'WOW! Another match point saved by Chris Evert!'

"Then, of course, she kept going in the tournament and she had everyone in tears," Collins says, laughing. "She had Lesley Hunt in tears. She had Françoise Durr in tears. Hardened pros! In tears!"

King made it back to the women's locker room before the wildfire news of Evert's miraculous escape against Eisel reached the other players. King excitedly told everyone, "That kid is our next superstar! She's the one! She is it!"

"You could tell by the way the crowd was connecting to her," King explains. "Even then, she was good under pressure. You can look at kids and see how they play pressure situations, how they respond. Do they like being on center court or would they rather be on Court Fifty-five at ten in the morning? She was a star. A star was born in my eyes that match."

As implausible as Evert's 4–6, 7–6, 6–1 comeback from six match points down against Eisel was, what the sixteen-year-old Evert did next was also astonishing. With the stadium crowds convulsing with cheers for her each time, Evert raged back from one-set deficits to beat Françoise Durr of France in the third round and Lesley Hunt of Australia in their Round of Sixteen match. Afterward, Hunt said through sobs, "I can beat Chris Evert but not twelve thousand people." When Durr returned to the locker room, she was upset that the pro-Evert crowd had cheered her mistakes and not just Evert's winners.

"I hope they're satisfied," Durr wailed.

Satisfied? No one could get enough of Evert. The *New York Times* called her "Cinderella in Sneakers" and New York's *Daily News* nicknamed her "Little Miss Sunshine." Barry Lorge of *Tennis* magazine swooned, "For 10 wonderful days, New York was a sentimental place and the U.S. Open was a great romance." As Evert walked the Forest Hills grounds with her mother, fans jostled to get close to the young player, grabbing the hat she wore off her head and knocking the sweater she'd slung over her shoulders to the ground. Billy Talbert, the U.S. Open tournament director, scheduled all of

Evert's matches on the stadium court after her Eisel win: "There'd be a riot if I didn't," he explained. The public's fascination with Evert was so high, Collins was assigned to do the first-ever national television interview with her on the second weekend of the tournament.

"There was so little tennis broadcasting done in those days, we didn't have a broadcast booth at Forest Hills," Collins says. "There was just an open platform with a table. So we got Chrissie up there, and I'm a pretty good interviewer, but boy, it was really hard. She was so shy, so reserved. Meanwhile, another match had started on the center court. Pancho Gonzalez was playing. He was still a force in those days. So there's Chrissie, she's seated facing the court, and I had my back to the court. And I'm sure, in the process of trying to elicit something from her, I probably raised my voice.

"So she's sitting there and you can just see she's thinking, 'When is this ever going to end?' I'm plowing on, I'm trying everything— oh, it was terrible—and all of a sudden we can sort of hear—but she can also *see*—the court has become very quiet as I'm still talking. She can see that Gonzalez is approaching the railing now. And he shouts, 'GODDAMMIT, BUD! Don't you realize we're playing a MATCH down here?'

"Well, poor Chrissie's eyes flew open like big saucers. The interview closed just like that.

"It was not a success," Collins says with a laugh.

Though King believed Evert was destined to be tennis's next superstar, it was vitally important to King that it not happen quite yet. Not in this semifinal she was now scheduled to play against Evert.

Even then, King was well on her way to becoming the most formidable, revolutionary female sports figure of the twentieth century. No one else comes close. If people ask King today why she sleeps in so late, she's liable to joke, "I'm still tired from the seventies." When King drove herself to become the first woman athlete to earn

$100,000 in a single year in 1971—one year before she and Evert played—it was considered such a watershed achievement that she received a congratulatory call from President Nixon.

Before King helped found the first all-women's professional tour in 1970, female tennis players were treated as second-class citizens. They often played at the same tournament stops as men, but were paid a fraction of the prize money and expenses. Their matches were rarely shown on television. King's pioneering work to create an all-women's circuit allowed Evert and Navratilova to walk into a tableau that would incubate and launch them into the lives of the worldwide sports stars and millionaires they became.

But it was a hard slog for King, full of sparks and personal recrimination.

Many women of King's generation managed to carve out extraordinary lives without ever looking like the insurrectionists they were. But King, who was born in 1943—eleven years before Evert and thirteen before Navratilova—was adamant about calling sexism and elitism by their names. She insisted on living loud, not settling for whatever success she could manage with some sleight-of-hand in the shadows. Artificial limits drove her mad. She refused to be shackled by tradition. She asked impertinent questions. As King's many crusades and accomplishments proved, she was not the sort of woman you told to shut up or go away.

"People always thought I was angry. I wasn't. I was determined," King says.

At the remove of thirty years, the particulars of life for American women back then or the details of the battles King fought can seem largely forgotten, even quaintly absurd. Before 1975, an adult woman couldn't get a credit card in her own name unless her father or husband signed for it. Back then, there was still a raging debate about whether women and men deserved equal pay for equal work, or equal opportunity for college athletic scholarships, admissions to law schools and medical schools. Once upon a time—not very long ago—serious people actually maintained that women were constitutionally incapable of running beyond 5,000 meters at the Olympics or flying a commercial jet plane, becoming a CEO, or running for president.

Even the import given to King's famous 1973 Battle of the Sexes match against Bobby Riggs seems faintly ridiculous now. But at the time, the match wasn't seen as some overhyped tussle. It was earth-shaking.

An estimated 37 million Americans watched the event on live TV, and 30,742 fans streamed through gates of the Houston Astrodome on September 23, 1973, to see King take on Riggs, an aging former Wimbledon champion who had proclaimed himself the world's biggest male chauvinist pig. Arguments about who would win had raged for weeks at kitchen tables, around watercoolers at work, inside bowling alleys and beauty salons. Countless wagers were made. Bosses promised their secretaries they'd make the coffee for a week if King won; husbands told their wives they'd do the laundry and wash the dishes. The Las Vegas bookmakers offered 5 to 2 odds that Riggs would prevail. The Smithsonian Institution requested the mint green dress King wore that night and put it on display.

Nearly everywhere King went during the overheated buildup to the match, women would grab her by the arm or look her dead in the eye and say, "I hope you beat Riggs's pompous ass . . . I hope you shut . . . him . . . up."

As *New York Times* reporter Grace Lichtenstein wrote at the time, "What captured the public's imagination was the challenge implied in Bobby Riggs's blabbermouthing: that this grand, ludicrous face-off could somehow settle all the questions posed by women's liberation."

Thirty years later, Lichtenstein hasn't changed her mind about the meaning of King's convincing 6–4, 6–3, 6–3 win. "The fact that what was really an inconsequential, made-for-television, silly matchup—an absolute circus—has gone on to attain this mythical status is remarkable, because it shouldn't have been a landmark of anything," says Lichtenstein, who traveled the women's tennis tour that year to write her highly entertaining book, *A Long Way, Baby.*

"All the Battle of the Sexes really proved was that a twenty-nine-year-old woman in the prime of her tennis career could beat a fifty-five-year-old has-been who happens to be male," Lichtenstein says. "But there's also no denying that somehow Billie Jean's victory helped validate the idea that women could hang in there, not just on the tennis court but on the job or in the home. It was proof not so much of physical prowess but of mental toughness. Feminists still had not yet reached out to the masses by then, but Billie Jean reached out, grabbed them by the hair, and made people take notice."

The effect was seismic. Other female athletes such as Babe Didrikson Zaharias, Althea Gibson, and Peggy Fleming had earned large American audiences before King. And soon enough, Evert's popularity would eclipse them all. But King, the turbo-charged daughter of a Long Beach, California, fireman named Bill Moffitt and a housewife named Betty, became America's first overtly political female sports star.

Part of what made King different was that she didn't focus only on her own individual athletic achievement. An entire *class* of female sports stars was created when King helped found the first all-women's pro tennis tour in 1970, along with eight other players and their indefatigable ally Gladys Heldman, the tough, brassy publisher of *World Tennis* magazine. Lichtenstein called them "a new breed of career women" who were carving out a place for themselves in what had been a strictly man's world—the province of the sports superstar. The way King and the rest of the Original Nine pulled it off was nothing less than a guerrilla action, a flat-out rebellion against a tennis establishment that Heldman's daughter Julie once said treated them like "nice little things to have around."

"We didn't care back then about winning the majors like they do now," says King. "We wanted to make a women's *tour*. We wanted to make a living playing tennis. We wanted to take tennis to the people. Women athletes were still treated like freaks. I can remember the male reporters, they just couldn't figure out why the hell girls wanted to do this. They'd say, 'Why are you, why are you—why do you think you can do this?' And we would say, 'Because we can.'"

King's groundbreaking work paved the way for Evert and Navratilova to become what she called "the brave new athlete" and "our first-generation true professionals." Evert's splashdown at the U.S. Open came just eleven months after the Slims Tour was formed in 1970. Navratilova made her tour debut in the spring of 1973, five months before King's Battle of the Sexes match against Riggs. Evert and Navratilova's eventual rivalry was akin to one long conversation that continued many of the arguments and dreams King had first laid out: What should the female athlete look like? How should she behave? Perform? Trade on her sex appeal? And would customers pay to watch them play?

Spared the worry about whether they could make a living playing tennis, Evert and Navratilova's generation was free to concentrate on optimum performance, which was another of King's goals all along. "Billie Jean made us athletes, and Chris helped make us celebrities," Navratilova once said.

While Navratilova was encouraged to play sports as a girl in Czechoslovakia—she said that one good thing about the Communists was that they believed men's and women's athletic success had equal propaganda value—discrimination was no murky abstraction to King. Much of her activism and outrage was born of personal experience. When King told and retold the same scalding stories over the years, her righteous indignation and hurt seemed fresh each time.

There was the national tennis official who gave young Billie Jean one fifth the travel money for a trip to England that he gave to a male player of lesser distinction. There was Perry T. Jones, the Southern California tournament director who pulled ten-year-old Billie Jean out of a group photo because she was not wearing the de rigueur white skirt all the other girls wore. "My poor mom, who had worked so hard to make me these beautiful white shorts, was absolutely mortified, but we didn't know any better," says King. "It was my first sanctioned tournament, you know?"

Frank Brennan, a New Jersey–based businessman who was an

early booster of King's career, looked at the practical short haircut that she favored as a sixteen-year-old and the thick eyeglasses she wore to correct her horrible 20/400 vision and told her, "You'll be a good athlete, Billie Jean, because you're ugly."

King was devastated. "He said it just like that. He didn't believe he was being mean. He just made the remark in the same way as he might say, 'You'll be good because you have a nice backhand, Billie Jean.'"

In 1968, King, Rosie Casals, Ann Jones, and Françoise Durr became the first four women invited to play for pay and travel the world for two years on George MacCall's National Tennis League, an exhibition tour. King says she enjoyed a warm relationship with the six men in their barnstorming troupe: Rod Laver, Roy Emerson, Fred Stolle, Ken Rosewall, Pancho Gonzalez, and Andres Gimeno. The conditions were often substandard, and the schedule was grueling. "But it brought us closer," King says. "We had a blast." The players often ate dinner together and went nightclubbing and dancing. They whiled away the long hours of travel by talking about their lives and telling jokes and musing about the future of their sport.

And yet, when King tried to enlist the male players' support for the women's battles for better treatment, arguing that a united front would benefit them all, she was stunned by the male players' rebukes. The business of tennis was changing dramatically. Beginning in 1968, the major tournaments such as Wimbledon and Forest Hills began accepting professionals for the first time in addition to amateurs, most of whom had been getting under-the-table (or "shamateur") payments for years. Now that everything was aboveboard, the men and women players were all fighting for better pay from the tournaments. They wanted more freedom to set their own playing schedules rather than being controlled by their national associations. King and the other women players soon found that they were even less welcome than before.

Arthur Ashe, the first president of the Association of Tennis Professionals players' union, which was founded in 1968, said:

"Men are playing tennis for a living now. They don't want to give up money just for girls to play . . . Why should we have to split our money with them?" Clark Graebner, another top American pro, said, "I'm just as happy never to see the girls. They're not very attractive. I wouldn't want my daughter playing on the tour." A third American star, Stan Smith, told the *Daily Mirror* of London, "These tennis girls would be much happier if they settled down, got married, and had a family. Tennis is a tough life and it really isn't good for them. It de-feminizes them. . . . [They become] too independent and they can't adapt to anyone else, they won't be dependent on any man. They want to take charge, not only on the courts but at home."

"I couldn't believe it," King says. "When tennis opened up, the boys didn't want us around—these were my best friends, by the way—and that was crushing. I cannot tell you how crushing it was. Fred Stolle flat-out told me, 'No one wants to watch you birds play anyway. They're not gonna *pay* to watch you birds play.' And Arthur Ashe—Arthur was a pig. He was a total pig. He never got over it until after he met his wife, Jeanne [Moutoussamy, a professional photographer]. Before that? He was a total pig.

"I went to them after they started the ATP because I couldn't believe they left the women out of the players' union. It killed me. I still don't like to think about it. It hurts. They never even bothered to respond, and it was never the same for me with them after that. I mean, I love them. We're all great friends—still. But when I see them there's just this, this . . . yearning, I guess, to be validated. And I *hate* that too.

"I still want to say, 'Why didn't you just include us? Why? Look at what we're all doing thirty years later. We're all still here, we're all still getting together anyway. So, *why?*' "

The final event that led to the women's professional tour that Evert and Navratilova inherited was player-turned-promoter Jack Kramer's announcement that his 1970 Pacific Southwest tournament would offer a $7,500 purse for the women and $60,000 to the men. Just as insulting, none of the women who failed to make the Round of Sixteen would be paid a dime for her work. But every player entered in the men's draw would.

King and Rosie Casals asked Gladys Heldman, the publisher of *World Tennis,* if she would privately approach Kramer and ask him to increase the women's prize money. Kramer not only rebuffed Heldman, but groused that if the women didn't like the arrangement, he wouldn't pay them anything. He later maintained in his autobiography that the unprecedented disparity between the men's and women's purses was "just good business."

"The only prejudice practiced in tennis against the women players is by the fans," Kramer wrote. "People get up and go get a hot dog or go to the bathroom when the women come on."

Heldman had heard enough. She had experience as a successful tennis event promoter and decided to set up her own women's tournament at the Houston Racquet Club in late September of 1970, the same week as Kramer's Pacific Southwest event. Heldman decided that total prize money for the tournament would be $7,500—$2,500 of it from Virginia Slims cigarettes, the company that eventually agreed to sponsor the entire women's tour because of Heldman's friendship with Joseph F. Cullman III, the chairman of the Phillip Morris Tobacco Company. The Original Nine players who signed on to compete in Houston that week were King, Rosie Casals, Nancy Richey, Kerry Melville, Judy Dalton, Val Ziegenfuss, Peaches Bartkowicz, Kristy Pigeon, and Julie Heldman.

The evening before play in Houston began, U.S. Tennis Association officials informed Heldman and King that any player who participated in the tournament would face an indefinite suspension. Which meant that they could be banned from playing even the U.S. Open or Wimbledon.

That same evening, the Original Nine met at Gladys Heldman's home in Houston and debated whether they should go ahead with the Slims tournament. Some of the women now weren't so sure.

"We had people saying, 'Well, we do have a lot to lose,' but I didn't give a damn, a lot of us didn't," King recalls. "I finally said, 'You know what? We have *nothing* to lose.'

"When we were trying to figure out what would be a reasonable prize money minimum for our tournament, we laid everything out. We agreed to be honest about what we were all making under the table. I remember I got $1,100 once for two weeks in South Africa, and I thought that was huge. Nancy [Richey] said, 'What? I'm lucky to get something besides a plane fare.' Someone else said, 'Are you kidding? I'm lucky to get a plane ticket!' Most of the others didn't get anything.

"So I said, 'Lose? *Lose?* What do *we* have to lose? What do we have now? We have fewer and fewer places to play. When we do play with the men, it's a twelve to one ratio of prize money even though we're playing in front of a packed house. So you guys think they're really giving us something? Me personally, I think they're giving us absolutely NOTH-ING. I think we have *nothing* to lose. There's a great chance that we ourselves are never going to make the big bucks, never going to have the adulation. We could fall flat on our faces if we start a tour. But are you willing to do it just because you think it's the right thing to do?' "

The Original Nine voted to play. Then King called the USTA back and told them the maverick Slims tournament would go on.

The date was September 23, 1970, and "Women's Lob"— Gladys Heldman's nickname for the new tour—was born. For all intents and purposes, the entire modern women's sports industry was launched that day as well.

By the time King played Evert one year later at the 1971 U.S. Open, the Virginia Slims tour had already grown to seven stops and $305,000 in prize money. In Navratilova's rookie year, 1973, total purses had mushroomed to $775,000.

By the time Navratilova retired from singles play in 1994, five years after Evert, the two of them had earned a staggering combined total of $30 million in prize money alone.

———————

Evert has always said that she wouldn't trade the era she began her tennis career for any other era. The Slims tour that she and Navratilova walked onto as teenagers was a freewheeling, rollicking, seat-of-the-pants place.

King was well established as the Slims tour's best player, its chief spokesperson, its leading innovator and policy maker, its lightning rod, quality-control monitor, locker room sheriff, and mentor. "Billie Jean groomed me and she groomed Martina," Evert said. "She pulled me aside when I was nineteen and told me I needed to be a leader, that I was going to learn the business of this tour, and that it was important, if I was going to be a top player, that I be out front."

Most of the founding players considered themselves a sorority of friends and groundbreakers, not just die-hard competitors, and they pitched in to make the new tour work. To defray costs, Ann Jones's husband, Pip, used to roll up the Slims tour's carpeted indoor court and drive it on a truck from town to town. Many of the players stayed during tournaments in private family housing rather than pay for more expensive hotels. There were no full-time trainers to treat the players' aches and pains as there are today. Nancy Richey once had a root canal in the morning in Denver, then played her match that night gargling scotch to kill the pain.

Because the USTA banned its officials from working Slims events, Peachy Kellmeyer, the Slims' first tour director, sometimes had to persuade people who happened to be at the arena to work as linesmen for the matches.

"One time we talked the Xerox repairman into calling the lines, but he gave himself away when he yelled 'Foul!' instead of 'Out!' " Kellmeyer says, slapping a hand on her forehead.

Dress designer and tennis raconteur Ted Tinling, the colorful Englishman who in 1949 fashioned the controversial lace bloomers for Gussy Moran that got him disinvited from Wimbledon for thirty-three years, was hired to design the Slims players' flamboyant dresses. "I put the sin into tennis!" Tinling liked to boast. King and Heldman shared Tinling's philosophy that the new women's tour had to be a spectacle as well as a sporting event to succeed. He dressed them like showwomen, not athletes. White outfits were out; fluorescents and sequins were in. "When these athletes today say, 'Oh, I'm an entertainer,' I want to say, 'Where were you thirty-five frigging years ago? That's how we sold the Slims!' " King says with a laugh.

Tinling's affectionate nickname for King was Madame Superstar. The two of them would often haggle over his designs for her. "Rosie was always in sequins—her dresses used to weigh ten pounds—Frankie [Durr] would have her boobs bursting out, and Margaret [Court] used to have these huge collars," King says with a hoot. "I used to tell Teddy, 'Give me some reflective mirrors, or *something*. I like MORE. You're not giving me enough!' "

The Slims players so desperately wanted the tour to succeed, they gave free clinics on the days of their matches, glad-handed sponsors at cocktail parties, and even stood outside arenas wearing sandwich-board signs in some towns, urging people to stop and buy tickets.

No player worked as hard to promote the tour as King. She'd often do her first interview of the day at six a.m. and her last at well past midnight, long after she'd played. She came back too soon after several of her six knee surgeries. ("Rehab? No one knew about that then," she scoffs.) Her ex-husband, Larry King, a tennis promoter and attorney, said Billie Jean was constantly plagued by allergies and sinus conditions, and played so often while taking antibiotic prescriptions that made her skin photosensitive, she eventually lost the pigment in her skin.

King's zeal was evangelical, her attention to detail daunting. As Jeanie Brinkman, the Slims tour's first publicity director, told journalist Barry Lorge, "Billie Jean was a magnet, attracting and repelling with strong force. The tour used to fluctuate with her. If Billie was on a rampage, tension was high. If she was happy, everyone was.

It was never tranquil with Billie around, but it took her personality to make the sport."

King remembers it as a great—if exhausting—time, even though she and Gladys Heldman had to battle the USTA the first three years.

If King has a nagging private regret, it's the one that many of her colleagues voice for her: "As great a player as Billie was, Billie spent so many hours and hours of her life building the tour, I don't think she ever really found out how many more titles she could have won," says former player Betsy Nagelsen. "It's hard to relate the magnitude of what she did for the rest of us, because you can't."

That King came along at the same time as the women's movement gave a special resonance to what she stood for. The new women's tennis tour was seen as part of a larger societal transformation that had just begun. Women would constantly approach King to say that they admired her, all the while identifying themselves as "Joe Smith's wife."

"Yes," King would say to them, "but who are *you?*"

It was a time of great foment in America, an era when so many facets of everyday life were thrown open for referendum, from American involvement in the Vietnam War to the demands being made by the civil rights, abortion rights, and gay rights movements. The Watergate scandal was deepening. The memories of the assassinations of Robert F. Kennedy and Martin Luther King Jr. were still fresh. The anarchy at Woodstock was too.

Even the role of athlete-activist that King embraced (and that Navratilova and Evert would reprise, in a different way) was new and controversial.

The Slims tour was founded just two years after the Black Power salute by African-American athletes at the 1968 Mexico City Summer Olympics, and just three years after Muhammad Ali was stripped of the heavyweight title and banned from boxing for refusing to fight in Vietnam. Some of the leading sportswriters of the day wrote unsparingly of King and Heldman's battles against the tennis establishment. During Wimbledon 1971, *Times of London* sportswriter Rex Bellamy harrumphed, "Here is another example of the game's servants attempting to assume the status of its masters."

On nearly every front, women's roles were being reconsidered and rewritten. But King didn't run from being aligned with feminists, as young Evert and Australia's Margaret Court did. To King, the battles were connected.

In the early 1970s, King marched in the streets with women's groups and played tennis exhibitions to help them raise money. In 1973, she helped found the first women's players' union, the Women's Tennis Association. In 1975, she and her husband Larry started World Team Tennis and persuaded most of the sport's stars to play side by side on coed teams. "Everything equal, see?" says King. She started the first women's sports magazine in 1975 too, reasoning that if the predominately male sports media wouldn't cover women athletes, she'd start a publication. "How else would people know what we sound like, what we look like, what we think, what we feel?" she says.

King was among the celebrities and activists who signed a prochoice petition that appeared in *Ms.* magazine in 1972, admitting that she had had an abortion. She got hate mail for weeks calling her a "killer." (*Roe v. Wade,* the landmark Supreme Court decision that legalized abortion in the United States, wasn't handed down until the following year, 1973.)

King testified persuasively on Capitol Hill for the passage of Title IX, the watershed 1972 federal law that paved the way for unprecedented access to college athletic scholarships for women, which weren't available to King when she was making Wimbledon finals but had been available to Larry. When they both played for California State at Los Angeles, Larry had all his expenses paid despite being the self-described seventh man on his six-man college team. Billie Jean was forced to pay her own way and get by on the hundred dollars a week she earned as a playground instructor. After she and Larry were married in 1965, Billie Jean helped put him through law school using her shamateur earnings, which she said never topped $7,000 a year.

Active as she was, King also candidly revealed what she disliked about the women's movement. She recoiled at the sometime absolutism or stridency she said she saw. "I *like* men," she said.

King enjoyed her friendship with women's leader Gloria Steinem but sometimes felt the women's movement was too abstract, too intellectualized, not action-oriented enough. In one particularly animated discussion in the early 1970s, King told Steinem, "Gloria, you're not using us right! Gloria, we're the ones! We can sell this movement! We're on TV. We sweat. We're real. We're fun! C'mon, let's figure this out! We're out here doing and proving all these same things that so many of you are only talking about. You guys keep thinking from the neck up, and it's the whole body—the whole body—that makes women powerful. And empowered."

Some years later, King passed Steinem on her way to the microphone at a banquet for the Women's Sports Foundation, another organization King helped found.

Steinem, knowing it would delight King, whispered, "Hey, Billie, guess what? I'm working out now!"

"*Yes!*" King said, tossing back her head to laugh.

As much as King attracted censure because of ways she dared to challenge the status quo, what prodded her more reluctant peers—even Evert—to join her was the dawning realization that their existence didn't necessarily improve as they sat out the gender and culture wars.

The experiences King spoke about were shared by all the women in ways big and small. Rosie Casals says, "The idea of a woman being a breadwinner was still new to people then." Jeanie Brinkman, the Slims tour publicity director, recalls being given strange looks on airplanes simply because she carried a briefcase. "That was something most women just didn't do yet," Brinkman recalls.

Julie Heldman never considered herself the out-front activist her mother, Gladys, and Billie Jean were. Yet Julie remembers being taken aback when Will Grimsley, a sportswriter for the Associated Press, sought her out the day after King defaulted during their match at the 1973 U.S. Open. "I was still flying really high because I had won," Heldman says. "Then Will Grimsley walked up to me and said, 'Were you wearing a bra yesterday?' It was one of the biggest wins of my career. And that's what he wanted to know."

Women athletes had become used to being treated with condescension or derided as mannish freaks, arrested tomboys, or some exaggerated horde of closeted lesbians. The players on the tennis tour who were lesbians had long gotten used to seeing the pronounced bigotry against them portrayed as some gross infringement of the heterosexual players' rights, not theirs. The greater crime seemed to be that the straight women players were being called lesbians too.

Grace Lichtenstein says it's hard to convey now how deeply entrenched such attitudes were, or how radical the women's tennis players' breakaway to start their own tour seemed. They were not only reaching for sports superstardom—that province previously limited to men. As Lichtenstein wrote, "They were defying all the false tenets of femininity that had plagued me and so many other girls. As a kid growing up in the 1950s, I accepted the concept of women athletes as freaks. I had been taught that to want to become an athlete of any kind was unacceptable. Girls were passive, noncompetitive, dependent. The notion of a sexy woman athlete was a contradiction."

Even Evert, apolitical and exalted for her femininity as she was, caught flak within a year of her debut for being too driven, too "calculating," too "cold." Tennis coverage of the day was routinely colored with descriptions of Margaret Court's "near virile" serve, Nancy Richey's "tomboy style," and King's alleged bitterness at not being born a boy.

Jim Murray, the *Los Angeles Times* Pulitzer Prize–winning columnist, once wrote: "King has never forgiven Nature for the dirty trick it played on her in preventing her from being a safety for the Green Bay Packers."

The idea that the women players weren't trying to be ersatz men—they were simply pursuing something they loved—was a distinction that was often lost. When *Sports Illustrated* writer Edward "Bud" Shrake was assigned to write about the two-year-old women's tour in 1972, he felt it important to assure readers that the players were "an amazingly good-looking group of people, especially when one thought of the stereotype of the woman athlete. Nobody had a beard. Nobody looked or sounded like Ernest Borgnine. . . . Nobody waddled. Not a lumberjack in the group."

Julie Heldman, a Stanford University graduate who later became a lawyer, a mother, and a U.S. Court of Appeals clerk, was one of the sharper wits and more sophisticated women on the pro tour. She was a top ten player who adored traveling the world. But when she began to tally up the cues she received from society, she felt frustrated. "All my life I've been programmed to quit. In high school, people said, 'When are you going to quit?' In college, they were saying, 'When are you going to quit and get married and have kids?' "

Swedish player Ingrid Bentzer, the first secretary of the Women's Tennis Association, is an accomplished woman who speaks seven languages. Constantly having to defend her femininity, she says, was wearying. "Back then, so many things could prick you. The most *stupid* things would come up. I always remember with my first husband . . . he had a girlfriend before me with skin like porcelain. She always smelled like perfume. And here I was, I smelled of BenGay liniment and I had calluses on my hands. I thought, 'Ahhhh, Bentzer—you're a jock.' As a woman, you'd get put into these funny, funny positions. Nowadays it's easy to look back and say, 'Well, that treatment was *crap!*' But at the time . . ."

At the time, many women faced with censure or rejection did quit. Others got discouraged about the fight for such contested terrain. Then along came Billie Jean King, jerking a thumb in her fellow players' direction and brazenly saying, "Follow me."

Given the resistance that King and her fellow female athletes faced, Bobby Riggs's male chauvinist pig act before the Battle of the Sexes match doesn't seem like a total farce but, rather, a cartoonish exaggeration of the prevailing attitudes of the time. The notion of "political correctness" hadn't been invented. Some British sportswriters still described Evonne Goolagong, the Aborigine Australian champion, as a "dancing delightful chocolate drop" in print. During the run-up to King's match against Riggs, one of Riggs's press conference stunts involved holding up a T-shirt with a large hole cut out for each nipple.

"I thought Billie Jean would look better in this than me," Riggs cracked.

Riggs himself wasn't politically minded. He was an inveterate hustler, a goofy showman chasing a paycheck, a podium-pounding quote machine. He had the added cachet of having already beaten Margaret Court, then the top-ranked woman in the world, in May of 1973 in a match that became known as the Mother's Day Massacre. Talented as Court was, she was notorious for choking. She accepted the match with Riggs for the $10,000 payday after King repeatedly turned him down, but was overcome by the hype for the novel match. Court admitted she played "in a daze." She lost briskly, 6–2, 6–1. Afterward King felt she had to play Riggs to restore honor to the women's tour. (Riggs tried to lure Evert into a showdown too, but Jimmy Evert said no.)

King has always had an amazing prescience, an uncanny knack for recognizing the importance of events even as they are happening. She would pick her paths and stick to them. But as much as King kept up a brave public face as she championed her causes, she says she often privately wept about her "tough bitch" label.

Over the years, King and Riggs went back and forth about the meaning of their Battle of the Sexes showdown. King would always say, "It was about *social change*, Bobby. It wasn't about a hustle. Don't you understand? This was historical, what you and I did." A day or two before Riggs died in 1995, King says she called to check on him. "One of the last things he ever said to me, in a very weak voice, was 'We did make a difference, didn't we?' Then I said, 'I love you.' And he said he loved me."

In time, King came to regard her 1971 U.S. Open semifinal showdown against sixteen-year-old Chris Evert as more important than her clash against Riggs. Few experts would agree. Both Bud Collins of the *Boston Globe* and Neil Amdur of the *New York Times* maintain that an Evert win over King that day would've simply been more great theater, not a deathblow for the nascent women's tour.

But even if it was King's own inflated sense of self-drama that sparked her panic attack the morning she was scheduled to play Evert, there was no disputing the elevating effect it had on King's performance. As King stood in the shower, wracked by her anxiety-induced sobs, she watched the water swirl down the drain and thought it was the perfect metaphor for the match she was about to play.

"My head started going through the history of what we'd done," King says, "and I just felt if I lost to Chris, everything we had tried to build was going to go down the drain. They'll say, 'Amateur Wins U.S. Open' and 'She's better than professionals.' Then we could not or might not have had our own tour. And if we don't have a tour, we are screwed, we are finished. I thought, 'I have to win. I have to win this match.' It's one of the hardest moments I ever had. The only time I cried about a match before or since."

Before long, the force of King's personality would have such an effect on Evert that Evert disciplined herself not to look at her across the net. King stood a mere five feet six, but her eyes burned like ingots; she was given to histrionics. She would work herself into such a seething pitch during matches that Evert admittedly came to experience her as "physically overwhelming" and "definitely intimidating."

But that wasn't true yet when they met at the 1971 U.S. Open. As they made their ceremonial walk from the women's locker room to the stadium court, Evert thought King meant it as a gesture of friendship when she told her, "You're riding the crest of a wave. Enjoy it while you can."

King was one of a few women players who had introduced herself to Evert and acted kindly to her during her giant-killing tournament run. Unbeknownst to Evert, King had also called a meeting of her fellow players earlier in the tournament—"Yep," King booms with that trademark, explosive laugh of hers, "another meeting! HAH!"—and chided them for giving young Evert the cold shoulder.

"I said, 'All right, you guys. How many of you said hi to Chris Evert?' " King recalls. "A couple of them said, 'Well, *she's* not very nice . . . She's such a snob . . . She's standoffish too.' I said, 'You guys, she is *sixteen years old*! And I don't even care how she behaves. We are older. We welcome the younger players. Didn't we talk about doing all this work to give the younger generations an opportunity? Look at her—she is *it*! You are going to be passing the baton to her. She is our next star! We have *got* to have her. So I don't even care if you like her. It's not about "like," it's about doing the right thing. And besides, *I* like her.' "

Then King told them: "What you guys are really upset about is, she's kicking our asses."

True to form, Evert didn't play like some stagestruck schoolgirl once she and King strode out and chair umpire Florence Blanchard leaned into the microphone and said, *"Miss Evert has won the toss and has elected to serve first.*

"Linesmen ready.

"Players, play."

With jets droning overhead from nearby LaGuardia Airport and the overflow crowd bursting into thunderous cheers every time Evert hit a good shot, she coolly rallied from a 0–40 deficit in the first game of the match to hold serve. She snatched the first two points off King's serve too. But King stiffened and smacked an ace. She outlasted Evert in a long rally to even the match. Then King celebrated by baring her teeth and screaming, "YEAH!" She slammed down her extra service ball and began pacing in a circle, three times around, like some caged cat at the zoo.

There was no conspicuous turning point, no glaring blunder that decided the match. Evert hit her share of passing shots and winners. But King, always a superb tactician, kept dinking back replies, making Evert generate her own pace on ground strokes. She pressured Evert enough to cause Evert's defensive lobs to float just long. Though normally a serve-and-volleyer, King stayed on baseline more than Evert anticipated, denying Evert a chance to find her rhythm and refusing to give her a target to lace her passing shots by.

The only hint of tension or frustration from Evert was the way she kept very deliberately tucking a long strand of bangs behind her ear, as if remaining calm enough to do that required some monumental act of self-control. A few times Evert muttered to herself following a mistake. On changeovers, Evert was often on the court before King, standing on the baseline, waiting, with one hand on her hip as if she was ready to get on with things.

But that was it.

King won 6–3, 6–2. But neither player really lost that day. Evert went home to Fort Lauderdale to a hero's welcome from her classmates at St. Thomas Aquinas High. The mayor of Fort Lauderdale sent her roses. She was trailed the next day at school by a reporter and photographer from *Life* magazine. And King—Madame Superstar, the self-described Old Lady—sent a congratulatory telegram to Evert during the unrelenting rains that delayed the women's final. King wrote, "When you left New York, the skies opened up and it poured rain. The heavens weren't happy you were gone."

"You know," Evert says, her eyes welling up with tears thirty-three years later, "Billie didn't have to do that."

King did it because she could. When the skies cleared, she beat Rosie Casals to win the U.S. Open final, then rolled to the Slims' next tournament stop feeling almost giddy. King thought, "After all our work to start a tour, we're going to be okay. A star was born this week."

CHAPTER THREE

ONE DREAM YOU WERE ALLOWED TO HAVE

As instantly impressed as King had been with Evert's game and comportment in 1971, she was thunderstruck by sixteen-year-old Martina Navratilova's raw athletic talent two years later when Navratilova arrived on the women's tour. On her first trip to England for Wimbledon that year, Navratilova watched her idol, King, and Rosie Casals pull up at a warm-up tournament outside London in a flashy car. Navratilova just stood there, staring, as the two stars swept by without noticing her. "This really is the big time," Navratilova thought.

Navratilova had never seen grass courts before she arrived in England. Wimbledon was the tournament she had always dreamed of as a child. When she finally walked inside the All England Club's black iron gates, she kneeled and touched the venerated turf. "I used to think the grass would be like it is on the soccer field," she marveled. "I never knew it would be knitted so close and short."

By then, Navratilova was acutely sensitive to the different quality of life beyond the iron curtain. She had made her first border crossing three years earlier, at age thirteen, to play a junior tournament in West Germany. When she returned home she began to notice for the first time how sad people really were. "They couldn't say or write or even read what they wanted," she said. "To get a pair of shoes was a major accomplishment. People had to wait in line for potatoes and pay the butcher under the table for decent meat."

Her first trip to America in 1973 stirred something even deeper in her. The vastness of the country and the seemingly infinite possibilities exerted a magnetic pull on her. "In America, it's like the sky is the limit—you are your own limit," she said.

Because the Czech tennis federation insisted that Navratilova play her first year on the short-lived women's tour that the USTA had started, and not the rival Slims tour, Navratilova didn't get to know Billie Jean King well until the following spring of 1974. At a tournament in Detroit, King paused to watch Navratilova practice and hustled over to give her some unsolicited advice on her backhand volley. Navratilova was thrilled.

Sometime later, the two of them shared a quiet car ride, and King told Martina something that shocked her.

"You know, you could be the greatest player ever," King said.

Navratilova stammered, "Really?" She was driving the car and she stole a look at King. Navratilova was still carrying the twenty extra pounds she had gained during her first visit to America. She did not look like a world-beater.

"Yeah, Martina, you could be the best player ever—I mean in the history of the game," King said. "God has given you this extraordinary talent. You're an amazing athlete. But if you don't work hard you are not going to make it."

"Are you serious?" Navratilova said, still studying King's face and waiting for the punch line.

"I am serious." King nodded. "Just think about it."

Then they fell silent again.

Emboldening moments like her conversation with King had begun to color Navratilova's thinking by the summer of 1975. The remarks about Navratilova's athletic ability and promise had become a familiar refrain. Some of the biggest names in tennis had noticed her.

Navratilova had been a fifteen-year-old alternate for Sparta, the most prestigious club team in Prague, riding the bench behind three more experienced players, when Jan Kodes, then Czechoslovakia's best player, surprised club officials by choosing Navratilova to be his mixed doubles partner in a decisive national league competition that was tied. "They said, 'Are you nuts'?" Kodes recalls. "But I said, 'I want Navratilova. I'd rather play with someone who is good near the net, who can smash well.' And we won [the decisive match]."

A year later, Australian champion Rod Laver saw Navratilova at a 1973 tournament in Toronto and told people she could be great someday, a compliment that rang in Navratilova's ears for months.

Navratilova returned to the professional tour in the spring of 1974 and won her first professional title in Orlando. She was so excited, she impulsively embraced a light pole near her courtside chair because, she said, there was nobody she knew well enough to hug. Before the year was over, Navratilova collected notable victories over some big names: Margaret Court, Evonne Goolagong, and Virginia Wade.

Still, Navratilova hadn't accomplished anything approaching the instant and unbroken success of her contemporary, Evert. Evert, then nineteen, was already a contender for the number one ranking in the world. Evert still resided on another plane. But Navratilova caught her attention. Navratilova's serve and her heavy ground strokes felt like cannonballs when they hit Evert's racket strings. Navratilova's backhand was flawed, but she already excelled at plucking off passing shot attempts and turning them into point-saving volleys. "I remember thinking she was the first young girl that came along who I thought had more talent than me," Evert recalls. "Thank God her backhand was still weak then."

What drove the robust early praise about Navratilova was the idea of what she might do, as well as the visceral sense she conveyed to anyone who watched her play. Yes, she was still raw and emotionally combustible, but here was a female tennis player somehow different and more physically gifted than anyone who had come before.

Mary Carillo was a high school junior in Douglaston, New York, and still a few years removed from her own tour debut when she saw Navratilova play for the first time at Forest Hills during the summer of 1974. "I remember watching her, transfixed," Carillo says.

Carillo, who is six months younger than Navratilova, had always yearned to play like Maria Bueno, the smooth Brazilian star of the 1960s with beautiful, fluid strokes. "I grew up very big on smooth, the art of it—that was a big deal to me," Carillo says. "I loved Billie Jean too, of course. Billie wanted to look like a dancer out there. She loved dance and she loved to study form and she was very aware of what she looked like in the air. Billie would finish shots and she wanted to look a certain way. That's a different mind-set and aesthetic from Martina's.

"There was something in your face about Martina rushing an opponent, even more so than Billie, even though they both played serve-and-volley. Martina was very choppy and harsh. With Martina, things happened in a hurry. It was percussive, frenetic, more of a jackhammer style. She'd be hitting these approach shots, just chipping and charging, and she'd sweep into shots, sort of take in the court as she ran in, lifting volleys off her feet. And I remember thinking right then that I had to change my idea about what I wanted to look like.

"I was kinda gangly," Carillo says. "I could not play like Martina. But I remember thinking, 'There's the prototype. There's the modern player.' It looked right, like, 'That's the way it's *supposed* to be.' "

Navratilova's two abbreviated seasons on the women's tours had given her a realistic idea of both her competition and her potential by the time she and her stepfather Mirek Navratil took their walk along the Berounka River in the summer of 1975. They were talking intently as they passed the stone and stucco houses in their village, by the trout fishermen casting near the banks, and on up toward Brdy Mountain, where they had often picked mushrooms and blueberries in the summer.

Navratilova was scheduled to leave for the 1975 U.S. Open the next morning. She was eighteen. She was fed up with her treatment by Czech sports officials. And she was talking to Mirek about defecting.

For Mirek, who married Navratilova's mother, Jana, when Martina was five, the conversation with Martina about defecting was intensely bittersweet.

Navratilova liked to joke that Mirek actually knew her before he met her mother. Martina was just three years old and running around the clay courts of her mother's tennis club in Revnice with a sawed-off racket that once belonged to her grandmother. Seeing Mirek pushing a wheelbarrow to help repair the courts, she ran over and hopped in. "Gimme a ride," she said. Mirek did. Soon he and Martina's mother were talking. They were both recreational players who had come to the modest five-court tennis club in Revnice that day to help with the spring cleaning. Jana had divorced Martina's biological father earlier that year. Before long, she and Mirek began dating. They were married two years later, and Mirek took such great interest and pride in Martina's life and her tennis game, she came to call him her father, not her stepfather.

It was Mirek who helped Navratilova believe she could be a great player or anything she wanted to be, and Mirek who would drive Martina to youth tournaments on the back of his motorbike, hours each way. (Navratilova's family never had enough money to buy a car until she bought them one with what she saved from the seventeen-dollar per diem the Czech federation gave her during her first two years on tour. At the time, she still wasn't allowed to keep any prize money.) It was also Mirek who landed nine-year-old Martina an important audition in Prague with her first coach, a former Czech Davis Cup player, George Parma, the entrée that launched Navratilova's tennis career.

Parma had told Mirek he was very busy and had little time for new players. But once he began to hit with Martina, the tryout stretched on for a half hour. When he strode over to Mirek to give him his verdict, Martina ran over to join them.

"I think we can do something with her," Parma said.

Soon, twice a week after school, Navratilova would take her racket and board a train from Revnice to Prague, transfer to a street-car, then make a two-mile walk to her practices at Klamkova Park, which had the only covered courts in the region. Her grandmother, Andela Subertova, lived just a few minutes' walk from the courts. Martina would often stay there on Friday nights, doing crossword puzzles with her grandmother and following her orders to eat her carrot salad because it would improve her eyesight for tennis.

Navratilova was offered the coveted invitation to train at the Sparta club after she won a state junior championship in 1972. It was a step up in competition. There, she had a chance to play alongside Kodes and receive coaching from Vera Sukova, a 1962 Wimbledon finalist.

Now, as she and Mirek walked and talked along the Berounka River just three years later, it seemed as if Mirek had helped her pursue her tennis dream so successfully, he might never see her again.

The cold war showed no signs of ending. Life under Czecho-slovakia's Communist regime was a stifling web of restraints. Tennis federation officials and their superiors at the national sports ministry were consistently leaning on Navratilova to play here, stay there, follow the rules, limit whom she talked to. Neither Mirek nor Jana were Communist Party members, a particular point of defiance for Jana, whose parents had been ordered by the Russians to surrender their thirty-acre family estate after World War II and move in 1948 into a smaller, two-story cement house they were forced to share with an unrelated family occupying the first floor.

"I hate Communism," Jana said.

Martina was born on October 18, 1956. She and her mother were living in one room on the second floor of the house when Mirek joined them, and they remained there when her younger sister, Jana, was born in June of 1963. Navratilova's grandparents lived in the other room on the second floor. The family estate they had lost had had its own clay tennis court and acres of apple orchards. The house they were forced to share lacked hot running water until Martina was twelve. Until then, everyone had to heat water for their baths on a coal stove.

The displacement of Navratilova's family by the Communists was not unique. Such things happened frequently throughout the Eastern Bloc. Nonetheless, says *New York Times* columnist George Vecsey, coauthor of Navratilova's 1985 autobiography, *Martina,* the confiscation of her mother's family property, heaped atop the other realities of life in the Soviet Bloc, left Martina with an ingrained sense of injustice—even entitlement. "She may not have had hot water until whenever, but the memory of having nice things goes beyond that," Vecsey says. "On her mother's side, they once had money. They used to look at that house with other people living in it with bitterness. It was part of their family heritage. And there was this sense in Martina, from a very early age, that things *did* belong to her, that she deserved to have certain things in life economically, psychologically."

That sense only heightened in Navratilova when she experienced something as galvanizing for her as the loss of the family home had been in 1948 to her mother and grandparents.

This time, the year was 1968.

For any Czech who was alive on August 21, 1968, the details of where they were and what they were doing are as indelibly imprinted as Americans' recollections of the moment they heard that President John F. Kennedy was shot. Martina's Sparta teammate,

Czech tennis star Jan Kodes, was fast asleep at his home in Prague, knowing he had an important league match in Stromovka the next day against Jan Kukal, his towering Davis Cup teammate. At four a.m., the telephone rang and Kodes's wife stirred and answered it.

"Are you kidding? Are you sure?" she said, suddenly wide awake.

"Let's sleep—I am playing Kukal tomorrow," Kodes protested. "Then my wife said, 'The Russians are here.' So we went to a window. We pulled the curtains apart. We lived in a corner building on a riverbank, near the Hlavkuv bridge. There is this parking lot by the Hlavkuv bridge, and I looked out of the window and the parking lot was full of tanks. They were moving across the bridge."

"Shut the window! Shut the curtains! HIDE!" Kodes's father-in-law yelled when Jan took another peek out the window. "When the soldiers get scared and see that, they start shooting," his father-in-law said.

Navratilova was roused from her bed that morning and given an equally stern warning. She was just eleven and staying at a friend's house in Pilsen, a town near the West German border. Navratilova had gone there to play a junior tournament. At six o'clock that morning her friend's father called home and warned them to stay inside. On his way to work he had seen Russian tanks in the streets and soldiers controlling the highways.

For Czechs, the news of the 1968 invasion was gut-wrenching. It was hope-smothering. The year had begun with such great promise. Reform-minded party official Alexander Dubcek had succeeded Antonin Novotny as the Communist Party leader in January. In February, the underdog Czech hockey team had defeated the Soviet Union, 5–4, at the Winter Olympics in Grenoble, sending thousands of Czechs pouring into the streets to celebrate. Navratilova, who played ice hockey each winter when the Berounka River froze, knew the names of all the Olympic heroes by heart.

By April, Dubcek had published an action program affirming his intention to provide "socialism with a human face." In late June, censorship was officially abolished in Czechoslovakia. The very next day, there was great excitement over the publication of "The 2,000 Words," a statement penned by dissident writer Ludvik Vaculik and signed by seventy prominent Czechs, calling for peaceful change.

Taken all together, that stretch of Czech history came to be known as the Prague Spring. Though Navratilova was only a school-girl, she noticed the stirrings on the streets when she traveled to the city for her lessons with George Parma. "You would have to have been deaf, dumb, and blind to miss what was going on," she wrote in her autobiography. "People were trying to recapture the old en-ergy they used to have before the war. There was a feeling of excite-ment in the air. People were holding mass open-air meetings in the town square, promising to work harder to help rebuild Czecho-slovakia, wanting only some small incentive, some reward, some freedom. Sometimes you'd go out in the morning and all the Russian banners would be turned around on the buildings as a modest protest."

To blunt the rising Czech nationalism, Soviet party leaders stepped up their rhetoric and actions. Dubcek took note and cooled his. The state-run Czech newspapers began to print stories heralding the good works of the Communist Party and exhuming old tales of the Russians liberating Czechoslovakia from the Nazis at the end of World War II. Czech leaders were summoned to Moscow and warned not to encourage any more foment, then sent back home. Communist Party rallies were organized; attendance by workers was expected. The Soviets ran military exercises in Sumava, Czecho-slovakia, in July.

"There was a lot of talk that the Russians would come in," Navratilova said. "But we never believed it would come to that."

Then on that August morning the country rose to the horrible growl of tanks, their treads noisily grinding up the roads, their tur-reted guns turning menacingly toward anyone who dared to sling a rock or a taunt their way. "Nobody was shooting where I was," Navratilova said, "but you had the feeling it could start any minute." Wenceslas Square in Prague, the city's historic central gath-ering spot, was pockmarked from mortar shells launched by Soviet tanks when thousands of people gathered during the first day of the invasion near the National Museum. Dubcek pleaded for calm.

When Mirek was finally able to get to Pilsen a few days later on his motorbike to pick up Martina, she wrapped her arms around his waist—tight—for the harrowing ride they made home. They picked their way for hours over the rutted roads, past the soldiers with machine guns and the Russians' loud, heavy machinery. Martina made part of the ride tucked inside Mirek's overcoat.

"It was just depressing to see everything," Navratilova said. "The countryside being ruined by these frigging tanks that came out of nowhere. Our lives were changed for good—well, not for 'good,' but forever. And I just remember being absolutely livid and feeling helpless and mad at the same time. And there was nothing you could do. Being an eleven-year-old girl, what can you do?"

Many Czech writers and historians have tried to capture the grimness and pathos of their closed society during those years. Vaclav Havel, the dissident writer who rose to president after being jailed several times before Communist rule ended in 1989, has written eloquently about the "entropy" of life under Communist oppression and the countless ways in which every man and woman is subjected to "a prolonged and thorough process of violation, enfeeblement and anesthesia." Others mentioned overwhelming feelings of timelessness, of hopelessness, numbing depression and haunting paranoia. Even as president, Havel used to carry what he called "an emergency packet" when he left the house each morning, just in case he was arrested and thrown in jail by political foes. All it contained were small comforts: cigarettes, a fresh T-shirt, a few books, a toothbrush and toothpaste, a laxative, and soap.

Navratilova has spoken achingly of 1968. She said she suddenly saw her country lose its vibrancy, its soul. When she and Mirek arrived home from Pilsen, she found everyone worried about what the Russians might do next. She eventually learned that her beloved coach, Parma, who had entranced her with stories about his tennis adventures outside Czechoslovakia, and the exploits of 1954 Wimbledon champion and Czech star Jarolsav Drobny, happened to be in Austria the day the Russians invaded. Parma decided to stay there.

For Navratilova, a girl whose biological father had stopped his sporadic visits to her a few years earlier, it was another blow. Not long after the Soviets invaded, Navratilova defeated a Russian girl in a tournament. When they shook hands at the net, Navratilova told her, "You need a tank to beat me."

Relying on instructions that Parma mailed him, Mirek took over Martina's training until she was invited to join Sparta. Mirek would practice with her and say, "Hit this one back now and imagine that you're playing Wimbledon."

"Wimbledon," says Martina, "was one dream you were allowed to have."

Navratilova had earned her first chance to compete abroad on the women's tour just months before Rod Laver tabbed her a rising star. She had captured her first Czech women's national championship in an upset over Kodes's sister, Denisa Vopickova, who had held the title eight years.

During her first few trips to the United States and a few European events in 1973, Navratilova found herself instantly drawn to Americans—their freedom, their ambition, their spirit. One of the first U.S. tennis players Navratilova met was Vitas Gerulaitis, the long-haired, blond, Brooklyn-born bon vivant. She thought, "Are all Americans like *him?*"

Navratilova always had a facility for languages, and she quickly set out to improve her English, picking up words and phrases from commercials and cartoons and then trying out the ones she liked in casual conversation: "I can't believe I ate the whole thing." "I'm on a seafood diet—when I see food, I eat it. Ha ha ha."

For Navratilova, the change of pace from Czechoslovakia, the intoxicating bursts of liberty, during her travels were dizzying.

She and Betsy Nagelsen, a sometime opponent and doubles partner, hit it off immediately. Navratilova stayed with Nagelsen and her parents on a 1974 tournament swing through Florida and was happy to find that Nagelsen's exuberance for sports matched hers. When the two of them weren't playing tennis, they were cannonballing into the pool or playing catch with a football and trying to see who could hit the streetlamps with a toss. "Martina was very popular with everyone as a kid, and so much fun, like, 'Life, gosh! There's just so much to do!' " Nagelsen says.

Nagelsen remembers Evert as a polar opposite. "When Chris and her mom came to stay with us during tournaments, Chris was perfectly happy to get her magazines and curl up on the side of the couch," Nagelsen says with a laugh. "I'd say, 'Chris, let's go play football!' It would be, 'No, thanks. I'm happy right here.' "

Navratilova's wide-eyed enthusiasm was endearing. Virginia Slims tour director Peachy Kellmeyer once traveled with Navratilova to Florida immediately after Navratilova had won a fur coat at a Chicago indoor tournament. "It looked like dog fur—God, it was ugly," Kellmeyer says. "It was the ugliest. But Martina was so darn proud of that coat she insisted on wearing it our whole flight to Florida and during the cab ride to my mom's home."

When Navratilova won her first car at another Florida tournament, Virginia Slims publicity director Jeanie Brinkman happened to look out her hotel room window and see an overjoyed Navratilova driving around the empty parking lot in circles. Laughing now, Brinkman says, "We finally had to say, 'Martina, it's time to come in now. That's enough.' "

Despite their differences, Navratilova and Evert quickly developed a budding friendship. Evert, still a very correct Catholic schoolgirl, instantly liked Navratilova when they exchanged hellos at Navratilova's first American tournament. They spoke a few weeks later at another event in St. Petersburg, Florida. Though Navratilova's memory of that second encounter was one of surprise—she couldn't believe Evert noticed her and said hello—Evert, laughing, says she couldn't have missed Navratilova.

"There might have been a thousand people milling around that day," Evert says, "and there's Martina walking around in the crowd in this one-piece bathing suit with these crazy tan lines going here and here and there, still twenty-five pounds overweight, eating a Popsicle. She was just oblivious, not even caring. Just as fresh and raw and naive and vulnerable as ever. And I was horrified for her. I thought, 'Oh my God! I wouldn't ever get in a bathing suit in front of even five people by a pool!' But she was just not self-conscious at all. That was my first impression. I thought, 'Wow. That girl's got guts.' And I just chuckled. It was cute. I mean, it was just a really cute impression that I had of her at that time."

Other Czech players who were allowed out of the country were far more inhibited than Navratilova. They were far more hesitant to defy orders or cut loose, or test the limits of what was permissible. "I did not dare," Kodes says. Hana Mandlikova, who is six years younger than Navratilova, was shocked and deeply suspicious when she ventured out on tour. Americans or Westerners often asked her questions that would've been considered intemperate or even dangerous to answer back home.

"People from other countries didn't know any better, and it's so hard to explain, even now," says Mandlikova. "At the start, I hated America. It was so different. People were so open, so brash, which is great, but I wasn't used to it. When I got used to it, I felt wonderful. You were free. You could be friendly. You didn't have to hide everything. But where I grew up, people talked with only their closest friends about politics or what you didn't like. No one knew who was spying on whom."

After the Soviet crackdown in 1968, everyday life for Czechs became even more constricted. Many who signed petitions supporting "The 2,000 Words" were punished. Doctors were forced into jobs digging ditches. Intellectuals were jailed. Vaclav Havel survived by working for a time at a brewery. More than 100,000 people, many of them Czechoslovakia's best and brightest, defected in the first twelve months alone, a brain drain that was felt for decades. Czech tennis players who traveled outside the country were accompanied to Grand Slam tournaments by supervisors, who were ordered to watch and write reports: With whom did players socialize? Where did they go? What was discussed?

Jan Kodes says that the players often traveled alone to minor tournaments but had to sign statements before leaving, promising to report anything "extraordinary." Athletes' passports were confiscated after each trip abroad and kept at a central office, then reissued just before they left for their next event. Travel permits had to be requested for each trip.

Every Czech athletic contest against the Soviet Union became freighted with even more political meaning. Every soccer victory was hailed; every Olympic triumph became legend. When Soviet tennis players came to Prague in 1971 to play Davis Cup, police and plainclothes security patrolled the grandstands to discourage trouble. Kodes says that he had a splitting tension headache throughout the two-day competition. He barely slept. Much of his first pressure-packed match against the Soviet number one, Alex Metreveli, was played in a steady rain and medieval gloom. When Kodes stroked a good shot the crowd at the I Czechoslovak Lawn Tennis Klub burst into ear-splitting cheers. When he lost a point, the Czech fans shrieked and slapped their foreheads.

"With Russia, it is a deep thing," Kodes says.

Kodes won two of his three matches to lead Czechoslovakia to victory that weekend. When he arrived at Wimbledon a few weeks later he wasn't surprised to learn that the two Russians he defeated had been kept home. Kodes knew how the system worked. He was also older, married, and more willing to navigate the shoals than Navratilova, who was ten years his junior. Kodes was traveling on the men's tour full-time when Navratilova started playing the women's tour, and it wasn't long before stories of her impetuous behavior floated back to him.

"If we go back to politics," Kodes explains, "there were two wings at the time: one represented the government and the other the Communist Party. The government wing wanted success and progress. The Party wing was ideological: 'Chop off heads. Prohibitions. Set examples for the youth. Foreign cars and rock 'n' roll are bad.' These were two extremes, and these two wings were fighting hard. That means that they caused each other trouble out of spite.

"Back then, they were fighting over Navratilova," Kodes says.

Navratilova broke the Socialist rules of travel almost from the start. She refused to limit her fraternizing to other Czechs or Eastern European players. Antonin Bolardt, a high-ranking sports official and Czech Davis Cup captain, griped, "Martina is avoiding the collective—she is friends with the girls from the West, those Americans." In 1974, Navratilova accepted an invitation to train for a few weeks with Billie Jean King and Rosie Casals in California. Betsy Nagelsen says, "It was funny to watch the transformation in Martina. She went from the girl I met who said, 'Let's go swimming!' to this girl wearing Gucci clothes and gold bracelets and driving fancy cars." Soon Czech officials began to mutter that Navratilova was too "Americanized," that she had her nose in the air.

At the 1974 U.S. Open, tour player Shari Barman introduced Navratilova to her father, Fred Barman, a genial man who had started as a mailroom clerk at Twentieth-Century Fox in Hollywood and worked his way up to become a show business manager. Barman had a lifelong penchant for Bentley cars and a stable of clients that included actors Peter Graves and David Janssen. His daughter Shari, in addition to playing the women's tour, sometimes worked as the assistant pro at the Beverly Hills Hotel, where she was Katharine Hepburn's hitting partner. Shari landed the honor partly because Hepburn liked her wit and partly because Shari conscientiously followed Hepburn's orders, warbled in that distinctive Connecticut Yankee voice, to keep the ball near her, for God's sake.

"She liked the exercise but didn't like to run," Shari says.

Before long, Martina had become fast friends with the Barmans. Fred Barman helped her negotiate a better financial deal with Czech officials when she turned eighteen. For the first time, Navratilova would keep 80 percent of her winnings and pay the rest to the Czech government as tax. She no longer had to live off the meager seventeen-dollar-a-day per diem she was being paid above hotel expenses, or make trips home carrying thousands of dollars in cash because the Czech officials insisted on receiving her prize money in American hard currency. (Hana Mandlikova, who began playing abroad at fifteen, was so anxious about losing her winnings, she kept the cash in a bag beneath her head while she slept on planes. On trips in and out of the country, she often hid American dollars in her shoes and belt to get past sticky-fingered Czech border guards.)

Navratilova, done with being a cash mule and flush with money for the first time, started to buy things like jewelry. Lots of it. In Los Angeles, some players took her shopping on Rodeo Drive and disco dancing at The Candy Store.

Even in 1975, Czech players didn't control their own schedules. But Navratilova bucked that rule too. In February, she chose to stay in the United States for an extra week to play a tournament in Amelia Island, Florida. She didn't seek official permission. Within days, she received a tearful phone call from her alarmed parents, saying she might be in trouble. Next came a terse telegram from the Czech tennis federation, ordering Navratilova to return immediately. Now Navratilova was scared and crying.

A tournament official intervened on Navratilova's behalf. Navratilova, thinking things were smoothed over, kept playing. She advanced to the final, where she lost to Evert, still a common occurrence. Navratilova flew home hoping her success would earn her a reprieve. But she was called in by federation officials and forced to defend herself.

Threats, not just reprimands, were hurled at her now.

"[Her] staying that extra week was an excuse for them to say her acts were egregious and so on," says Kodes. "The whole problem was that the state wanted to demonstrate its power over the people. Everything was directed by some kind of violence. Small-time officials who wanted to appear important told her, 'We will give you a lesson.' Other officials wanted to show how good they were and possibly write a detailed report on her. Antonin Bolardt started it all because he became the boss of national-level sports. He was building a Communist career. He wanted to please the higher-ups."

Navratilova said all the right things at the disciplinary meeting. Vera Sukova, the Czech women's national team captain and coach who was feeling enormous pressure from her superiors because of Navratilova's behavior, urged her afterward to behave, to play the game.

Navratilova's parents were more distraught. They warned her, "You can't do whatever you want."

"Why not?" Martina said.

Had Navratilova listened to those around her, the escalating tensions might have abated. Her life might have been totally different. "You would have probably never heard of me," she once said. She was accumulating successes at a faster pace now. In 1975 she and Renata Tomanova led Czechoslovakia to its first-ever Federation Cup title, with Sukova as their coach. Navratilova was routinely advancing farther into tournaments too—finally notching her first win over Evert in 1975 in a tense 3–6, 6–4, 7–6 quarterfinal match in Washington, D.C. Navratilova was so nervous on match point, she knocked a volley off her racket frame and sagged with relief when it fluttered over the net for a winner.

Told Navratilova was so excited she didn't sleep at all that night, Shari Barman says, "Chris probably didn't either."

Four weeks later, Navratilova went on a giant-killing run and beat Margaret Court, Virginia Wade, and Australian star Evonne Goolagong in succession at the U.S. Indoor Championships in Boston. Bud Collins, in an impish nod to Navratilova's extra weight, gave her a nickname that stuck: "The Great Wide Hope."

Evert, by now the world's number one player, asked Navratilova to be her doubles partner. Navratilova was flattered and said yes. They were young, traveling the world, and trying to figure out who they were. "We used to discuss everything together then," Evert said. "I used to tell her all about my problems with boyfriends, and we really got to know and care about each other." At a tournament in Philadelphia, Evert and Navratilova shared a pepperoni pizza the night before playing their semifinal against each other. Navratilova narrowly lost, 7–6, 6–4, then practiced with Evert the next morning to help her prepare for the final. "I used to turn to Chris a lot for help and advice in those early years in America, and she was always so understanding," Navratilova said.

In early May, the men's and women's tours both happened to be in Rome on consecutive weeks for the Italian Open. Navratilova and Evert were among a few players who decided to practice together at the Cavalieri Hilton, where they were staying. One day, journeyman pro Dino Martin, the son of the entertainer Dean Martin and a sometime pop singer himself, sidled up to Evert and said, "You know who I really like?"

"Who?" Evert said, her heart fluttering. She had always thought Martin was cute.

"I really like that Martina."

"I looked at him and blurted, '*Really?*' " Evert recalls, laughing at the memory. "What I was really thinking was 'Don't you . . . um . . . like me?' I remember just then, Martina was going by eating a big apple, and there's Dino, who was real strong, looking at her and telling me, 'Yeah, I'm really turned on by those muscles of hers, you know. I'm really turned on by her.' And I was like, 'Okay, okay, okay . . .'

"At that time, Martina still always had this story about having a boyfriend back home in Czechoslovakia. So I said, 'God, Martina, Dino's really cute and he likes you and he wants to go out with you!' " Knowing that actor Desi Arnaz Jr. was Martin's best friend, Evert had what she thought was a brainstorm. She told Navratilova, "Wouldn't it be fun if the four of us went out on a double date?"

The next time Evert and Navratilova were playing in Los Angeles, Martin and Arnaz picked them up in Martin's sports car after Evert had just appeared on *The Dinah Shore Show*. And off the four of them went—to a drive-in movie.

Despite Evert's efforts to play matchmaker and Martin's choice of venue, sparks did not fly. Navratilova and Martin may have been the only dates at the drive-in who actually watched the movie. Navratilova says, "I was still trying to figure out my sexuality then."

Navratilova and Evert's next stop after Rome was the French Open in Paris, the first Grand Slam of the year. Navratilova, just a few months removed from her last chiding from Czech officials, was allowed to compete. But once again she didn't stay with the Czech players, who were put in a hotel forty-five minutes from the tournament. Navratilova was seeded second in the singles draw behind Evert. They were playing doubles together, and Navratilova decided to stay at the same luxury hotel that Evert and many of the other seeded players chose. Evert, who had only a slight awareness of Navratilova's troubles with Czech officials, thought nothing of Navratilova's decision. Navratilova knew the hotel was outlandishly expensive, but she didn't give it a second thought.

"I thought I deserved it," Navratilova said.

When Evert and Navratilova tore to the 1975 French Open finals in both singles and doubles, it was a happy surprise to both of them—especially when they beat Olga Morozova and Julie Anthony for the doubles title, giving Navratilova her first Grand Slam crown of any kind. (It was Evert's fourth.) In the singles final, Navratilova seized the first set from Evert, then faded just as dramatically to a 2–6, 6–2, 6–1 loss. It was the first, but in many ways the most unremarkable, of the fourteen major finals they would play.

Navratilova flew home and was shocked to learn that she was in trouble again—this time because of her lavish hotel arrangements. More threats were made. Czech officials suggested that Navratilova wouldn't be allowed to go to Wimbledon with her parents and sister as planned. Again, permission finally came. But Navratilova was sullen.

"I can't live like this," she said.

Czech officials knew Navratilova had a realistic chance of making the Wimbledon finals in singles, doubles, and mixed doubles with Kodes. Kodes believes they were trying to extend Navratilova an olive branch by allowing her family to join her at Wimbledon. But Navratilova didn't regard the gesture as a concession. Weary of the clashes, she asked Fred Barman to fly from Los Angeles to London and make secret arrangements for her and her entire family to defect in London. And Barman did. The tentative plan was for Navratilova's family to go to the U.S. Embassy when Martina was done playing. As the Wimbledon fortnight went on, however, Barman learned that Navratilova's family was waffling. Martina would play her matches during the day. At night, she and her parents would resume their emotional discussions. When Martina lost in the quarterfinal round to Margaret Court, she and her family quickly had to decide what to do.

"The bottom line was, we chickened out," Martina said.

Hana Mandlikova was playing at the Czech national championships in Pilsen two weeks later, and she vividly recalls the shock that rippled through the tennis facility when Navratilova and her family walked in. "There were stories going around that they had defected," Mandlikova recalls. "People looked as if they had seen a ghost."

Getting permission to leave the country as a family was so rare, Kodes explains, it was almost taken for granted then that anyone who did get out of Czechoslovakia would leave and never come back. Kodes suspects that he earned party officials' trust when he and his wife didn't seek asylum after he fought for her to make a rare trip with him to a 1970 tournament in Japan. Nor did Kodes ever defect.

"The truth is that if someone tried to play a trick on me, took me to Bartolomejska [secret police headquarters], and slapped me a few times, I would do it too," Kodes says. "But I was not brave enough. I did not have a reason that pushed me to emigration. I was born in Prague. I love Prague. My family is there. From 1970 to 1975, that was the peak of my career."

Navratilova's career lay in front of her. After the Pilsen tournament, Vera Sukova called and told Navratilova that she had been yanked from a scheduled trip to France. Soon Czech officials were suggesting that Navratilova might not go to the U.S. Open in a few weeks.

Back at their Sparta club in Prague, Kodes ran into Navratilova's father, Mirek, who told Kodes the news.

"That's nonsense. That's impossible. That's stupid!" Kodes said. "If she is one of our best players, a ban will not solve anything."

Kodes made an appointment to see Antonin Himl, a moderate federation official who ranked just below Martina's chief antagonist, Antonin Bolardt. Five years earlier, in 1970, Himl had supported Kodes's controversial request to be allowed to build a new house with his tournament winnings, pointing out, "Since we allowed Kodes to earn this money, he should be allowed to spend some of it."

"Considering he did this in the presidium of KSC [the Communist Party], you could call this a heroic deed," Kodes says.

What Kodes was about to do now for Navratilova was similarly principled—an act of compassion from one athlete to another, a show of conviction made without regard for his personal risk.

"This is not rational!" Kodes told Himl when Himl received him. "What am I supposed to say? I played mixed doubles with her in the Wimbledon semifinals. I will arrive at the U.S. Open. Someone will ask me where Martina is. Should I say that you did not let her come because she is friends with the Americans? Should I say that she is sick? What?"

Himl replied that there were "behind-the-scenes opinions" that Navratilova would defect. Himl said Navratilova had shown "tendencies" that suggested Billie Jean King, Rosie Casals, and a few other players had an "influence" on her.

"The Western world wants to steal her," Himl said.

"If she is not stolen now, she will be in two, three, or five years," Kodes shot back. "You won't be able to stop it. You would have to lock her up. I consider it nonsense to restrain an athlete like this from her career. She is an extraordinary talent."

Based on Kodes's intervention, Himl—whom Kodes considered a good-hearted man, a sportsman first and Communist apparatchik second—said he would allow Navratilova to go to the U.S. Open, as well as one New York tune-up tournament before that. But Himl set a condition that Navratilova regarded as ominous: she was told that she had to return immediately after the U.S. Open to finish high school. That meant skipping the women's fall tour.

Navratilova, now eighteen, wasn't sure when she'd be allowed out of Czechoslovakia again if she did return. She couldn't know if the Berlin Wall would ever fall or the iron curtain would lift. Choosing to defect in 1975 meant risking never seeing her family or homeland again—a reality that Navratilova was reminded of constantly in coming years.

All of that lay ahead as Martina and Mirek walked along the river the night before she left for the 1975 U.S. Open. Finally, Navratilova said, "I think I want to stay over there."

Mirek said, "I was going to tell you the same thing."

Looking at her, Mirek added, "Don't say a word to your mother. Just go. If you're going to do it, stay there. No matter what we say, don't let us talk you into coming back. We may have a gun to our head when we talk to you on the phone. Someone could be listening.

"Remember," Mirek stressed, "if you go, stay. There is no circumstance under which you'd be able to come back."

CHAPTER FOUR

CHRIS AMERICA

As Navratilova felt pushed to the brink of taking drastic action to ensure her tennis future, Chris Evert had the more pleasant problem of adjusting to instant success and stardom. Evert won twenty-three tournaments in her first three years on the pro tour, still the women's record for the Open era. In 1972, her second season, Evert was already a contender for the number one world ranking that Margaret Court and Billie Jean King had exchanged during the 1960s. But Evert's snowballing popularity was based on her appearance and personality as much as her athletic achievements. She was seen as a welcome respite from the firebrands in her own sport and the at-large feminists of the day. She was still teenaged and wholesome, polite as she was pretty, trained by her no-nonsense father and chaperoned on tour by her doting mother, who seemed to have a smile and a kind word for everyone.

The only people Evert seemed to threaten or dismay were the other women players. "That's true," says Jeanie Brinkman, the Virginia Slims tour publicity director, "but you can't be a women's libber if you're not yet a woman."

The traditional opinions that Evert voiced at the start of her career—"Man is still the breadwinner no matter what the women's libbers say . . . My goal is still to win Forest Hills or Wimbledon, but my greatest goals in life are to have a happy marriage and have some nice kids . . . I don't think the [women's] equal pay protest is a good idea"—were the antithesis of King's philosophical positions and the maverick spirit of the Virginia Slims tour. A great deal was made of Evert's traditional femininity too, and Evert conceded, "I carried it to the hilt. I probably overcompensated . . . I still thought of women athletes as freaks, and I used to hate myself, thinking I must not be a whole woman. The nail polish, the ruffles on my bloomers, the hair ribbons, and not wearing socks—all of that was very important to me. I would not be the stereotyped jock."

Professional women athletes were still treated like strange, mysterious creatures when Evert arrived on tour. The few autobiographies of female athletes, including King's, featured obligatory passages about how menstruation affected athletic performance (the consensus: it depends on the woman) and what women talked about in the locker room as opposed to men (dating, but not sex, Evert maintained in her 1982 autobiography, *Chrissie*).

Margaret Court's politics were even more conservative than the young Evert's. "Margaret makes a great roast lamb, you know," Court's husband, Barry, told a reporter after he and Margaret returned to the tennis tour in 1972, following a break for the birth of their first child. But excepting Court, the early stalwarts of the Slims Tour such as King and Rosie Casals, Betty Stove and Julie Heldman, Ann Jones and Ingrid Bentzer, were independent, strong-minded women who said what they thought and did as they pleased.

"People said it was radical, but it felt normal to me," says Casals, King's most loyal sidekick. When Casals was asked by a male reporter to name the most difficult thing about being a woman athlete, Casals gave him the once-over and deadpanned, "You ever try to play tennis with two apples on your chest?" Told another time that some people considered female athletes unladylike, Casals, who was known to enjoy a good cigar, said without a trace of irony, "If some people say we're unfeminine, well, I say screw 'em."

As much as Evert's early conservatism put her out of step with the progressives in the women's locker room, it put her in near perfect sync with tennis's old guard, the largely country club set that still ran the sport and attended the tournaments. Before the Open era of tennis began in 1968, most tournaments were small affairs hosted by elite private clubs for the enjoyment of their members. The clubs had little interest in heeding King's call to "take tennis to the masses." Tennis was still a boutique operation. Before 1968, professionalism was still a dirty word in the sport, same as it was at the Olympics. Impeccably behaved "gentlemen" champions like Australia's Rod Laver remained the gold standard.

By Evert's arrival three years into the Open era, tennis was changing at breakneck speed. It was a contentious time. The under-the-table payments stopped. The sport was taking off as a full-blown business, and everyone seemed to be grabbing or trying to maintain a piece of the action—the national associations, the tournaments, the players, their newly organized unions, and the agents who began shadowing the athletes like pilot fish, lured by the booming prize money.

Between 1968 and 1976, it seemed as if someone in tennis was always boycotting something or suing somebody else over some thing or another. Players feuded openly, depending on which philosophical camp they were in. Men's star Jimmy Connors sued the ATP and several promoters, claiming they constrained his ability to make a living. The Slims leaders were irritated that Margaret Court and Britain's Virginia Wade, the very proper daughter of an Anglican bishop, sat out the early fights against the Establishment but were now riding on the Slims players' coattails, collecting prize money after the hard work and risks and suspensions had been endured.

Evert, the heir apparent to Court and King, felt caught in the middle. "When I was sixteen or eighteen, people would ask me questions on issues or whatever, and I would feel I had to answer," Evert says, "but at the same time I would also think, 'Leave me alone. I don't want to get involved in this.' Billie Jean was the perfect person to articulate what things meant for women. But me, I was in my own little teenage world of tennis and boyfriends. I was more concerned about getting my first serve in. My parents weren't the type to discuss politics at home. They were more worried about putting food on the table for their five kids. I'd go play tournaments, unpack my little suitcase when I got home, and go back to being my tenth-grade self. I didn't have posters of tennis players on my wall. I still liked the Monkees and Bobby Sherman."

Evert was amazed that people found her "cold" and "calculating" then. "If I wasn't that warm," she says, "it's because I was petrified of people."

The irony is that Evert accomplished some things on the court that were revolutionary. Part of her appeal was her way of seeming everything to everybody. She was both the antidote to bigmouthed feminists and the personification of the feminist dream of the career woman who could have it all. Athletically, if not yet politically, Evert epitomized one of King's arguments: the idea that a girl, given the same encouragement and resources as a boy, was equally capable of great achievements. But Evert also showed that a traditionally feminine woman could be a sports champion. She made people comfortable.

Evert was the teenage prodigy who made teenage prodigies the norm in women's tennis, and she navigated the passage to adulthood better and with more enduring success than anyone since. Evert was professional tennis's first American-born ingenue. As she grew older, she was the first female player of the Open era to put sexual fizz into the office of World's Greatest Tennis Player—granted, in a wholesome, Grace Kelly way. To tournament promoters and television executives alike, Evert was the ideal athlete for the television age, a perfect combination of good looks and talent. Women wanted to be her. Men wanted to see her.

But put Evert in a press conference in those early days, and she often became cautious, even wooden. Sports commentator Mary Carillo says, "I actually think Chrissie was the beginning of the downfall of media access in tennis. Because before she came along, that locker room was full of grown-up women who had fought for change and demanded things. They were formidable women with grown-up ideas and attitudes. Educated women. Women who for years and years had begged for coverage from the press. Then along came Chrissie, who was so young and so shy she needed handlers. She didn't know how to handle certain situations at sixteen, seventeen. So the tournament people, the Slims people—everybody—they literally walked her to her press conferences. They told her whom she had to talk to, what questions to answer."

Even the time-honored getaway line of the modern press conference—"Last question"—started with Evert, Carillo says. "And once Chrissie got that treatment, it sort of became standard."

Evert was still so acutely self-conscious as a teenager that she would watch her younger sister Jeanne wear the latest fad clothing item to school first to gauge the reaction before jumping onboard herself. On tour, Evert was uncomfortable with many of the questions reporters hurled at her, especially personal inquiries such as, "Do you have a boyfriend back home?" She felt driven inward even more by the nicknames she started picking up: the Ice Maiden, the Icicle, Little Miss Pokerface. She detested them. She was no longer some Cinderella in sneakers—not to the women she was beating regularly, and not to the press, which had never seen a female athlete quite like her. She found the mixed signals confusing and inhibiting.

For a long time, she would think, "What would Chris Evert do?" before speaking.

"In a lot of ways, I was given a [public] personality before I had a chance to develop one myself," Evert says. "Even today when I do corporate appearances, people always say to me, 'My God, I had no idea you had a sense of humor!' They're so surprised. But I couldn't play my best tennis if I let everything out. It would have been nice to be free and loose on the court, to have that exchange with the crowd that Billie Jean or Martina had. But I couldn't. So my control became associated with winning. But it was also one of the things that allowed people to put me in little boxes that were hard to escape. And it hurt."

After her dramatic comeback over Mary Ann Eisel at the 1971 U.S. Open, Evert had the temerity to give *Tennis* magazine a detailed rundown of what her veteran opponent should have done differently—an added if unintended humiliation that her veteran opponent surely didn't need. Evert also told reporters that just before she saved the first of those six match points against Eisel, she was already thinking about how she would look as she walked to the net a loser: "Would I be cute? Sad? Tired?" Then Eisel's serve came floating up at her like "a huge balloon," just begging to be put away. "So," Evert added, "I picked a spot and hit my two-handed backhand."

Such comments were construed as proof of Evert's self-absorption, not her youth. After each of her three comeback victories at the 1971 Open, she found the locker room "quiet as a morgue" when she walked in. The mood toward Evert didn't change when she took a break from high school and ventured back on tour in the spring of 1972. She ended up crying in the bathroom of the women's locker room in Dallas after King vanquished her in a quarterfinal match. Evert was hurt because some of the other players had congratulated King on her two-set romp as if she had won the U.S. Open all over again.

Though Evert's talent was enough to make her unpopular among her peers, something else worked against her as well.

About a month before the Dallas match between King and Evert, Billie Jean and her husband, Larry King, had flown to Florida to formally recruit Chris to take a stand against the USTA and play on the upstart Virginia Slims tour. But when the Kings arrived at the Everts' Fort Lauderdale home, they were told that seventeen-year-old Chris wouldn't be joining them. Only her father, Jimmy Evert, would meet with them.

After taking a seat on the Everts' living room sofa, Billie Jean launched into her best pitch. She told Jimmy that his daughter was the future of the game and a definite superstar. She emphasized the long view of the split from the USTA to him, ticking off the ages of the established women stars and highlighting how the Slims circuit was being built to benefit Chris's generation. Seeing Jimmy was unmoved, "I went into my beg mode," King jokes. "I have a very good beg mode, you know."

Still, Jimmy Evert didn't budge. He told King that his loyalty remained with the USTA, which had helped Chris as a junior player. He said he didn't want Chris to be suspended, as the Original Nine Slims players had been. And that was that. The meeting ended cordially and the Kings left, disappointed. When the USTA cobbled together a rival tour months later, hoping to drive the Virginia Slims circuit out of business, Evert and Evonne Goolagong were its two big stars.

Billie Jean King genuinely had no hard feelings—she was never someone to let a little word like "no" stand in her way—but some of the other Slims players were cold to Evert for a great while because of her USTA allegiance. The one beef King did have with Evert—and it would last years—sprang from Evert's frequent statements that she had helped bring a new "femininity" to the women's tour. King felt such comments disparaged the women who came before Evert. "I bitched nicely a couple times to Chris," King says, "and she apologized and said, 'Oh, I'm so sorry, Billie. I'd never want to hurt you.' So she was good to me. But she kept doing it and I finally figured it out: Chris needed to do that for Chris. She'd flirt with the guys and so on because that feedback was important to her."

The low-key USTA tour lasted less than a year before peace was brokered with the better-funded, more competitive Slims tour in 1974. Both tours merged into one, and King again tried to smooth the way for Evert, inviting Evert to be her doubles partner as a show of acceptance.

Evert's previous decision to spurn the Slims circuit for the USTA was among the things that stamped her as a hidebound Establishment girl, a label that took her a long time to live down. The USTA had not only failed to address the women players' demands for more equitable treatment or prize money but actively tried to obstruct the new opportunities that Gladys Heldman and the players were creating for themselves. And starting the Slims tour wasn't easy. Heldman said that during her initial search for sponsors she got twenty nos before her first yes. Without Evert as one of its cornerstones, the USTA Tour wouldn't have existed even as briefly as it did.

In many ways, Evert's endorsement of the USTA was seen as support for exactly the conventional molds the progressive women athletes were trying to transcend. "And I didn't help myself when I did other stupid but innocent little things, like picking Bobby Riggs to beat Billie Jean," Evert says, rolling her eyes. "They still show that interview on TV, and every time I see it I go, 'Ugh.' "

Still, the public didn't hold Evert's positions against her. Most fans had little knowledge or stake in tennis's internecine battles.

When Evert traveled to England to play her first Wimbledon in the summer of 1972, it was her first major tournament since her sensational U.S. Open debut ten months earlier. From the moment the Wimbledon draw was announced, Evert's possible semifinal meeting with twenty-year-old Australian sensation Evonne Goolagong was hyped.

Goolagong was the other new star of 1971, a sublime player from Australia with silky movements and gorgeous strokes. With her tousled hair and easygoing smile, Goolagong was as mirthful on the court as Evert was perfectly creased. Goolagong's story was even more remarkable than Evert's: She was one of eight children born to an itinerant Aboriginal sheep shearer and his wife, and for a time they lived in a shack with a dirt floor. She began playing tennis in Barellan, a small rural town in New South Wales. When Evonne was thirteen, her parents accepted an invitation for her to live and train with Vic Edwards, a prominent Australian coach who ran a Sydney tennis academy, and he soon became Evonne's legal guardian. Goolagong's ascent was swift. She won the 1971 French Open and Wimbledon titles as a nineteen-year-old, then followed Edwards's longtime plan for her to skip the U.S. Open six weeks later—a decision that cost Goolagong the chance to play Evert during Evert's breakthrough run.

By the eve of the 1972 Wimbledon tournament, the European press was declaring the potential Evert-Goolagong showdown the most eagerly anticipated women's tennis match since the fabled 1926 contest between Suzanne Lenglen and Helen Wills, the Goddess and the American Girl. Lenglen was a dramatic Frenchwoman who sometimes liked to swig brandy out of a flask on court during changeovers and favored ermine-trimmed capes. Wills, an iron-willed Californian, had crossed the Atlantic on a steamship in 1926 to play her in Cannes. Lenglen prevailed, 6–3, 8–6, in a hard-fought battle that, as one correspondent wrote, "made continents stand still and ranked as the most important sporting event of modern times exclusively in the hands of the fairer sex."

The hyberbole notwithstanding, Evert and Goolagong did not disappoint. But by the end of a fortnight, the memorable Wimbledon semifinal they played wasn't the only talk of the tournament. The London tabloids breathlessly reported that Evert—America's chaste girl next door—had struck up a romance with another newcomer, Jimmy Connors, tennis's bad boy.

She was seventeen. He was nineteen. And they were calling it love.

Whatever negligible chance Evert had of keeping her romantic life out of public view ended with the news of her relationship with Connors. It was the event that catapulted Evert out of the sports section and into the gossip columns and celebrity magazines.

On the surface the romance looked like the classic case of the good girl falling for the incorrigible boy (an oversentimentalized arrangement that has left a lot of good girls flinging their fists against their pillows and crying, "Why, why, why?"). Evert admits that she was "obsessed" with her relationship with Connors at first. Like any infatuated teenager, she'd arrange her whole days, including her practice times, around when she thought Jimmy might call. "Remember, Chris wasn't just a Catholic girl—she was a *cloistered* Catholic girl," Grace Lichtenstein says.

On one of their first dates, Connors took Evert to the Playboy Club in London. Dating Connors allowed Evert to pop the sort of emotional wheelies she wouldn't have dared try on her own. Evert's pairing with Connors also had just enough symmetry—the shared tennis futures, the same inexhaustible drive to win—to leave some people rhapsodizing that it was a storybook romance.

But not everyone saw it that way.

If the uptight wing of tennis's old guard had a nightmare vision of the sort of rabble that would come crashing through the gates once the Open era of tennis began, Jimmy Connors was it. His antic-filled pro career began in 1972, five years before an even more voluble American, eighteen-year-old John McEnroe, began perfecting his scornful lines on pro chair umpires and grimacing through matches as if he were fighting a bad case of acid reflux.

Unlike McEnroe, the son of a successful New York lawyer, Connors was not a child of privilege. He did not have a close relationship with his father most of his life. He learned tennis on public courts, as had Evert and Billie Jean King. Connors was taught by his maternal grandmother, Bertha Thompson, whom he called Two Mom, and by his hard-driving mother, Gloria Connors, who traveled the tour with him. Gloria and Two Mom had been nationally ranked as young women, and Connors revered them both. Connors's family legend holds that Gloria cleared the land for a tennis court behind their East St. Louis, Illinois, home while she was pregnant with Jimmy.

If the Chris America/Ugly American angle to the Evert-Connors romance wasn't tantalizing enough, there was another subplot: Jimmy Evert had dated Gloria Connors briefly when he attended the University of Notre Dame and she attended nearby St. Mary's College. As children, Chris and Jimmy had exchanged awkward hellos at a few junior tournaments before Gloria sent her son off to Los Angeles at age sixteen to train full-time with retired tennis star Pancho Segura. Effective as Segura was, Two Mom always maintained that Jimmy already possessed a barbed-wire attitude and game when he moved to Los Angeles and that Segura just applied some spit and polish. One of Gloria's favorite boasts was that Jimmy was the first male world champion developed by two women. Not only that, Gloria bragged, but they had given him a ruthless power game.

"I taught him he had to be a tiger—if he didn't kill, he'd get killed," Gloria Connors said. "When Jimmy was a youngster, if I had the chance I'd hit the ball down his throat. 'See, Jimmy,' I'd say, 'even your mother will do it to you.' So I guess I have to take the credit and the blame for his court behavior."

There was plenty of both to go around. Connors skyrocketed to number one by 1974, just his third year on tour. He also constantly offended sensibilities. He was arrogant, rude, self-serving, and vulgar. His career was full of skirmishes—most of them fights he picked, then seemed determined to flog to a bloody conclusion. He and his equally truculent pal Ilie Nastase, a Romanian star, were the first players to turn tennis matches into preening, machismo, expletive-filled spectacles. At any moment Connors was liable to give the finger to the crowd, lapse into snide off-color banter, or celebrate a good point with a primal yell and a couple of pelvic thrusts, his fists clenched at his sides.

When something displeased him, he was infamous for jerking his hand up and down his racket grip, as if he were masturbating. He had small eyes that peered out beneath a Prince Valiant haircut and a mouth that seemed perpetually tilted sideways in a half smile, half sneer. He uttered boasts before Grand Slam tournaments such as "There are going to be 127 losers and me." And he swore he didn't give a flying rip what anyone else thought.

"I believe if you're going to be a schmuck, be a schmuck," Connors said.

Not surprisingly, Connors had few friends. He preferred to travel and dine in the company of his mother, Segura, and his business manager, Bill Riordan, a reformed alcoholic and ex-boxing promoter who talked like a carnival barker and cooked up star vehicles for Connors like winner-take-all matches in Las Vegas.

"When the history of tennis is written," Riordan declared, "this will be known as the Jimmy Connors era!"

During Jimmy's debut at Wimbledon in 1972, Gloria Connors shouted so loudly for her son—"Kick 'em in the slats, Jimbo! Yippee!"—that one of Jimmy's irritated early-round opponents, Nicky Kalogeropoulous of Greece, finally asked Mrs. Connors, "Would you kindly shut up?"

Eventually, the chair umpire did the same.

"Cool it, Mom," Jimmy said.

Martin Amis, writing years later about tennis's lust for "personalities," noted that players other than Connors somehow managed to be "interesting" without being "assholes." Even Ted Tinling, the sharp wit whose tenure in tennis dated back to Suzanne Lenglen's reign in the 1920s, mourned the ill-tempered behavioral trend that Connors and Nastase started and McEnroe perpetuated.

"People used to commit tennis murder with so much more grace and charm," Tinling sighed.

Tinling was no prude. His assessments of people were often laceratingly funny and deadly accurate. He once said that Argentine beauty Gabriela Sabatini "looks like Marilyn Monroe, walks like John Wayne." He uttered the truest line about the nerve-shredding experience of watching a Navratilova match: "She goes from arrogance to panic with nothing in between." Asked at a tournament if he had seen the petulant Czech star Hana Mandlikova, Tinling snorted, "You mean Lady MacBeth? WHO CARES!"

But Tinling always called Evert "our most gracious champion." He thought she hung the moon.

The idea that the perfectly behaved Evert would fall for Connors—let alone stick up for him as she did, cooing, "He's the best first love a girl could ever have"—only confirmed in many people's minds that Evert was nothing but "a silly girl," *Tennis* magazine writer Peter Bodo observed. Evert insisted that off the court there was an impish, tender side to Connors that only the women in his life saw. After Two Mom died, Connors played his 1975 Wimbledon final against Arthur Ashe with a tearstained letter from his late grandmother inside a plastic bag tucked into one of his socks. He read from it during changeovers. "That's the Jimmy I fell in love with," Evert told a friend.

When members of the ever-mischievous British press spied Evert and Connors together on the Wimbledon grounds during the opening week of the 1974 tournament, they recognized a good story and they pounced. Evert and Connors were asked to pause for a picture, and Connors slung his arm around Evert's shoulders, tilted up his chin, and smiled rakishly as the shutters clicked. The photos appeared in newspapers around the world the next day. Before long, *People* magazine was doing its first feature on Evert and Connors, and the British press nicknamed them "the Lovebird Couple."

Evert told the reporters that she and Connors first began talking at the Wightman Cup dinner before Wimbledon started; now she and Jimmy were inseparable. "Finally," Evert said, "I have something besides tennis to love."

Connors nodded and said, "For me it's definitely love. She's a great girl."

By the next day Connors was backpedaling furiously.

"I only met the girl twelve days ago," Connors protested when reporters descended on him again. "That's hardly long enough for anyone to fall in love."

It wasn't just Evert and Connors who were blindsided by the first-day tabloid coverage—their horrified mothers were as well. The London tabloids practically had the two teenagers about to marry. When reporters went looking for a second-day quote from Evert to pair with Connors's remarks, only her mother was talking.

"There is no question of wedding bells," Colette Evert said. "Tennis is still first with Chris."

E vert was getting a crash course in celebrity. As if to prove that tennis was indeed her focus, she pushed Goolagong in their semifinal thriller before Goolagong won, 4–6, 6–3, 6–4. For the first time in her career, Evert wasn't the crowd favorite—Goolagong, the Wimbledon defending champion, was. Evert became rattled as Goolagong surged back from a one-set, 0–3 deficit to win seven straight games and force a third set. "It was one of the few times in my career I really let a crowd get to me," Evert admits. When she returned to the locker room, she angrily sent her rackets clattering to the floor. Thinking about the vociferous crowd reaction, she asked herself, "What did I do to upset them?" Then she began to cry.

Reporters never knew that. Newspaper accounts of the match were all raves. David Gray of the *Guardian* wrote: "There could hardly have been a semifinal full of higher excitement or deeper emotion. . . . There could not have been a better advertisement for the new order of the game. . . . The stage is set for the grand tennis rivalry of the '70s."

But no epic rivalry, just a very good one, ever took hold between Evert and Goolagong. Talented as Goolagong was, she never shared Evert's or Navratilova's bloodlust for competition and titles. Goolagong never again duplicated her 1971 year-end number one ranking, and she never played all four Grand Slams in the same year after 1973.

Goolagong married an English businessman named Roger Cawley in 1975. They settled down in Hilton Head, South Carolina, and Goolagong left the tour in early 1977 to have their first child, a daughter named Kelly. The Australian Open became Goolagong's sinecure in those trimmed-back years. She won four straight titles between 1974 and 1977, a time when many top players still didn't make the long trip to Melbourne.

In short, Goolagong ended up gliding into the domestic life that Evert had always envisioned for herself by age twenty-one or twenty-five. Meanwhile, Evert, confronted with the actual prospect of going through with marriage to Jimmy Connors, backed away.

Evert and Connors, lost in the first romance of their lives, quickly chafed at the constant chaperoning by their mothers. Chris had worked hard to graduate high school a semester early so she could turn pro on her eighteenth birthday in December of 1972. By the spring of 1973, eight months into her relationship with Connors, Evert was fighting with her mother about never being allowed to be alone with him. She and Colette were barely speaking by the end of an eight-week trip to Europe. For the first time, Chris's game began to suffer.

Evert lost to players she never lost to before, and she lost titles in uncharacteristic ways. She was serving for the French Open title against Margaret Court and lost in three sets. She dropped the Wimbledon final to Billie Jean King after losing the first set, 6–0. Grace Lichtenstein, who was there, compared King's seething, virtuoso performance to "a shit-kicking guitar riff by Jimi Hendrix. It was the loveliest, meanest set of tennis I'd ever seen."

In September, Evert lost yet again to Court—this time in three sets in the semifinals of the 1973 U.S. Open. Once back in Fort Lauderdale, knowing she wouldn't see Connors for weeks, Evert rebelled against her parents for the first time in her life. She wrote them a note explaining that she desperately missed Connors, then hurried to the airport and took a flight to Los Angeles to see him.

It was the same night that King played her Battle of the Sexes match against Bobby Riggs, and Evert remembers the pilot announcing the set-by-set scores to cheers and groans as their plane streaked across the country.

Evert's parents were stunned, but they reacted calmly. When Chris finally came home, it was agreed that she could begin traveling the circuit on her own, in the company of her sister Jeanne or her best friend, Ana Leaird. Two months later, in November of 1973, both Evert and Connors won the South African Open. Afterward, they visited a nearby diamond mine and bought Chris an engagement ring with part of Connors's tournament winnings. Then Connors dropped to one knee as he slid the ring onto Chris's finger and proposed.

Colette noticed the ring immediately when nineteen-year-old Chris stepped off the plane in Florida.

"I don't think you should let your father see it just yet," Colette said. "Don't you think Jimmy and your father should talk first?"

Evert had a ring on her finger. She had a wedding on the horizon. And the first seven months of 1974 were a blissful period for her and Connors. Their careers began to skyrocket at precisely the same time. They won their first Wimbledon titles on back-to-back days, and Chris likened it to "a fairy tale" when she and Jimmy danced the traditional first dance at the Champions Ball, the spotlight on them and "The Girl That I Marry," the song the bandleader chose, playing.

But their victories also underscored how realistic their bristling tennis aspirations were. So did the cues of those around them. When Evert's parents and Gloria Connors sat down to discuss a wedding date, Gloria was staunchly opposed to a midsummer wedding, telling the Everts, "Nobody wins Wimbledon on their honeymoon." November 8 became the chosen date.

Connors and Evert still hadn't reconciled how much longer Chris would play after they were married. It was Connors's preference that Evert quit soon and travel with him. She and Connors picked out a house in Los Angeles, but Connors took his time closing the deal. When Evert called him at Dino Martin's home one night to talk about where their purchase stood, she heard female voices and giggling in the background. She recalls, "I just got the feeling that maybe I wasn't the only one in the picture."

After Connors demolished Ken Rosewall a few weeks later in the final of the U.S. Open, 6–1, 6–0, 6–1, for his third major title of 1974, Evert saw the stack of messages for Connors back at their hotel—some of them from starlets. Later that night, Connors spent most of his victory dinner at the opposite end of the table from

Evert, reveling with his mother and Pancho Segura and Bill Riordan. "You know," Evert thought to herself, "maybe this is something he needs to go through on his own."

"It wasn't so much a matter of falling out of love as facing reality," Evert recalls. "We both had our careers. Neither of us wanted to quit."

Five weeks before the wedding, Evert and Connors had a six-hour phone conversation late one night.

"Do you think that maybe we should put this off a little bit?" Evert finally asked Connors.

"What do you think?" he said.

"I don't know if we're ready," Evert said.

Connors agreed.

Evert and Connors initially said they had just decided to postpone the November wedding. But by December of 1974, Evert had stopped wearing her engagement ring altogether and gave it back to Connors, who wore it on a chain around his neck.

The pull between them would last years. They continued to date now and then until 1978. When they checked into a California hotel once for a quiet weekend, the hotel's management, thinking they had eloped, hung a banner outside welcoming them, which soon prompted a call from gossip columnist Rona Barrett.

Evert still blames Connors for her finals loss to Billie Jean King at Wimbledon in 1975. With Evert leading King 3–0 in the third set, Connors caused a commotion by walking into the Centre Court stands with actress Susan George, who was then living with actor Jack Jones. A shaken Evert lost the next six games and the title. Not wanting to diminish King's win, or feed the tabloid reporters' appetite for scandal, Evert denied seeing Connors and George's entrance at all.

"Oh, I saw them," Evert now admits. "Flashbulbs were going off. People were standing up to look. You couldn't miss it."

The next day Connors said that he and Evert were through.

By the time of her broken-off engagement to Connors, Evert had already started a personal migration that would take her far from the sheltered, cautious girl she had been at the start of her career. Evert was never merely carried along by her success. She was bright. She thought things through.

She gave an interview to the *Los Angeles Times* in October of 1974, the same month she and Connors ended their engagement. Evert, still only nineteen, said, "I'm going through a stage where I'm trying to analyze how important my career is to me and how important other things are. I'm listening more now and I'm more aware. . . . Billie Jean King is so independent and she's for equality and sometimes I listen to her and I could listen for hours. It kind of infiltrates my mind and I start to question all the things I've been brought up on. I read magazines like *Ms.* and *WomenSports*, and it's like all us girls are together, you know—sisterhood."

Evert's appropriation of a women's movement buzzword like "sisterhood" was notable. By 1975, Evert was elected to her first of eight terms as president of the WTA, and she had joined King's calls for equal prize money and a possible women's boycott of Wimbledon if the All England Club didn't comply—two stances she had avoided two years earlier. Before long, Evert had stopped wearing makeup during matches, calling it "ridiculous" because mascara "runs in about five minutes." She kept pushing back her long-stated plan to be married and out of tennis from age twenty-one to twenty-five or beyond. "I want to marry and have kids someday—just not *now*," she wrote in her diary in 1976. "I love tennis. It's my life."

Evert's learning curve was accelerated when she began traveling alone on tour. She called those first few years her "college education." Many of the women tennis players were fast friends, and Evert liked the range of characters in the locker room. Most of them were different than anyone she'd ever known.

At any given moment, Rosie Casals might be in one corner planning an excursion to a museum or concert, and Navratilova might be strolling by with her latest dog. (*Boston Globe* writer Bud Collins says, "I remember asking Roy Emerson once, 'What kind of dog is that Martina has, a long-haired Chihuahua?' And Emmo said, 'That's not a dog. That's a rat with a perm.' ") Françoise Durr of France could be playing one of her loud bilingual Scrabble games with Betty Stove of the Netherlands, who spoke six languages. Kristien Kemmer might be showing Evert the latest halter dress she bought. Ingrid Bentzer of Sweden might be walking around the dressing room stark naked with a cigarette dangling from her mouth, raucously holding forth on any number of topics in what Bentzer jokingly calls her "pompous Swedish way."

"Chris, being so Catholic, had been held in a very tight rein," Bentzer says, "and if you ask me now, would she have been the champion she was without that discipline, I would say no. But I also think when Chrissie first arrived she had a different outlook on things than some people, and in those early years, especially, she became more open-minded. All the big personalities were still out there on tour, and I think that was a very important addition to her character. She sort of added on, grew into her own skin, and she was able to let that flippant side of herself out. And it turned out she was terribly funny. She had a big heart. She was true to her friends. And oh, we had such a lot of fun."

Evert often struggled to reconcile what she impulsively wanted to do versus what her strict upbringing and daily trips to Mass had taught her as a girl. As Bentzer says with a laugh, "For Chrissie, it was the old dodge with all Catholic girls. Chrissie was always drawn to dangerous guys. The naughty guys. Being European, I had different attitudes about a lot of things, including sex. Chrissie would always walk around the dressing room with her bra and underpants on, and I was always teasing her, 'Are you going to shower in your underwear?' I was more like, 'Yes, this is an arm, this is a breast—*who cares?*' I would constantly tell her, 'It's all right, Chrissie, you're not a bad person if you do this or that.' She'd say, 'Oh, Ingrid . . . I just can't.' I'd say, '*What?* What *is* the problem? For God's sake, Chrissie, would you get a life?' "

vert didn't date anyone else for a while after her split with Connors. But partly to shake the doldrums, she and Jeanie Brinkman, the Virginia Slims publicity director, made a resolution to do something exciting in every city they visited in 1975. To celebrate her twenty-first birthday, Evert splurged and bought herself an expensive lynx coat. "And I got a less expensive fitch coat—which is a polecat," Brinkman says, laughing.

In Washington, D.C., Brinkman—always looking for a publicity stunt to promote the tournament—suggested that Evert invite President Ford's son Jack to one of her matches. And Ford accepted. As Ford and Evert posed for pictures in the interview room after her match, Brinkman coyly whispered, "Aw, go on, Jack . . . Give her a kiss on the cheek." Ford did, and the photographers caught it. Ford and Evert had dinner at the White House late that night and saw each other a few more times during the week, raiding the presidential refrigerator several times. Then he and Evert dated for several more months. "He was one hot man," Evert says.

When the tour rolled on to New York, Evert signed a modeling contract with the Ford Agency, which Brinkman had helped her land. They were nearly done celebrating that night at 21, the swank Manhattan restaurant, when the maître d' politely told them that they would have to leave soon. The restaurant was reserved for a movie premiere party for actor Burt Reynolds. On her way out, Evert scrawled her phone number and a message to Reynolds on a cocktail napkin, telling him she'd like to meet him, then asked the maître d' to give it to him.

Later that night, Evert's phone rang.

"Hi. This is Burt."

At the time, Reynolds was the top box office attraction in America, and he had posed for a centerfold for *Cosmopolitan* a few years earlier. When their schedules finally permitted a first date, Reynolds, a fellow Floridian, arrived to pick Chris up at her parents' house in Fort Lauderdale. Evert remembers that her mother spent just a little more time getting ready than usual and her father looked even neater than he normally did. Reynolds arrived with two other couples in a caravan of three Rolls-Royces. Over the next year, they dated, Evert visited Reynolds on the movie set of *Semi-Tough,* and Reynolds sent Evert a necklace with a diamond-encrusted number one pendant. Later, he gave her another necklace with "Babe," his nickname for her, spelled out in diamonds. They caused a stir when Reynolds attended some of Evert's matches at the Virginia Slims Championships in New York.

"Write whatever you want. I'm not saying a word," Evert said coyly when some reporters trailing after her asked questions about her relationship with Reynolds.

By then, tennis was enjoying its greatest boom. It was glamorous. It had cachet. A Neilsen survey released after the 1974 U.S. Open revealed that nearly 34 million Americans considered themselves at least occasional tennis players, a threefold increase in just four years. Another poll found the number of Americans who followed tennis had jumped from 17 to 26 percent in 1974, placing it just behind pro football, baseball, and basketball.

Evert, King, Navratilova, Goolagong, Court, and Wade were all battling for titles on the women's tour. Newcombe and Connors, Ashe, Nastase, and Borg were all clashing on men's tour. Soon Tracy Austin and John McEnroe would join them. As Connors said, looking back on those years, "A fan would look at their draw sheet and have a hard time knowing which match to choose."

Numerous players—not just Evert—mingled with entertainers and celebrities. McEnroe, an aspiring rock musician, eventually took guitar lessons from Eric Clapton and hung out with fellow iconoclasts Jack Nicholson and Mick Jagger. (Their advice: "Don't change.") At Wimbledon one year, Borg needed an escort of six English policemen to protect him from the mob of shrieking schoolgirls that rushed him on his walk from the court to the locker room. Connors's mouthpiece, Bill Riordan, spoke of Connors recording some songs with Paul Anka and perhaps quitting tennis for a show biz career.

Among the women players, Evert was the unsurpassed star.

"As a celebrity and an athlete, she had begun to move to a different plane outside of sports, and she wanted that," Jeanie Brinkman says. As Evert matured from a girl into a woman, sportswriters' stories strayed beyond her matches. They frequently commented on her good looks or coquettish behavior. They wrote that she won matches "without disturbing a hair out of place"; that she "perched prettily" atop her courtside chair. Some stories read like mash notes or sonnets:

Her long fingernails were polished a pale pink. She wore a small diamond on a gold chain around her neck and silver earrings, pierced. Against her streaked blond hair and golden tan, her eyelashes were so dark they appeared to have been dipped in an ink well.

Look at her. Not a drop of perspiration.

"Oh God," Jeanie Brinkman howls. "We would get into these press conferences and Chris would say something that I thought was, you know, maybe moderately funny—*maybe*. And these male sportswriters would laugh so hard you would have to pick them up off the floor. I'd send Chris up about it all the time and she'd just laugh at me and say, 'I know, I know.' "

Evert was finally starting to show some spontaneity and a sharp sense of humor, not just the tough competitiveness underneath the imperturbable exterior. She wasn't offended when someone remarked on her looks. *Tennis* writer Peter Bodo accurately pegged her as someone who "highlighted the difference between two kinds of feminism: the one that accepts, enjoys, and sometimes trades on the differences between the sexes while still insisting on equality, and the branch whose constituents believe that our traditional concepts of femininity are confining, socially imposed burdens."

George Vecsey puts it more plainly: "To me, Chris was always a great analyst of what she did, and she had all the poise of some great, great strip queen. She just had this way of taking the whole hall into her—I mean, she played to the back row, she played to the front row, she played to the women, she played to the men. She liked the little eyebrow-raising jokes, or being told how she looked good in tennis dresses."

Madison Avenue took notice. Companies lined up to offer Evert endorsements. Andy Warhol, a friend of a friend of Brinkman's, asked Evert to be part of a series of portraits that he was doing on athletes, including Pelé, Jack Nicklaus, and Muhammad Ali. "I like my Warhol painting and I guess he was brilliant, but the sitting with him was totally unmemorable," Evert says. "He hardly said a word." Brinkman, who first met Warhol at the parties he and Margaret Trudeau threw at The Factory, his art studio in New York City, is more blunt: "I sat next to Andy Warhol at the Ali-Frazier fight at Madison Square Garden, and it was the most boring night. He was always nervous. Very furtive. Always skulking around."

Evert joined the top players who signed with the World Team Tennis summer circuit in 1976, enticed by the six-figure guarantees. The WTT's promoters encouraged the sort of showmanship and camaraderie that the early Slims Tour was known for. Many of the players were attracted by the novel opportunity to enjoy playing tennis as a coed team sport. Evert played two seasons for Phoenix and one year for the Los Angeles Strings, though it required skipping the French Open.

If the Slims Tour was Evert's "college education," then the WTT was spring break.

"I made up for lost time, believe me, when I was on my own," Evert says. "I was a party animal. That was my release."

Evert smoked pot for the first time during those years. In addition to continuing her busy dating life, she was living and working in close quarters with stars from the men's tour now too. The summer she played for the Los Angeles Strings, Evert agreed to accompany Connors's old pal Nastase on his first date with supermodel Cheryl Tiegs, after much pleading. Laughing, Evert recalls, "He was telling me, 'Chrissie, Chrissie, oh, Chrissie, you've gotta help me, please, please, you've gotta come with me.' Then, of all places, he took us to a strip bar."

Evert and Stephanie Tolleson, a Team Tennis teammate in Phoenix, accepted an invitation from the Amritraj brothers, Vijay and Ashok, to share some authentic Indian takeout food at their hotel one night on a visit to New York. When they got to the Amritrajs' room, the two brothers, who were born in Madras, were seated cross-legged in their underwear on the bed. "I guess they were so comfortable with us as teammates, they didn't bother to get dressed," Evert says with a laugh. "We had to tell them, 'Uh, guys . . . could you, uh, please put on some clothes so we can eat?' "

Evert briefly dated Vitas Gerulaitis, who took her to Manhattan's infamous Studio 54 and points beyond. "Weird places," Evert says with a smile. "I'll never forget, one time Vitas took me to this place and he and I were sitting at a table. This girl at another table just kept looking at Vitas and looking at him, and finally Vitas says, 'Oh, no. I think maybe I dated her once.' Then he says, 'Oh, God, she's coming over.' Sure enough, she came over. She sat down. And then she leans forward and—in this really deep voice—says, 'Hi, Vitas.'

"Well, I didn't know it was a transvestite bar!" Evert exclaims. "Vitas had no idea who she was. But we had a big laugh about that for a long, long time. 'So, Vitas, you, uh, dated her, huh? Oh, right. Uh-huh, Uh-huh . . .' "

If Evert's off-court life was expanding, she remained as driven as ever on the court. When she returned to the women's tour she reverted to the same strict routine of room-service meals, practice, play a match, get a massage, and sleep. She never dwelled on victories too long. "You're just so afraid to let any slice of happiness in," she said, "because the minute you do, someone comes along and beats you."

Evert's absorption with winning remained total. But for the first time she began to question the toll tennis was taking on her.

When Evert won her second Wimbledon title in 1976, it was her first since her breakup with Connors. She went to the Wimbledon ball with her mother, danced the traditional first dance with the men's champion, Bjorn Borg, and left shortly afterward. Evert, now twenty-one, returned to her empty hotel room and sat on the bed for a long time, sad that she had no man in her life anymore with whom to share her victory.

Her feelings hadn't changed when she returned to defend her Wimbledon crown in 1977. With Navratilova and Billie Jean King eliminated from the tournament, Evert actually approached her semifinal against British star Virginia Wade with some rare calm. "I really had Virginia's number then," Evert says.

She lost anyway, with the Centre Court crowd again rising up against her and for their countrywoman.

By match point Evert felt so out of sorts, so uncharacteristically disengaged, she mistook a linesman's half-raised hand as an out call and began her walk to the net to shake Wade's hand even as Wade proceeded to return her shot. Evert had the right to ask for a replay of the point, but she conceded it and hurried off the court.

On her walk to her post-match press conference with Jeanie Brinkman, Evert was so disconsolate and weary of the grinding pressure, she suddenly couldn't bear the idea of going through the ritual post-match autopsy. She stopped abruptly in the hallway, pressed her back against the wall, and slid down to the floor. Then she began to sob, and Brinkman knelt down and tried to console her. One of the things Evert cried was, "I'm not a machine."

"It was so painful, the memory still gives me a shiver," Brinkman says thirty years later.

Evert always considered herself someone who played tennis not to lose rather than to win. She once said the reason she drove herself so relentlessly was that she absolutely loathed having to endure the overjoyed look on her victorious opponent's face as she walked toward the net.

"I *hate* that," Evert said.

An oft-told story about Evert captures her perfectly: She was sitting in the Wimbledon locker room one year when Paula Smith, a journeyman player, returned after a loss and said, "Thank God my happiness doesn't depend on a tennis match."

"Thank God mine does," Evert shot back.

For three days after her loss to Wade, Evert stayed in her bathrobe at her London hotel, stuck in a deep depression. Just to punish herself, she watched the BBC replay of her loss to Wade. Two days later, with Queen Elizabeth watching at Centre Court, the thirty-one-year-old Wade won her first Wimbledon title on her fifteenth try, touching off a national celebration. Wade was Britain's first Wimbledon champion in eight years. And Evert remained in her room, still sulking and eating whatever the hell she liked.

"Fried food, things that are bad for you, things that make you break out—you name it," Evert says. "I just let myself go."

To see her right then, no one would have known that Evert was number one in the world, the owner of a 54–2 record that year, someone touted as one of the most admired women in sports. Bud Collins got a tip that Evert had trashed her hotel room after the loss to Wade. "And Chrissie confirmed it to me," Collins says. Evert found herself crying two to three times a day for another two weeks. "I thought I was losing control," she said. "It gets old—tennis all year, the strain of staying number one, people always at your heels. I had been going nonstop for seven full years."

Near the end of 1977, Evert announced that she had decided to take a break from the tour. Her sabbatical would stretch on for four months, into early 1978.

While her rivalry with Goolagong was destined to be relatively short-lived, and Billie Jean King's career was fading, Navratilova was slowly, steadily gaining on Evert.

Even if Navratilova had a few tamped-down secrets of her own.

CHAPTER FIVE

COMING TO AMERICA, COMING OUT

When Navratilova and her father, Mirek, returned to their home in Revnice after their walk along the river, Navratilova tried to occupy herself, packing for her next morning's trip to the United States. She didn't dare hint to anyone that she was thinking of defecting. She took nothing extra in her suitcase. She made no cryptic remarks to her mother or to her twelve-year-old sister, Jana, let alone the friends she might never see again. She just tried to stay busy around the house that night, patting her dog on the head, taking a good long look at her grandmother, who was then in her seventies. The next morning Navratilova said her goodbyes, same as always. As her plane climbed out of Prague, the world that she was leaving behind pulled away from view and shrank in size until the details were a blur.

Navratilova wasn't positive that she was going to defect as her plane banked and headed west across the Atlantic. But her convictions about her tennis potential were strong. She had watched her friend Evert rise to number one with barely a wrong step, and she was not too proud to admit that Evert was her measuring stick. Billie

Jean King was still Navratilova's idol and mentor, and the impressionable Navratilova mimicked her, right down to getting a permed hairdo once. But Evert was Navratilova's contemporary, the front-runner she would have to chase down and overtake. When Navratilova finally beat Evert for the first time in January of 1975 in the quarterfinals in Washington, D.C., the breakthrough worked an alchemy on Navratilova's self-image.

"I knew I could be number one then," Navratilova said, "because I had just beaten the number one player in the world."

It didn't seem to matter to Navratilova that she had won only two career titles in the thirty-six pro tournaments she had played, or that Evert, by contrast, had already amassed thirty-six titles in just forty-nine events.

Navratilova thought she could compete with Evert. If anything, Evert gave a face, a rough blueprint, and some stolen momentum to her own dreams. It didn't matter that it was Evert's face. When Navratilova looked at Evert and all that Evert had done, she superimposed herself, and their past results or current rank had no claim.

A few weeks after the Washington win, Navratilova defeated Evert for a second time, this time in the semifinals of a Chicago tournament. But Evert promptly started another winning streak against Navratilova that reached eight matches and lasted nearly a year. During that span Navratilova pried only two sets off Evert. She had improved to the point where she and Evert were starting to meet regularly in finals. But once there, the relationship between them snapped back to what it had always been: Evert was still dominant, and still unthreatened enough by Navratilova to play doubles with her. And Navratilova told herself that the one-sidedness of their rivalry was only temporary. She was happy to be enjoying the best year of her career in 1975 despite her escalating fights with the Czech sports officials.

Her family's decision not to defect at Wimbledon made it clear to Navratilova that if she was going to leave Czechoslovakia, she'd have to do so alone.

When Navratilova's plane touched down in New York for her

U.S. Open warm-up tournament in Westchester County, she was already emotionally wrought. Thoughts of defecting were consuming her by now. She didn't merely lose in the quarterfinals to Dianne Fromholtz. "I got wiped out," Navratilova said. The shock of her early ouster brought everything into urgent focus: Navratilova realized that if she suffered another early loss at the U.S. Open, time would abruptly run out for her. She had strict orders to return to Czechoslovakia immediately after the Open to finish high school, which presumably meant skipping the rest of the tennis season.

Navratilova was just eight weeks away from her nineteenth birthday. She was in the midst of her finest year to date as a pro. When she tried to imagine the coming years, the thought that kept barreling through her mind was the same: "If you go back, your life will never be your own."

And so, after her loss to Fromholtz, Navratilova picked up the telephone and called her business manager, Fred Barman.

"Fred, can you help me?" Navratilova said. "I want to stay."

Until Navratilova's phone call, Fred Barman's only experience with international intrigue was handling the finances for actor Peter Graves, the star of the hit TV show *Mission: Impossible*. But Barman's daughter Shari, one of Navratilova's friends on the tennis tour, says, "To me, my father was the perfect person to handle things for Martina. He loved her. She knew she could trust him. He's the sort of person who dots all the i's and crosses all the t's. He also spent his whole childhood and adult life in Hollywood, and, you know, anything can happen here. In Hollywood you always have to be ready for anything."

Fred Barman did try to anticipate every eventuality once Navratilova decided to defect. But he also admits, "I was paranoid. In retrospect, I can see that some of it was not necessary. But I was in charge of this eighteen-year-old girl, and I felt the responsibility like she was my daughter. I heard what the Communists did in those days. There were stories—if you were a dissenter, if you tried to defect, they would put you in a diplomatic car, jab you with a needle to sedate you, whisk you to the airport, and that person would never be seen again. It was a scary time."

Barman's first move was to call an attorney he knew in Washington, D.C., who discussed Navratilova's case privately with some of his contacts at the FBI. Barman, meanwhile, began working with the Immigration and Naturalization Service in New York City to begin secretly processing the paperwork for Navratilova's defection.

The understanding was that Navratilova would formally request asylum when she was finished playing the two-week U.S. Open. As Navratilova moved through the draw the first week, somehow managing to win each match, the defection process took on a cloak-and-dagger feel. She was told by her FBI contact not to breathe a word about her plans to anyone. Between matches she was frequently at her Manhattan hotel, meeting with people who were working on her defection, desperately hoping her Czech minders didn't notice. Barman says that at one point the FBI assured him and Navratilova that there was no cause to worry, the FBI was protecting her.

"From what?" they asked each other, eyes wide.

By the time Navratilova beat Margaret Court in the quarterfinals to advance to a semifinal showdown against Evert, the plan was set: Navratilova had an appointment later that evening at the Immigration and Naturalization Service's otherwise deserted office building in Lower Manhattan. Again Navratilova played a strong match—barely losing, 6–4, 6–4, to drop her career record against Evert to 2–11. Unbeknownst to Evert, still her doubles partner, Navratilova and Barman and the Washington-based attorney slipped into a back entrance at the INS shortly after six o'clock that evening, then took a lurching old freight elevator to one of the building's empty top floors, where they were met by an INS agent. As the elevator ascended, Barman studied Navratilova's face. He was struck by how matter-of-fact she looked.

"I don't know how Martina really felt inside, but she took it all blasé, like she wasn't afraid at all," Barman says. "But I was quite concerned. Nobody else was there. The agent took us into this long room, and it had a hallway here and a hallway there, and it had a door at the end. We were shown into this office. Martina sat down in front of this metal desk and the attorney and I sat behind her. The first thing the INS guy does is take off his jacket, and he's got this great big gun. I thought, 'Aw, geez—I *hate* guns.' Then he says to her, 'Can I see your passport?' So she gives it to him. Then he said, 'I'll be right back.'

"Well, I panicked," Barman says.

Barman didn't trust the agent's explanation that he would return after making a photocopy of Navratilova's passport until the man came back and slid Martina's passport across the desk.

The INS agent then asked Barman and the attorney to leave the room. "Which I didn't want to do either," Barman grouses. "But he had the gun."

Out in the hallway, Barman couldn't hear what Navratilova and the agent were discussing. As he and the attorney waited, two more men walked down the dimly lit hallway and introduced themselves as FBI agents. Again, Barman was skeptical. When one of the agents said he had been born in Czechoslovakia and he was there in case Navratilova needed an interpreter, Barman no longer believed their story at all.

He tersely asked to see their FBI identification, which the agents calmly produced. Then one of the men showed Barman his gun, saying it was a special weapon only FBI agents carried. "I wouldn't know the difference," Barman shot back. "Anybody can steal a badge or steal somebody's gun."

The agents now offered to call someone who could vouch that they were indeed from the FBI, and Barman says, "I pretended to go along with it" when they picked up a nearby phone and made a call. Barman's mind was racing: How did he know what number these men were really calling? "So I turned my back to them when they handed me the phone and I hung up on purpose," Barman says. "Then I called my own FBI guy and asked about these guys. And he said, 'Yeah. They're okay.' "

As that was happening in the hallway, the INS agent in the room with Navratilova was still filling out forms and asking her basic questions: Why did she want to leave Czechoslovakia? What were her plans in the States? He asked about her and her family's views on Communism. "That was really insulting," Navratilova told journalist Peter Bodo years later, her indignation still fresh. "My parents, for example, were thrown out of school for not being Communists and paid their price way back in the 1940s and '50s."

Shortly after ten p.m., Navratilova and Barman were told they could leave. Again they were warned by the INS agent to keep quiet about Navratilova's plans, for her own protection.

The next morning at seven-thirty the telephone rang in Navratilova's hotel room. It was a CBS television news crew, asking her for an interview right away in the hotel lobby.

"Now?" Navratilova said, not piecing anything together.

When she hung up, her phone quickly rang again.

"Why did you do it?" her Czech coach, Vera Sukova, cried.

"Do what?" Navratilova stammered.

"Why did you defect?" Sukova said. "It's in the *Washington Post*. You defected!"

Sukova said she was on her way to Navratilova's hotel to talk her out of it, and she hung up.

Now Navratilova was afraid.

Quickly she called Fred Barman and blurted, "They found out!"

"Get the hell out of there—now!" Barman said.

For Navratilova, for Barman, and for Jeanie Brinkman, the next twelve hours were a blur. Because of the leak to the *Washington Post* (the source of which Navratilova never discovered), Navratilova was on the run. "We wanted to make sure the Czechs wouldn't somehow try to snatch me," she said. After ending his frantic phone call with Navratilova, Barman immediately phoned Brinkman, who had an apartment in Greenwich Village. Brinkman dressed hurriedly, flagged down a cab, and rushed over to the Roosevelt Hotel, where Navratilova was staying.

"We had it planned that she would take no tennis rackets, nothing, so nobody would know she was a tennis player," Brinkman says. "When I got to the hotel, she was waiting, and it was actually very sad in the way she was standing in this back alley with something over her head to hide who she was."

Barman and Brinkman decided to take Navratilova to the U.S. Open tournament site at Forest Hills. Brinkman figured as soon as Navratilova made her announcement public, no foreign agents could try to grab her, but the hours before that would be the most dangerous. Turning to Navratilova, Brinkman explained, "I'm going to put you in the locker room until we can get a press conference. You'll be safe there because there's security."

As Brinkman and Martina sped toward Forest Hills in a taxi, they were "literally shaking." Brinkman says, "We were even going to change cabs because we thought that would be better if we were being followed. Then I thought, 'You know, maybe I've watched too many movies . . .' But at that moment, you don't know. You just don't know. So we ended up not switching cabs, but I was thinking, 'What the hell am I going to do if someone does tries something?' I'm five feet two. Through it all, Martina was very still. Very quiet and still."

Navratilova had considered defecting for months, but she had never thought it through this far. She had taken pensive walks around Revnice. She had looked at the church steeples and stone houses and chalets, the nearby mountains and the river, and she asked herself if she was willing to abandon her family and all that was dear and familiar to her. But neither she nor Brinkman anticipated the pandemonium they encountered when they walked into the press tent for Navratilova's jammed news conference at Forest Hills shortly after eleven a.m. that Saturday.

Navratilova was wearing a patterned sweater and pair of slacks. As she made her way to her seat and picked up the microphone that was set atop a table, the shoulder-to-shoulder row of television cameramen blinked on their bright lights and the swarm of print photographers started firing their camera shutters. Every time Navratilova showed the slightest bit of emotion—a sigh, a small smile, the hint of a tear—the shutters clicked loudly in unison. The reporters who were questioning Navratilova were jostling for space and competing to be heard. "You have never seen such a cacophony of people screaming and yelling, throwing sentences at her," television journalist Jack Whitaker remembered. The reporters shouted out their overlapping questions to Navratilova in two languages, and Navratilova, speaking in a thin, clear voice, tried her best to explain her decision. Sometimes she struggled to keep her composure.

"I had no idea what a splash it would be," Navratilova later said. "After Baryshnikov, there was Navratilova."

When Billie Jean King rose that Saturday morning and heard the news of Navratilova's defection from a friend, she thought, "Oh my God . . . this is it. She did it." King was the only person in tennis whom Navratilova had told that she planned to defect. Shari Barman and Rosie Casals later went to Navratilova's hotel room to collect the clothing and tennis equipment Navratilova had left behind in her haste. Jan Kodes, who was also playing in the U.S. Open, heard the news flash about Navratilova's defection on his car radio. He called her hotel as soon as he could get to a telephone.

"I was told she was gone, she had already checked out," Kodes says.

Iva Drapalova, a young Prague-based Associated Press reporter who happened to live in Revnice, Martina's hometown, saw the bulletin that Navratilova had defected on the news wires that Saturday. Drapalova went to interview Navratilova's family the next day.

"I talked to her grandmother, but Martina's dad [Mirek] was not at home," Drapalova says. "He called me later and he was very angry. I did not dare quote him. He cried, '[Czech sports official Antonin] Bolardt took my daughter away!' I ended up quoting the grandmother instead."

Evert, who would play and win the U.S. Open final later that Saturday against Evonne Goolagong, was at her Manhattan hotel when Navratilova's hastily arranged press conference took place. Though she and Navratilova had been doubles partners for four months, Navratilova hadn't told her about her defection plans. Navratilova had spoken only vaguely to Evert about her travel restrictions and troubles with Czech officials—and even then only a few times. So when Evert heard Navratilova had defected, Evert's first thought was "Oh God, I hope she knows what she's doing. She's so vulnerable. She's either very idealistic or very ambitious. I can't imagine not seeing my family."

Brinkman had similar concerns as she and Barman watched Navratilova plow through her press conference. At times the surreal scene felt like an out-of-body experience.

"My biggest memory is Martina had to keep excusing herself because she had to go to the ladies' room," Brinkman says. "You have to remember, Martina was a very naive girl. A very sweet, curious, dear naive girl from a closed-off Communist country. She handled that day remarkably well. But to look back on all of that through the eyes of an American—particularly at this juncture in time, thirty years removed from that day—it doesn't have the same enormous emotional resonance as it did then. Back then, it was a very odd time. It was the cold war. It was a very dramatic thing she had done. I remember thinking it was so sad, so very, very sad, that it had come to that."

In 1975, defecting meant forever. There was no hint that the Eastern Bloc would be broken up, that the borders would ever be flung open, the concertina wire all gone.

Asked now if Navratilova had any inkling what lay ahead, Brinkman winces and her voice grows soft.

"How *could* she?" Brinkman says.

Over the next few days while arrangements were made for Navratilova to stay temporarily in the home of some Czech friends in upstate New York, she remained in hiding at the FBI's suggestion at Brinkman's tiny apartment in Greenwich Village, which consisted of two rooms with a galley kitchen, a Murphy bed, and a pullout sofa. The night of Navratilova's Forest Hills press conference, Brinkman received a phone call at home from a U.S. government official telling her that her phone was being tapped. "He also said there was a car with an FBI agent outside the apartment to protect us, just in case, and that if we were in trouble I could phone them," Brinkman says.

Fred Barman sat with Navratilova and Brinkman that first night. For a while, the three of them tried watching TV, hoping to take Martina's mind off the circumstances. But Navratilova remained very quiet. Brinkman, hoping to ease the tension, finally suggested that they venture just across the street to get something to eat at one of her neighborhood haunts, a tavern called Jimmy Day's. Brinkman had many friends there and thought it would be safe. Her friend Ross was the bartender that night, and he saw them walk in.

"We hadn't said a word about anything to anybody. Not a soul," Brinkman says. "But when we walked into the bar, Ross yells out to me, 'Hey, Frank'—he always called me Frank—'Hey, Frank, someone was in here looking for you.' So I said, 'Who?' And he said, 'I think it was the KGB.' "

Navratilova bolted out of the bar and ran back to Brinkman's apartment.

"Well, it was just a joke, but poor Martina," Brinkman says. "We finally caught her, brought her back, and eventually had a nice meal."

Later that night as Brinkman and Navratilova were preparing to go to sleep, Brinkman got a phone call from a man she had met at a cocktail party given by Mark McCormack, the founder of IMG, the sports management company.

"This guy had asked me if I would show him around the Village sometime that week," Brinkman says, "and I had completely forgotten it because he was married and I had no interest. The only problem was it was Spiro Agnew—the vice president! He's calling to ask me out to dinner and he doesn't know the phone is tapped by federal agents! So I'm sitting there, just listening to him—'Hi, Jeanie, it's Ted Agnew . . .'—and I couldn't *tell* him. I just kept saying, 'Dinner. Uh . . . No, no thank you. No . . . No, no . . . No. No.' "

When Navratilova's parents finally reached her by telephone a couple of days after her defection, they asked her to come home. But, remembering what her father had told her the night before she left—*If you do defect, stay there. Don't come back, no matter what we say*—Martina consoled herself with the thought that, deep down, her family understood.

Then she went back to work within two weeks, trailed by an FBI bodyguard and unsure of what her reception on tour would be.

To Navratilova's relief and surprise, she received a standing ovation at the first event she played in Atlanta, then again in Charlotte, North Carolina. By then, the Czech sports federation had issued a statement that read: "Martina Navratilova has suffered a defeat in the face of the Czechoslovak society. Navratilova had all the possibilities in Czechoslovakia to develop her talent, but she preferred a professional career and a fat bank account."

Her maternal grandfather, an irascible man whom Martina feared as a girl, was quoted in a news story the same day as saying, "Oh, that little idiot, why did she do that?" When reminded of his comment by a *People* magazine reporter a few days later, Navratilova broke into tears.

Navratilova continued to travel for weeks after her defection with FBI protection. In Denver, Navratilova's hotel room phone rang one day and, to her surprise, it was Vera Sukova. Sukova had been sent to Colorado by Czech authorities with orders to try to persuade Navratilova to return home. Feeling obliged to give her former coach a face-to-face explanation, Navratilova agreed to meet in the hotel coffee shop with Sukova and an official whom Sukova described as a Czech embassy representative.

When Navratilova told Fred Barman she had agreed to the meeting, he was livid.

"I didn't like it," he says.

The fears about Navratilova being snatched were no joke. Brinkman recalls a vague story about an Eastern Bloc gymnast who had tried to defect but disappeared. In 1950, some members of the

Czech national ice hockey team were jailed for an alleged plot to emigrate during the world championship that year in London. They were about to travel there to defend their title, but the players were arrested at the airport shortly before their departure for England. Czech authorities alleged that the team had first contemplated a group emigration during a tournament in Switzerland in 1948, the year of the Communist putsch in Czechoslovakia, but ultimately decided to return home. This time, goaltender Bohumil Modry was accused of leading the 1950 conspiracy. He was sentenced by the Communist regime to fifteen years in prison and served his time in uranium mines. The radiation caused Modry's premature death at age forty-seven

When Sukova arrived at the hotel for her meeting with Navratilova, Barman and the FBI bodyguard accompanied Navratilova downstairs, then stood in the lobby, out of earshot but watching intently.

Sukova told Navratilova that it was still possible for her to go home. The embassy official assured Navratilova that if she returned before her travel visa ran out at the end of October, she would have the freedom to manage her tennis career as she pleased. But, the official added, if Navratilova returned after her visa expired, she would go to jail for two years.

Navratilova dwelled only on the threat.

"I was more afraid of what the Czechs would do to me than any Americans," she said.

Sukova warned Navratilova that she was under surveillance. The embassy official said that he had been followed by an American agent all the way to Denver—a story that made Navratilova scoff. But as Barman stood across the lobby with Navratilova's bodyguard, Barman learned the embassy official was indeed being tailed. "We knew someone else was watching the meeting, but we didn't know which person in the lobby was also the FBI," Barman says. "So to keep ourselves amused, the other agent and I were standing there saying, 'He's the one. No, wait—he's the one!' Finally, the next day I think, we were told who it was. He was a short guy, a Native

American–looking guy. But we never saw him. So he was doing his job very well."

Navratilova talked calmly with Sukova and the Czech official for more than two hours. There were no tears, no heated moments. When they were through, Navratilova said she hadn't changed her mind. "Not one ounce," Barman says. Everyone shook hands and the meeting broke up.

Navratilova went on to win the tournament.

Navratilova felt sympathy for Sukova, whom she suspected would suffer reprisals at home because she had not persuaded Navratilova to return. But Navratilova and her former coach never discussed possible implications for Sukova that day in Denver, or when they passed each other at tournaments over the years and nodded their hellos. Vera Sukova died of a brain tumor in 1982. To this day, Navratilova has never discussed the fallout Sukova faced with her husband, Cyril Suk, who was then president of the Czech Tennis Federation, or their daughter Helena, who eventually became a top player. "I suppose it's too painful," says Helena, who was only ten when Navratilova left.

Cyril Suk learned of Navratilova's defection at his home in Prague when he turned on Voice of America radio. Suk buried his head in his hands and sat down. He never believed that Navratilova's defection was absolutely necessary. Nor did Kodes, her former mixed doubles partner.

"It is not true that Americans who appropriate her now taught her to play tennis—they taught her shit," Kodes says. "I say that because I am and I have always been a patriot. We taught her to play tennis here in the Czech Republic."

Suk, like Kodes, was upset. He feared that the state would withdraw support for tennis in Czechoslovakia, and he worried what might happen to his family. Navratilova was immediately declared a nonperson and her name was no longer mentioned in news accounts or record books. (In coming years, newspaper editors in the state-run Czech media would slyly keep their countrymen abreast of her accomplishments with carefully worded stories such as: "The four semifinalists of Wimbledon are known. They are Chris Evert, Andrea Jaeger, and Evonne Goolagong." Any Czech who could count to four would know the last semifinalist's name.)

A few days after Navratilova's defection, Antonin Himl, Vera and Cyril's boss at the Czech Sports Federation, the man who approved Navratilova's final trip to the States, called Sukova. He asked her to come to his office and take the Federation Cup trophy that the 1975 Czech team, led by Navratilova and coached by Sukova, had won just a few months earlier. "I can no longer have it here," Himl explained.

"So the trophy was in our home, sitting on my magnetophone," says Suk.

"It was like a hot piece of coal no one wanted," Helena recalls.

Kodes, still Czechoslovakia's number one male player, was spared punishment, though he had argued for Navratilova's freedom to travel. But, hearing there were reprisals against Vera to come, Suk swallowed hard and made an appointment to see Antonin Himl. "When something happens, each society looks for a scapegoat to blame," Suk explains. "The easiest thing was to blame it on the national coach. So Vera was the main culprit. Vera was denounced. But we used to solve all things together, and I wanted to make sure my wife knew that I backed her completely, not that I will build my own career and she will be left behind."

When Suk met with Himl, Suk gave him an ultimatum: "If my wife is harmed, I will abdicate my position too. Do not commit this injustice."

To their relief, it worked. Though the harassment and social shunning that Vera Sukova faced would continue for a year, she and her husband were not fired, and Czechoslovakia's tennis program was not dismantled.

"I think I took a few good steps in my life," Suk says, his voice catching and eyes tearing up, "and taking this stand for my wife was one of them."

If Czechs viewed Navratilova's departure with emotions ranging from sadness to jubilation at how she had thumbed her nose at the Communist system, Navratilova's first year in America was a similar jumble of emotions. Her early exhilaration—"I never had anything before and I enjoy everything I have now," she said—was offset by behind-the-scenes distress, some of which she was loath to acknowledge for years.

Navratilova was free, rich, and steadily improving as a tennis player. But she was also nineteen, alone, and living out of a suitcase. As the months passed, the reception Navratilova enjoyed from American crowds grew more conflicted.

She burst into tears when a heckler at a January 1976 match in Los Angeles shouted, "Russian go home!" at her. But Billie Jean King gave her a fortifying pep talk. "Crying? There's no crying in professional tennis!" King said, nudging Navratilova till she got a smile.

King also tried to calm Navratilova during a doubles match they played when Navratilova wouldn't stop complaining that the chair umpire was mispronouncing her last name.

"Guess what—if you win enough, they'll get it right," an exasperated King finally said.

"You think so?" Navratilova blinked. She hadn't thought of that.

"I *know* so," King said.

Navratilova was a curiosity now in nearly every tournament town she played. Sports editors who previously wouldn't have devoted a column inch to women's tennis dispatched writers to see how Navratilova was adjusting to a life that had gone from black and white to Technicolor. British newspapers mentioned how she was "stateless," calling her "the Girl from Nowhere."

"I'm homesick for my parents and my sister, but I'm having a ball," Navratilova insisted three months after her defection.

Publicly, anyway, Navratilova was resolute. Over and over she pronounced herself happy, fulfilled, possessing no regrets. She repeatedly insisted that her parents and sister had not suffered any penalties for her decision. She constantly stressed that her decision to defect had nothing to do with politics. She worried that if she said anything critical of the Czech regime, it might create difficulties for her family.

Only years later would Navratilova reveal that when she spoke to her parents on the phone that first year, their conversations often ended with tears on both ends of the line. "There were times I just wanted to go home," Navratilova said. Only belatedly did Navratilova admit that her parents knew their chances of ever getting a job promotion ended when she left. Her sister had been prevented from getting into high school for a year, and she wasn't welcome at some tennis tournaments she tried to enter.

For the most part, Western reporters bought Navratilova's highly edited accounts. Many came away struck by her enthusiasms and amused by her eager absorption of all things American. "Those first few months, she really was like a kid in a candy store," Shari Barman says.

Navratilova still had her appetite for Big Macs and ice cream. She liked to show off her knowledge of American football, baseball, and basketball. "I'm going to take a quick shower so we can get the doubles on quickly, and then we can all go watch the Super Bowl," Navratilova told a tournament crowd in Landover, Maryland, after winning the singles title. She was so eager to assimilate that she traveled with a dictionary and studiously looked up English words she didn't recognize.

Navratilova already had her trademark bluntness. Speaking to a reporter about the chore of attending the pretournament cocktail parties for sponsors, Navratilova said, "The only way to survive strangers is to have a few drinks." Asked by another interviewer if she had noticed any negative features of America, Navratilova said, "Oh, yes. I hate that there is still discrimination here, that in some country clubs blacks and Jews are not allowed."

It even made Navratilova happy to know that she could voice such opinions and face no repercussions in her new country.

"I'm free at last," she told a friend.

In time, however, the portrayals of Navratilova's Westernization became an increasingly sensitive subject to her. Even when reporters didn't ask about her spending habits, Navratilova sometimes volunteered how she went "the whole Beverly Hills route" and got vanity license plates for her Mercedes that read X-CZECH, or how Barman set up a business for her and Navratilova named it Brat, Inc.—a nod to Rosie Casals's nickname for her, "Navrat the Brat."

When Navratilova began keeping her prize money at the start of 1975, she had bought herself one unremarkable gold bracelet for seventy-five dollars during a shopping trip in Sausalito. After her defection, numerous news articles began to detail Navratilova's fondness for excessive jewelry. She was tweaked for her shopping sprees at Neiman Marcus and the Rodeo Drive shops near Barman's Beverly Hills home, where Barman and his wife had invited her to stay after her defection.

A December 1975 *New York Times* story was typical: "The Czechoslovak-born star has become a walking delegate for conspicuous consumption. She wears a raccoon coat over designer jeans and a floral blouse from Giorgio's, the Hollywood boutique. She wears four rings and assorted other jewelry, including a gold necklace with diamond insert. . . . The usual status-symbol shoes and purse round out the wardrobe. She owns a $20,000 Mercedes Benz 450SL sports coupe. She is fluent in American slang. . . . As an undisciplined gourmand, she is overweight."

A New York *Daily News* article the same week also mentioned Navratilova's Rolex watch and Gucci handbag, but now the gold rings on her fingers had ticked up from four to five.

Ted Tinling thought he recognized what was happening with Navratilova. Like her, he had always reveled in his stateside visits. "Whenever I'm in America," he said, "I feel I've come off the side roads at last."

Tinling said that after he emigrated to the United States in 1974, he too went through a cycle of exhilaration to "mental turbulence."

"It's a delayed reaction," Tinling said. "After nine to fifteen months, the euphoria begins to wear off."

Navratilova was hardly the first nouveau riche athlete to indulge in excesses once in possession of money or freedom. British golfer Tony Jacklin splurged on leopard-skin bedspreads and furs. New York Knicks star Walt Frazier said he had a flamboyant alter ego named Clyde who favored Super Fly outfits and wide-brimmed hats. Boxer Sugar Ray Robinson traveled with an enormous entourage that included a barber and a golf pro. Czech star Hana Mandlikova, who began playing the women's tour three years after Navratilova's defection, said she bought whatever caught her eye at first, regardless of the price. Mandlikova was only fifteen when she made her pro tour debut, and she grew so lonely as she traveled the world that she spent as much as $2,000 a month on phone calls. She used to leave her hotel room television on all day and all night just to have other voices in the room.

At first, Navratilova was too flush with her newfound freedom to exercise too much restraint or introspection. It's not her nature anyway. She had big plans and she wanted to get on with them. When she signed a reported $150,000 contract to play Team Tennis for the Cleveland Nets in 1976, she proudly wore the number one diamond pendant that Nets owner Joe Zingale had given her. Zingale believed that Navratilova would soon be the top-ranked player in the world. "And I do too," Navratilova had said.

Navratilova still spoke cheerfully about her friendship with Evert. They had made nightly trips to some Tokyo discos on a tournament trip to Japan. She noted how playing Evert eleven times in 1975 taught her a lot, even though she lost nine of the encounters. "I have to be more patient," Navratilova said. In Los Angeles, a reporter asked Navratilova if 1976 could be the year she dethroned Evert, and Navratilova nodded and said, "I proved I can beat Chris and beat all of them. But I have to do it more consistently."

Only now and then did the rest seep in.

"Sure I get sad," Navratilova told an Australian reporter in December of 1975, staring at her first Christmas since her defection. "Wouldn't you be sad if you didn't know when you'd see your parents again?"

By then, another secret was tugging at Navratilova too.

———

Though Navratilova had told people she had a boyfriend back home in Czechoslovakia and that she might marry someday, she came to realize she preferred the company of women. At the time, a handful of the top players were lesbians. Though they were discreet about their love lives or partners, Navratilova noticed that homosexuality was not regarded in the West as some grave psychological disturbance, as it was back home. In Czechoslovakia, Navratilova said, gays were still often sent to mental institutions.

Not long after her September 1975 defection, Navratilova had her first sexual experience with a woman whom she has never described beyond "somebody older than me, a woman I met in the States." In her autobiography, Navratilova wrote: "It seemed so natural. I never panicked and thought, 'Oh, I'm strange, I'm weird, what do I do now?' . . . The next morning—voilà—I had an outright, head-over-heels case of infatuation with her. *When will I see you again? What will we do with our time together?* I was in love, just like the storybooks, and everything felt great."

To Navratilova's dismay, the relationship ended after six months. She was heartbroken. In the first ten months of 1976 she didn't win a tournament. Her early euphoria about her move to the States gave way to troughs of deep unhappiness. All the progress she had made as a player in 1975 began to slide away, even though she had recommitted to losing weight and dropped twenty pounds.

In March of 1976, after arriving in Los Angeles to play the Virginia Slims Championships, an irritable Navratilova said she was tired of talking about leaving Czechoslovakia.

"Why? Why? Why? Why do people keep asking me about my defection?" Navratilova sharply asked a *Los Angeles Herald-Examiner* reporter. "I answer the same questions a hundred times a day. No, I don't have any regrets about it. Yes, I'm very happy now. Yes, my parents are just fine and no one is harassing them back home . . . I don't understand what the big fuss is over me."

Navratilova began to mention here and there how being declared a nonperson back home had hurt her. "You realize you don't have a country," she said. She spoke of the pang she felt every time she filed a visa application and had to write "stateless" on the form because she was still enduring the routine wait for her American citizenship.

In April, while in Florida for the *Superstars* competition, she was introduced to thirty-two-year-old professional golfer Sandra Haynie. Haynie was a lot of things the nineteen-year-old Navratilova wasn't—steady, settled, already a major title winner in her sport, an athlete touted for her equanimity and professionalism. She remembers Navratilova "as very outgoing. And fun. Very willing to learn, and laugh, and just join in with everybody." By June, Navratilova and Haynie were talking often. Navratilova sought Haynie's advice on everything from the unflattering portrayals of her spending habits to how to improve her composure and killer instinct during matches.

Navratilova had always been demonstrative on the court. "A holy terror," she once admitted. Her matches were often emotionally charged, switchback-filled experiences. She rushed the net and lunged for balls. She'd toss her head back in disgust, slap herself on the thigh, bang her racket on the ground during a changeover, and scream at the sky. She'd stride up to chair umpires, shrieking about some line call and pointing frantically to where she thought the ball had bounced, acting if those points weren't merely lost or squandered—they had been murdered. And right before everyone's eyes!

"HOW COULD YOU CALL THAT OUT?" she screeched, her eyes beseeching.

Navratilova has always had a high-pitched voice, but it trills even higher, up toward crockery-shattering range, when she's upset. It was nothing for her to scream things at herself during matches too—"How about a lob? . . . Hit the ball, you chickenhead!"—oblivious to how she was making fans laugh out loud.

Many times Navratilova's outbursts were harmless. But by the middle of 1976, her increasingly dark moods seemed to rule her, sometimes sabotaging sure-looking victories.

Haynie says, "It was bad, because when she was into that or

questioning line calls, it became a couple lost points, then it became a game, then it became three games. It just mushroomed."

At Wimbledon 1976, Navratilova suffered a near meltdown during a match against Britain's Sue Barker when she thought a linesman had missed a call. "Are you *British?*" Navratilova demanded to know, then asked that the linesman be removed. Though Navratilova held on to win the match, Evert beat her in the semifinals a few days later, 6–3, 4–6, 6–4. And Navratilova's career record against her fell to 3–15.

Navratilova and Evert went on to win the 1976 Wimbledon doubles title together. But a little over a month later, Evert scratched from playing doubles with Navratilova at the U.S. Open, citing tendonitis in her right hand. Navratilova was upset to find this news out by reading it in the newspaper. Before long, she and Chris weren't playing doubles together at all.

"I couldn't handle it," Evert admits. "Martina was getting better. Martina was a threat. With all the practicing we were doing together, I felt she was getting a little too good of a read on my game."

Navratilova arrived at the 1976 U.S. Open in late August still having not won a singles title all year. She was exhausted from the jam-packed World Team Tennis schedule she had just played. She was lonely. Her wrist hurt. She was prickly.

To make matters worse, when Navratilova arrived at Forest Hills, she found that everyone wanted to talk about the first anniversary of her defection. As Navratilova walked the grounds, she became conscious that she was retracing her steps to the women's locker room where she had hidden out that first day, surrounded by security. The press tent was still there too, looking the same as it did during her tumultuous press conference. Before long, Navratilova said, she began to have flashbacks.

"It all kicked in: 'It's been a year and this is it . . . This is where I am,' " Navratilova said. "I had nobody to lean on. I couldn't see my family, they couldn't see me. I was all alone. I was nineteen, which is still pretty young . . . I felt the whole world was against me."

Haynie had agreed to come see Navratilova play, but she didn't

Sixteen-year-old amateur Chris Evert became an overnight sensation during her 1971 U.S. Open debut before Billie Jean King ended Chris's upset-filled run in the semifinals. The *New York Times* called Evert "Cinderella in Sneakers." AP/WIDE WORLD PHOTOS

TOP Chris, 17, at home
with her tennis-playing
family in 1972. Front row
(*left to right*): John, 10;
mother Colette; Jeanne, 14;
father Jimmy. Back row:
Drew, 18; Clare, 4.

AP/WIDE WORLD PHOTOS

RIGHT Martina
Navratilova, 16, on only
her second visit to the
United States from
Czechoslovakia,
impulsively celebrated
winning her first pro title
in Orlando by hugging a
light pole near the court
because, she said, she
didn't know anyone there
well enough to hug.

PRIVATE COLLECTION OF

BETSY NAGELSON MCCORMACK

Chris prepares to return a shot in the very first match she and Martina ever played, on March 22, 1973, in Akron, Ohio. Evert was already an international star; Martina said she was just hoping to make Chris remember her name. PAUL TOPLE/AKRON BEACON JOURNAL

Chris, the first tennis superstar to come along in the television age of sports, was celebrated from the start of her career as a perfect combination of traditional feminine looks and athletic ability. EVENING STANDARD/GETTY IMAGES

Sweethearts Jimmy Connors, 20, and Chris, 18, pretend to ignore their chaperoning mothers, Colette Evert and Gloria Connors (*far right*), during a break at the 1973 French Open. They called off their engagement five weeks before their 1975 wedding. AP/WIDE WORLD PHOTOS

Eighteen-year-old Martina was stunned by the commotion she encountered when she announced her defection on September 7, 1975, at a raucous press conference at the U.S. Open in Forest Hills, New York. "After Baryshnikov, there was Navratilova," she later said. AP/WIDE WORLD PHOTOS

Haunted by flashbacks on the one-year anniversary of her defection, nineteen-year-old Martina sobs after suffering a stunning first-round upset at the 1976 U.S Open; she lost to Janet Newberry (*right*). "It all kicked in: This is where I am . . . I have nobody to lean on," Martina said. AP/WIDE WORLD PHOTOS

The Duchess of Kent applauds as Chris and Martina, by now good friends as well as rivals, hold up their women's doubles trophy at Centre Court, Wimbledon, after winning the 1976 championship. They also won the 1975 French Open doubles title together. AP/WIDE WORLD PHOTOS

Chris and British tennis star John Lloyd emerged from their wedding at St. Anthony's Church in Ft. Lauderdale, on April 17, 1979. An estimated 1,000 fans gathered outside the church to catch a glimpse of the newlyweds, who were married a whirlwind nine months after they met.

LEFT Chris's loss to Martina at Wimbledon in 1982 foreshadowed the stunning reversal in their rivalry. It was Navratilova's first Grand Slam title after she began training with basketball star Nancy Lieberman, who encouraged a "Kill Chris" mentality. TONY DUFFY/GETTY IMAGES

BOTTOM Martina and Chris walk out onto Wimbledon's Centre Court to play their 1982 championship match. Martina never lost to Evert in a Wimbledon final.

WALTER IOOSS, JR./ SPORTS ILLUSTRATED

TOP Nancy Lieberman (*left*) and Renee Richards cheer Martina from the friends' box at Wimbledon in 1982. They were the original two members of Team Navratilova, the support team that helped Martina reach legendary heights in her career. WALTER IOOSS, JR./ SPORTS ILLUSTRATED

RIGHT Martina's win over Chris at the 1983 U.S. Open, the only Grand Slam tournament Martina had never before won, was hailed as the victory that proved she had indisputably replaced Chris atop the women's game, and was there to stay. MANNY MILLAN/SPORTS ILLUSTRATED

arrive in New York in time for Navratilova's first-round match against Janet Newberry. It had rained constantly that day, pushing their start time from eleven a.m. to well after six p.m. Navratilova's request for a one-day postponement was denied. It was cold and dank when they finally hit the court. Only a fraction of the crowd remained.

Newberry, a workaday pro, was competing in just her fourth event after knee surgery, and she was not Navratilova's equal. But Newberry came roaring back from a 1–6 pasting in the first set to eke out the second, 6–4. Navratilova hadn't practiced in the two weeks before the Open, figuring she'd play herself into shape. But she was making too many errors and she couldn't stop. Before long Newberry was serving for the match at 5–3, and she started Navratilova's tournament exit with an ace.

Navratilova was already crying as she shook Newberry's hand at the net. She sat down heavily in her courtside chair and buried her face in a towel. Then she kept crying.

And she kept crying . . .

Soon Navratilova's shoulders were heaving and her sobs had grown so distractingly loud, so hysterical, that Newberry stopped gathering her things. She walked over, tenderly slung an arm across Navratilova's shoulders, and leaned over to ask if she was all right. When Navratilova was finally ready to leave, Newberry accompanied her off the court. One reporter wrote that it looked as if Newberry were assisting an old woman across the street.

A still shaken Newberry later said, "I hope I never see anyone in that condition again."

As Fred Barman made the long walk back to the locker room with Navratilova, she leaned on his shoulder and cried the whole way as reporters trailed them at a respectful distance. "I've never seen her like this," Barman said after Navratilova disappeared into the dressing room, where she remained for a long time, still crying.

"This whole year for Martina has been like a kid taking her first trip to Disneyland," Barman said. "Here's a young kid who was imprisoned just a year ago."

Evert, the closest tennis had to a sure thing, won the tournament.

The day after her loss to Newberry, Navratilova flew with Haynie to Dallas and bought a house. They had decided to live together.

And life began for Navratilova yet again.

CHAPTER SIX

BIRTH OF A RIVALRY

The prospect of living with Haynie and having a home of her own appealed to Navratilova. "The house was the first thing I owned in America that meant anything to me," she said. "Finally I had roots and security." Navratilova quickly made friends with the families and kids in her new Dallas neighborhood, sometimes joining them for street games of tag football. She proudly wore a T-shirt that read ON THE EIGHTH DAY GOD MADE THE DALLAS COWBOYS. Navratilova had just turned twenty years old, and she was still given to the odd or impulsive purchase. "Is that a Pac-Man?" tennis player Mary Carillo asked incredulously on one visit to Navratilova's home, staring at the huge video game that sat like a piece of furniture in the living room.

But, slowly, Haynie was having a calming effect on Navratilova. She listened to Navratilova talk about how frightened she had been in the months after her defection and her fears that someone might try to snatch her in the middle of the night. When Haynie, who had taken an injury break from the golf tour, resumed traveling now and then in 1977, Navratilova disliked being home alone so much that she bought a pistol to protect herself.

"Well, it's okay if you want to keep it in the house or in the nightstand by the bed," Haynie said, "but, uh . . . let's just not keep it under the pillow."

People on the tennis tour began to notice a change in Navratilova. If tennis is not the most mentally tortuous of sports, then golf—with its inevitable humbling of even the greatest players—is. Haynie was able to help Navratilova understand that her approach to being a professional athlete needed to change. She gave Navratilova advice on how to handle defeat, how to deal with the press, how to control her emotions in competition, how to improve her diet. By the start of 1977, Navratilova had dropped from 167 pounds to 145. She was gathering herself for another run at Evert, same as she had begun in 1975. When Navratilova defeated Evert in Washington, D.C., for the second straight year—and only the second time in a final—Evert considered it significant. "This is a new Martina," Evert told reporters. "But it's good. It gets my game up."

The next three times she and Navratilova played, Evert was ready. She swatted Navratilova aside in straight sets in Seattle, beat her in three sets in Los Angeles, then outlasted her for a third straight win in a rollicking, three-set final in Philadelphia that, by the end, had the crowd shrieking with every volley Navratilova stabbed back and gasping at some of the passing shots that Evert blazed by Navratilova at the net.

All the traits that would eventually characterize Evert and Navratilova's rivalry were slowly beginning to emerge like a photograph developing in a darkroom pan. The contrasts in their games and public images were all beginning to sharpen. Their personalities were becoming familiar. Navratilova attacked, Evert counterpunched, hoping to wear Navratilova down like water over a stone. Navratilova was the athletic wonder who sent serves screaming off her racket, Evert the clinician who could have played in a lab coat. Navratilova raged at herself. Evert never let on what she was feeling. That was the hell of it.

Evert absolutely loathed making mistakes—so much that her reputation for playing immaculate tennis was a significant part of her aura. Her opponents, Navratilova included, began routinely to say that Evert *didn't* make mistakes—which, of course, was untrue.

But Evert's opponents' belief in her perfection exerted the same sort of pressure. Soon they would strive to be too fine and spray their shots to the back wall even before Evert needed to hit a winner. And Evert knew it. She was constantly taking a measure of her opponents' emotions in the locker room before a match, in midmatch, or after matches. She intently watched the other players' advances through the draw.

Exhilarating as her Philadelphia win over Navratilova was, Evert was more interested in what to make of it. Her career record against Navratilova was still a lopsided 18–4. Yet, when Evert saw her good friend Steve Flink, the writer for *World Tennis,* after the match, it was she who began tossing questions at him once they were talking alone.

"Chris felt she had pushed herself to her limit in that Philadelphia match," Flink says. "She knew she had played well and Martina had played well and yet she had barely won. It was not far from when Martina began to make her move and, in retrospect, it's interesting, Chris saw it coming. And she wanted to deal with it realistically."

"How close do you think Martina was to her best?" Evert asked Flink. "Where do you think she is right now? How much better can she get?"

With Evert gone on the four-month break that she took after her second 1977 loss to Virginia Wade, Navratilova embarked on the most imposing run yet in her five-year career. She won a record seven consecutive tournaments and thirty-seven matches to start 1978 before Tracy Austin, then fifteen but still just five feet tall and ninety pounds, upset her in Dallas. By midsummer, Navratilova had snapped the four-year stranglehold the idle Evert had on the weekly number one computer ranking. Yet to Navratilova's dismay, she wasn't universally hailed as some prodigal talent who had arrived at long last. The cynics said that this was just another streak in a career already full of them. Wait till Evert gets back, they said. This is just the latest transformation by a woman who, for better or worse, seems to go through quite a few of them. It won't last, the skeptics predicted.

Tempering the praise were Navratilova's occasional head-scratching losses, like her 1977 Wimbledon quarterfinal fall against Betty Stove. "I thought Martina was ready to win Wimbledon that year," Bud Collins says. And Flink agrees.

Navratilova's on-court emotional swings were becoming less disastrous now, but they hadn't totally disappeared. At that same 1977 Wimbledon tournament, she stunned her mixed doubles partner, Dennis Ralston, by dissolving into tears on Centre Court when they fell behind 1–4 in the third set against Stove and Frew McMillan.

"Martina, what's wrong?" Ralston asked.

"We're going to *lose*," Navratilova wailed.

"Well, we haven't lost yet!" Ralston snapped.

Because Navratilova's 1978 winning streak happened in the enormous vacuum created by Evert's absence, there was an asterisk placed on everything she did. By early summer, by the luck of the draw, Navratilova and Evert still hadn't played each other, though Evert had returned to the tour in March. Both of them skipped the French Open in May because of World Team Tennis. Everything was funneling the two of them toward a July reckoning at Wimbledon. But unlike their first career Grand Slam final at the 1975 French Open, which was played on Evert's best surface, clay, Navratilova would this time face Evert on grass, a quicker surface that favored Navratilova's serve-and-volley game.

Evert, never one to miss a chance to plant some psychological tremors, again let Navratilova know that she was conceding nothing. A weekend before Wimbledon, they played what amounted to a preliminary bout on grass in the final at Eastbourne, a quaint little

English seaside town with a faded boardwalk, a pretty white bandstand, and a conspicuously large number of senior citizen homes, the front porches populated by residents dozing in chairs with blankets strewn across their laps.

On a previous tournament visit to Eastbourne, Navratilova had actually griped that the squawking of the seagulls wheeling overhead disrupted her concentration. But on this occasion Navratilova contradicted the notion that she wasn't mentally tough enough to beat Evert at all, let alone defeat Evert in a tight match. Navratilova rallied from a 1–4 third-set deficit to dig out a 6–4, 4–6, 9–7 win.

Navratilova headed to the hallowed grounds of Wimbledon believing she was on the verge of something big.

For serious and casual tennis enthusiasts alike, Centre Court at Wimbledon is the cathedral of the sport. The Championships, as the tournament is simply called by its host, the All England Lawn Tennis and Croquet Club, have been contested in southwest London since 1877, interrupted only by Europe's two World Wars. Court Two, the most famous of the bandbox side courts, is nicknamed the Graveyard of Champions because of all the upsets that have happened there. The tournament is the only Grand Slam where fans queue up and sleep on the street the night before, hoping to get a ticket for the next day of play.

Within the timeless space of the Centre Court itself, the acoustics seem to magnify every exultant shout and every groan of despair. It is not like the raw and loud U.S. Open, where the fans never seem to shut up. Points at Centre Court Wimbledon begin in the same absolute still and quiet that befalls a concert hall when the maestro turns to the orchestra and raises his baton. But during and after points—then, the British star Virginia Wade says, players are confronted by a wall of sound when they strike a great shot, withering gasps when they blunder away an important point, and patronizing "ahhhhs" when they flub a makeable volley. Surprises are received on Centre Court with the same sort of tittering that ripples through a courtroom after a shocking revelation.

Wade believes tension comes into play more on Centre Court than any other court in the world because "the crowd is slightly hysterical there. And there's a great aura about that court. You can walk in it in the middle of winter when it's empty with no lines or anything, and it *speaks* to you. There are a lot of spirits growing in that grass. It's a heavenly, spiritual place."

For Navratilova, Wimbledon had always been a touchstone, the terminus of her dreams when she was a child in Revnice, hitting ball after ball back to her father. Before she ever imagined herself going to the United States or overtaking King or Evert, Navratilova dreamed of winning Wimbledon. She saw herself hoisting the trophy over her head like Czech star Jarolsav Drobny did in 1954 or her own mixed doubles partner, Jan Kodes, did in 1973 after his three-set singles win over Soviet star Alex Metreveli. On that day, a thrilled Navratilova, then just sixteen, had waited excitedly for Kodes to come off Centre Court and jumped up to give him a peck on the cheek.

At Wimbledon in 1978, Navratilova and Evert rumbled into the championship match to no one's surprise. In the days leading up to the final, Navratilova resented the repeated questions about the presumed fears fluttering around in her head. She insisted, "I'm not the same person I was a year ago. I don't think it will come down to nerves."

Hearing that, Australian star John Newcombe, who was working as a TV commentator for the match, laughed and said he hadn't thought he was going to be nervous for his first Wimbledon final, either, "until the umpire said, 'Play.' When I looked down, my racket was shaking in my hand."

Navratilova was indeed tight. She betrayed it when she broke into a nervous laugh after she and Evert made their entrance onto Centre Court and she self-consciously dipped into her curtsy to the Royal Box a half beat too soon. After that, Navratilova kept looking at Evert for cues for when to resume their walk to their courtside chairs and where to pose for the traditional pre-match photo at the net. She let out deep gusts of breath as she awaited the start of the match, as if trying to calm herself. Once it started, Evert, playing in her fourth Wimbledon final, seemed nervous as well, even though she stormed to a 6–2 first-set win.

Navratilova made too many unforced errors to have a chance in the opening set, but a telling pattern had been established. She was charging the net at literally every opportunity and exerting the sort of relentless psychological pressure that Evert was noted for—albeit in a dramatically different way. Instead of allowing Evert to turn the match into a ground stroke war, Navratilova kept attacking and crowding the net. She changed the rhythm of the match from the tick-tock of long rallies to something closer to a frenzied Rachmaninoff symphony. Flurries of points were over in seconds. Whole games flew by. Navratilova kept probing each point for a ball to chip back and come charging in behind, and she kept driving her volleys deep to either corner. She didn't care if she was serving or Evert was. Her tactics didn't change.

Navratilova kept up a running dialogue with herself throughout the first and second sets too. "Oh no—not *him* again!" she blurted, eyes wide, after the same baseline linesman made a second straight close call against her. But whatever Navratilova was feeling didn't destroy her. This was Wimbledon. For a change, the anguish seemed to spur her along instead. She started to convert more of Evert's defensive lobs into overhead smashes. She was clawing back into the match, letting Evert know she was in a dogfight.

The day before the match both Navratilova and Evert had been questioned at length about how such good friends could handle being rivals. Evert explained she always tried to put a blank face on whoever her opponent across the net was—something Haynie had been counseling Navratilova to do for months. But Evert and Navratilova were only eighteen months removed from being teenage doubles partners who used to sit on their chairs during changeovers, cracking up as Evert read from a joke book that she liked to sneak on court in her racket bag. Wimbledon final or not, some of that camaraderie was still there.

With the winds gusting in the second game of their second set, Navratilova completely whiffed on an overhead smash, leaving Evert standing stock-still in the frontcourt and just staring at Navratilova. She tried to stifle a laugh as an embarrassed Navratilova slapped a palm to her forehead.

Four games later, Navratilova guessed that Evert was about to hit a crosscourt forehand and took off on a left-to-right sprint along the net—only to have Evert inadvertently smash a shot off her left temple. As a horrified Evert ran in toward her, Navratilova staggered two steps along the net, clutching her head, and theatrically fell to one knee. And the crowd laughed. "I'm all right," Navratilova assured Evert with a smile when she stood back up. When a relieved Evert playfully cuffed Navratilova on the head a few times before walking back to resume play, the crowd laughed again.

"I think when she hit me that woke me up," Navratilova said.

Navratilova fought off three break points to hold serve in that game. Her power advantage was slowly beginning to reveal itself. Evert was playing the second set for the title, but Navratilova was playing to stay alive. The urgency on both sides was evident. But Navratilova's poise was even more striking. Serving at 5–4 to extend the match, Navratilova closed out the second set at 40–30 by outlasting Evert in a tense rally.

Navratilova had refused to blink.

The crowd bellowed its approval.

They had now played an hour and a half, and there still was no hint of who was going to win.

In coming years, Navratilova would look back and call this match against Evert the most important of their eighty-match rivalry. Resolute as Navratilova had just been in the second set, the smart money remained on Evert as the match rolled into the decisive third set. "She's the hatchet woman with the cold, cold heart—she says so herself," Bud Collins said on TV.

The third set was a spellbinding tug-of-war. Even a month after the match, Navratilova claimed she could remember every point. Navratilova broke Evert's serve in the opening game and shot off to a two-games-to-nothing lead. Evert reeled her back in. All the paradoxical traits that opponents often cited about Evert—her striking tendency to actually hit harder rather than more tentatively when she was down, her habit of making her conservative game less conservative under pressure—were surfacing now.

Evert set her mouth in a taut thin line and tried her best to close Navratilova out. She left Navratilova swiping futilely at a dizzying array of shots—backhand service return winners she struck off Navratilova's booming serve, some bulletlike ground strokes that hugged the lines, short balls that she smacked on the run past Navratilova at ridiculously sharp angles.

Navratilova stared down at the grass, muttering.

Evert won four straight games in all, breaking Navratilova's serve at love in the last to seize a 4–2 final set lead. She was now just eight points from victory. The match had assumed the familiar feel of so many of Evert's previous matches—until she uncharacteristically missed a forehand. That gave Navratilova a glimmer of hope for a service break. Then Evert watched helplessly as Navratilova got her first lucky bounce of the day—a ball struck by Evert that slapped the top of the net, slithered along the tape for an agonizing instant, then plopped back onto Evert's side of the court as if exhausted.

Given that boost, Navratilova inched back to 3–4, then 4-all. When Evert squandered a break point with another mishit shot, Navratilova sprinted to her courtside chair on the changeover. Navratilova was forcing Evert to play her game now.

Evert barely held serve at 5–4 in the most suspenseful game of the match, somehow running down a drop volley by Navratilova and then bending low enough on a full sprint to dig out a backhand that she daringly sent crosscourt for a winner. "That takes great nerve and great ability!" John Newcombe raved.

Evert seemed to have shoved the pressure back across the court at Navratilova. And Navratilova—still holding a 4–20 lifetime record against Evert and teetering on a threshold where she had faltered so many times before—gathered herself for a last furious push.

And it happened.

Over the next thirteen points Navratilova and Evert played, Navratilova surrendered only one. It was as if everything Navratilova was ever going to be—or not—rose up, burst forth, and found expression in her game. She was playing with a kind of instinctive confidence now. Her volleys were unerringly struck, infallibly placed. She looked relaxed. She moved to snag Evert's shots as if she could read her mind. Her serve, always a blur, became nearly unreturnable. She leveled the match at 5-all with a love service game, then broke Evert at 15–40 to pull ahead. It was as if the court were tilting to one side beneath them. Evert tossed her head, furious at herself. They were at match point now, and Navratilova dashed to the net again, driving a half volley to left frontcourt that Evert came running, running, running in to get— only to see the ball skid under her racket frame and dribble away.

Navratilova cut loose a shriek at the net.

"I can't believe it," Navratilova kept saying, looking around Centre Court and repeating the words, her mouth covered with one hand. The crowd was standing and applauding. She and Evert were both smiling when they hugged at the net. Again, Evert playfully tapped Navratilova on the head as they walked off, Navratilova's head tilted against Evert's in relief.

To look at them, it was hard to tell who had won and who had lost the match.

Navratilova said, "I didn't know whether to laugh or cry or scream."

Just before the Duchess of Kent handed Navratilova the 1978 championship plate on Centre Court, she quietly asked her about her parents in Czechoslovakia. Navratilova told the duchess that they had gone to a town near the German border where they could intercept the West German broadcast of the match.

"My only regret is my family couldn't be here to share this with me," Navratilova later said to reporters.

But it helped—a little, anyway—that her victory was a popular one. In England the next-day headlines read "The Nowhere Girl is the Queen of Wimbledon" . . . "The Ecstasy of the Exile" . . . "Mighty Martina!"

Immediately after the match, Sandra Haynie happily made her way to the tiny locker room for the seeded players, hoping to quickly congratulate Martina and leave. Haynie found only Evert there. Navratilova was still at her press conference. Trying to be respectful, Haynie sat down without a word on a small settee, thinking she'd wait quietly until Navratilova returned. To Haynie's surprise, a downcast Evert walked over and softly said, "May I sit here?" and motioned to the open spot beside her.

Haynie said sure and asked Evert if she'd like her to leave.

"No, no," Evert replied. And for a while, that's all that was said.

"She was upset," Haynie says, "so I didn't say another word to her. She just kind of collected herself for a couple minutes. Then she said, 'Okay. Thank you,' and she stood up to go, and that was it. But when I saw Chris later she said, 'Thank you for that.' I said, 'What?' She said, 'I just knew that you, of all people, would understand how I felt, even if you're a golfer and not a tennis player.' And that meant a lot to me. Because she was right."

Evert was genuinely happy for Navratilova. "I think she felt I was too good a player not to have won a Grand Slam title yet," Navratilova said. But months later, Evert would explain there was another reason for her ambivalence about losing the match.

Waiting for her in the Wimbledon tea room was British heart-throb and tennis star John Lloyd.

As a young woman, when Evert tried to picture herself as a wife, she always thought that she would have to marry another top player because only he could understand or tolerate what tennis demanded. But the difficulties she and Jimmy Connors had had in reconciling their careers disabused Evert of that notion. Not long after she began dating Lloyd during the Wimbledon fortnight, Evert said she no longer believed she would have to be with a player ranked number one or three or even five in the world.

"How about number thirty-two?" she was asked.

"Let's not get ridiculous," Evert shot back.

Evert was a star, all right, with the full complement of star perks, star headaches, and a star's ego. For the most part, Evert liked her status. "She got away with *mur*-der," Ingrid Bentzer says with a laugh. "But it wasn't all her fault. People let her. Chrissie has a warm heart. But when she was on top she could just walk all over people. She needs a bit of resistance, then the good Chrissie comes out."

Sometimes Evert asserted her rank just for laughs. At opening ceremonies for the 1978 Federation Cup tournament, Evert couldn't resist when Tracy Austin, still just fifteen years old, turned to Evert and whispered, "Who's the new girl on the Soviet team?"

"Nikita Khrushchev," Evert deadpanned.

"Ahhhh," Austin said.

In 1980, Mary Carillo, who was still trying to extend her injury-marred career, nervously walked out to play Evert in a doubles match at Eastbourne. On their way to the court, Evert turned to Carillo and amiably said, "Boy, Mary, it's been a long time since we've played, hasn't it?"

Carillo said, "Actually, Chris, this is the first time we've ever played."

Evert shot Carillo a sideways glance and said, "So . . ."

Droll pause.

"How does it feel?"

On other occasions, Evert's star turns were dead serious. The same competitive streak that made it hard for her to concede a single point made it difficult for her to tolerate being in someone else's shade for long. As president of the players union and the sport's leading female star, Evert was a power broker in every sense of the phrase. Evert had a deserved reputation for being diplomatic in public. But, privately, she would air her feelings out.

Pam Shriver tells a story about being forced into singles and not just doubles play for a U.S. Federation Cup team one year because Navratilova, by then a U.S. citizen, was injured. When a reporter suggested to Shriver that her ability to handle her unaccustomed singles role could be the most important factor in a U.S. team victory, Shriver agreed—only to find Evert banging on her hotel room door at seven a.m. the next day, waving the newspaper at her and saying, "Most important on the team, huh? Is *that* what you think?"

Evert always said that her blossoming romance with John Lloyd contributed to her late-match drift in her 1978 Wimbledon final against Navratilova, an assertion Navratilova challenged. "I always played better the times I was falling in love," Navratilova said. But Ingrid Bentzer, who introduced John and Chris to each other at Wimbledon, agrees that "almost immediately, both of them were totally cross-eyed with each other.

"It was near the time Princess Di and Prince Charles were married," Bentzer recalls, "and it [later] became something of a fairy tale . . . the English acquiring Chris Evert."

John Lloyd was the best male tennis player in Britain, a country not used to having any. He was a blond, blue-eyed pinup boy who reached the finals of the Australian Open the year before but found the crush of women and girls shrieking for him at Wimbledon that same year so distracting, he blamed them for his thudding, five-set loss to Germany's Kari Meller in the second round. Just one match earlier, Lloyd had inflamed hopes by upsetting fourth-seeded Roscoe Tanner, the rocket-serving American.

"It's nice to have a fan club," Lloyd told reporters, "[but] these girls come here knowing nothing about tennis. They just want to study my legs. As I'm about to serve, they say: 'Let's take a photo of him' and 'Isn't he lovely?' I know Borg and the other top players have had to master this, but at the moment I cannot close my ears to it."

As penance, he became known thereafter as "Legs Lloyd."

Evert had wanted Bentzer to introduce her to Lloyd after reading a newspaper interview he had given a few weeks before the 1978 tournament. Lloyd talked about how the constant travel on tour made having a personal life difficult. He said that he wished he could meet somebody that he could fall in love with, someone who would travel with him and share his life. The story—not to mention the accompanying photo of a shirtless Lloyd—caught Evert's attention.

"I had been feeling the same way about the tour for some time," she said. Evert, now twenty-four, was four months back from her four-month break. On her way to Wimbledon, she had told her friend Stephanie Tolleson, "No one understands what it's like. I'm number one in the world and I'm unhappy."

When Evert and Lloyd were finally introduced by Bentzer in the Wimbledon tea room, Lloyd said, "Lovely to meet you," and Evert's heart sank. Evert had never heard a man use the word "lovely" before, and as Lloyd walked away, she looked at Bentzer and moaned, "Oh no. He's gay!"

"He most certainly is *not*," Bentzer growled. "He's British."

The three of them agreed to meet a few nights later at a trendy London disco called Tramps. "I felt terribly superfluous," Bentzer says. Within three months, Evert and Lloyd were talking marriage. By Christmastime they were engaged. Their wedding took place on April 17, 1979, just nine months after they met, at St. Anthony's, Evert's childhood church in Fort Lauderdale, just around the corner from the Holiday Park tennis courts she was reared on.

The wedding was one of the city's social events of the year. Nearly a thousand fans gathered outside the church, hours before the ceremony, hoping to catch a glimpse of Evert and Lloyd. The press clamored unsuccessfully to be allowed in. Navratilova and Billie Jean King were among the 125 invitees who attended the wedding. At times the day unfolded like a fire drill gone bad. Evert realized on the way to the church that she had forgotten her bouquet at her house, and the entire wedding party had to turn around and go back. Bentzer threw everyone into a panic that morning when she started to get dressed for the ceremony and realized she'd forgotten to bring her undergarments. Once at the church, Stephanie Tolleson, one of Evert's bridesmaids, gave Evert a kiss and wished her good luck, then turned to make her walk down the aisle, tripped on the carpet, and fell flat on her face. When Tolleson stood up, her hair was a mess. As she limped off, Evert couldn't stop laughing.

Just before walking Chris to the altar, Jimmy Evert threw back a couple of stiff shots of liquor.

The reception went off without a hitch—if you don't count the bomb threat that someone called in.

Still, everyone raved that the bride and groom looked great and a fabulous time was had by all.

Looking back on her whirlwind courtship and marriage to Lloyd, Evert unsparingly said of herself, "All my life I pictured myself as one day becoming a cute little housewife. It was another variation of the way I saw myself in tennis, as a little walking, talking tennis doll. So when I grew disenchanted with tennis, I grabbed for that other idealized little image."

But Evert couldn't loosen her grip on tennis. When the weather proved too cold during the first few days of her honeymoon with Lloyd in Bermuda, Evert wanted to cut the trip short and fly back to resume their stay at her parents' home in Fort Lauderdale. "Was that an omen or what?" Evert says. "I literally said, 'Whoops! Honeymoon's over! I want to go back to Florida and start training again.'"

Evert had often wondered if she'd be able to combine marriage with her devotion to her career. At the Italian Open a few weeks after her wedding, Evert wondered if she had just experienced another foreshadowing. Suddenly Navratilova wasn't the only looming threat. Evert's attention was arrested by a sixteen-year-old girl with long pigtails that drooped down either side of her narrow face like basset hound ears, a blond American girl with a nerveless game and ferocious attitude who traveled with her mother and still dressed in pinafores trimmed in gingham and lace.

"Tracy Austin wanted to be Chris, and Chris didn't like that," says Rosie Casals. "There's only one Chris."

CHAPTER SEVEN

THE PERFECT STORM

Evert hadn't dismissed Navratilova as a rival when Tracy Austin came along. But she didn't need to fixate on Navratilova once she slipped into another listless cycle following her first Wimbledon win. Navratilova strained her shoulder in the fall of 1978 and used the nagging injury as an excuse to float through the rest of the year—a "cop-out," she admits. Pam Shriver, then just sixteen years old and as gangly as a newborn colt, handed Navratilova a shocking defeat in the U.S. Open semifinals in September. Evert beat Shriver in the final, and kept methodically moving forward.

"Chris was smart enough to see just how big a threat Martina was," says Mary Carillo. "She was already looking at her and thinking, 'Well, I don't do that, I don't hit that shot, I don't *want* to hit that shot, and—Oops!—there's another thing I don't do. And that over there? You couldn't *pay* me to do *that*.' Chris sized all of that up pretty quickly. She knew there was all this raw talent, raw energy, and raw power in Martina, and I think she was smart enough to know that Martina could be a perfect storm one day. The question with Martina was always when."

"But Tracy was different. Tracy had this nerveless Chrissie game."

After her win over Shriver, Evert didn't lose a match the rest of 1978. She beat Navratilova the last three times they played to edge her for the year-end number one ranking that was voted on by the press and the International Tennis Federation's three-member board. Navratilova was still number one in the WTA computer rankings, but she was unhappy that Evert won the other two honors. "I think I deserved it," Navratilova said. "I dominated for eight months, and Chris only did for three."

Looking ahead to 1979, Navratilova added, "I want to be number one in the mind of every single person on this earth."

Navratilova and Sandra Haynie parted ways after nearly three years together. In February of 1979, another player on the tennis tour asked Navratilova if she'd be willing to talk to novelist Rita Mae Brown, the bitingly funny lesbian author of the underground hit *Rubyfruit Jungle,* for a new book Brown was researching. Navratilova agreed. When Brown and Navratilova finally met for lunch, Brown questioned her at length about life in Czechoslovakia for a fictional character she was thinking of creating. Navratilova found Brown intellectually stimulating and "amusing as hell." They fell out of touch for a few months, then got back in contact again—this time after Navratilova called Brown. They agreed to meet in Chicago for what Brown later termed "a lunch that never ended." By the summer of 1979, they were seeing each other.

Brown, then thirty-three, was twelve years older than Navratilova, and she rapidly pushed her to broaden her worldview, taking her to museums and cultural events, talking to her about literature, politics, and her days as a controversial member of the women's and gay rights movements. As mind-expanding and politicizing as that time was for Navratilova—"My self-image [before Brown] was that of an athlete, unconnected to the world of activism and meetings and writings and ideas," Navratilova wrote in her autobiography—Brown did little to encourage Navratilova's training habits. Grace

Lichtenstein, who shared the same literary agent as Brown for a while, says, "I don't think Rita Mae could bear playing second fiddle or sitting like a little wifey in the stands, rooting for her girlfriend, you know?"

On some nights when Brown traveled with her, Navratilova barely arrived at the arena in time for her matches. Whether from hubris or the ambivalence that Brown encouraged, Navratilova began experiencing some of the ennui toward tennis that Evert had. Evert had always spoken of being married and having kids and retiring by age twenty-five. She thought she wanted more balance in her life. Navratilova thought her life would change drastically after she won Wimbledon, but she felt that nothing much had. The state-run Czech media was still banned from mentioning her name. Navratilova was still years away from getting her U.S. citizenship. She still ached to be reunited with her family.

Noting that Evert had gotten a hometown parade the first time she won Wimbledon, Navratilova told a *Times of London* reporter, "I never had that sense of belonging. I didn't get any of that. When I won Wimbledon the first time, something was missing."

It was Rita Mae Brown's considered opinion that Navratilova wouldn't find what she was searching for in a trifle such as a tennis match.

Little did Navratilova know that by the time she and Evert arrived in Rome for the 1979 Italian Open, Evert was sinking into a crisis worse than whatever angst Navratilova felt.

As much as the differences between Evert and Navratilova enlivened their rivalry, the same contrasts created some helpful distance between them. Evert, who admitted, "I lived most of my life in fear," was drawn to Navratilova's abandon and risk-taking and unapologetic bluntness. She envied Navratilova's athletic ability. Evert says she never had a problem reconciling Navratilova's homosexuality with her own conservative upbringing. "I think it's because my parents just never made a big deal about that sort of thing,"

Evert says. "They never said a bad word about gay people, not even when I first began playing the tennis tour. My mother treated everyone the same, and so I did too."

Navratilova, torn from her country and family and everything she had known as a girl, craved the self-control, public affection, and sense of community that Evert enjoyed. Navratilova said, "When I was a kid a long way from home, Chris and her mom were nice to me." She admitted, "I wanted to be more like Chris because I wanted the crowds to like me more. I played tennis in an exciting way—it was a good contrast with the two of us—and I thought I was just as good a human being as Chris was. So I thought, 'Why don't they like me?' Of course, I didn't come across as well as I could have . . . [And] Chris was such a perfect girl next door, the image. I just didn't know what I was up against."

Like Evert, Navratilova was sensitive about what was said or written about her. Navratilova always had a deep sense of injustice. She saw herself as a person of integrity. The constant tension between being true to herself and doing what would make her passage through life easier sometimes wore on her.

"I don't think Martina wanted to be straight," says George Vecsey, Navratilova's coauthor. "But I think she probably obsessed on the idea [of being] mainstream, loved, accepted the way Chrissie was. Martina didn't want it at the price of changing anything about herself, or doing anything about it. It just would've been nice for her to have everything she had *and* be Miss America."

Tracy Austin was an entirely different creature. Whereas Navratilova found playing Austin quite similar to playing Evert, Evert found playing Austin disturbing. Austin's baseline game and attitude were distractingly similar to her own. Evert was already pondering the life change her marriage had brought. Then along came Austin, whom the twenty-four-year-old Evert quickly came to regard as a younger, better, spookier version of herself. Austin had the same traditional feminine look, the same two-fisted backhand, the same unbreakable mind-set. Austin was exceedingly smart too. Her father was a rocket scientist.

Austin, though just sixteen, also had the arrogance of a pro champion long before she was one. Her coach at the time, Dutchborn Robert Lansdorp, the best ground stroke teacher in the game, is a tall, imposing man with a shaggy head of white hair and a baritone voice that seems to rumble up from deep in his barrel chest. He laughs when asked if all number one players have a bit of diva in them.

"Diva, diva . . . I do not know this word 'diva'—but I know the word 'bitch,' " Lansdorp booms. "And I'm telling you, it's almost the bigger the bitches [they are], the better they play."

Lansdorp laughs and adds, "You almost try to build this sort of egotistical, self-centered, I'm-the-greatest kind of person because you sort of want them to have that, you know? That's what they *have* to have. But then you kind of regret it a little bit later because once they get to that point, you think, 'Why aren't they just a little more friendly, a little nicer, more compassionate?' But they are just *such* bitches! They are."

He wags his head and smiles.

"It's very difficult," he sighs.

Lansdorp is renowned as a pitiless taskmaster. "If you want to puke, do it in your lunch bag," he would yell at players during practice. Yet Lansdorp says Austin asked more of herself than he did. Austin would drive herself to the point of exhaustion. Even in practice, she would bound after balls she had no chance of reaching. "She just couldn't let it go," says Lansdorp. He once took Austin ice skating when she was ten and accidentally fell on her, breaking her leg. Not long afterward, Lansdorp found Austin back on the court at her club, her leg still in a cast, hitting volleys while sitting in a chair.

"She was the first woman to come along tougher than the Ice Maiden," Lansdorp says.

The notion of failure—even against Evert—never seemed to enter Austin's mind.

"When you ask me that, it's like you think I thought, 'It's Chris Evert on the other side' when I don't *care* who's on the other side,"

Austin says. She is sitting in her impeccably decorated living room in Rolling Hills, California, more than two decades after she first played Evert, and she is still speaking in the present tense. "If I play her, I have to dissect her game, same as any person I'm playing. I have to figure out how I can win, what's the best way to win. I *want* to win. And I will do anything I can—I will dive on the ground, I will stay mentally tough. Whatever it takes. So, no, I wasn't intimidated by her."

That was probably a new experience for Evert.

"I guess," Austin says with a shrug.

Austin was well known in tennis circles long before she first defeated Evert. She had been touted as a phenom on the cover of *World Tennis* magazine when she was three. When she took her first look at fellow teenager Steffi Graf, the future twenty-two-time Grand Slam champion from Germany, she dismissively told reporters: "We have a hundred like her back in the States." By age thirteen, Austin had taken a set from fifty-eight-year-old Bobby Riggs and she had won so many age-group titles and exhibitions that *Tennis* magazine ran a story suggesting Austin was pound-for-pound the best female player in the world.

At the time, Austin tipped the scales at eighty pounds.

At sixteen, Austin launched what became a full-blown psychodrama for Evert by beating her in the final of the 1979 Italian Open, rallying from a 2–4 deficit in the final set to snap Evert's six-year, 125-match winning streak on clay. It was the most significant title of Austin's career thus far, and Evert claimed to be more relieved than stunned that her streak had ended. But when she got back to her hotel room with her husband, John, Evert cried. They stayed awake until four a.m., talking. It was as if Evert had gotten her first glimpse at her own mortality, and she was shaken. "I felt it was the end of an era," she says.

Lloyd, who played in the men's Italian Open two weeks later, was fighting his own demons. In Britain, Lloyd had resided comfortably among the top two or three players in the country, he played Davis Cup and enjoyed a nice bit of renown. But as he and Evert moved from their whirlwind engagement to their wedding to their first six months of married life, Lloyd began a grim losing streak that clanked to ten, then fifteen, then nineteen consecutive matches. "John was a little awed when he and Chrissie married," says their coach Dennis Ralston. "He was overwhelmed by it all."

The more Lloyd lost, the more pressure he put on himself and the worse he played. His tournament runs became vicious cycles of shaky optimism giving way to abject embarrassment replaced by brutal self-recrimination. Before long, he wasn't just losing. He began to quit at the hint of adversity. "And Chrissie just couldn't wrap her mind around tanking," Ralston says. "The idea was completely foreign to her."

At the Italian Open, Lloyd was ahead of Australian Phil Dent, 6–2, 3–0, when he hit a shot that bounced just a few inches out of bounds. After that, Lloyd hung his head. His movements became halfhearted. He kept muttering, "Oh, it's no good . . . Stuff it . . . I can't play." He didn't win another game in the match, losing 6–2, 3–6, 0–6. Evert, who was watching from the stands, was livid.

Evert had skipped playing a tournament to support Lloyd, and the only other person she'd ever done that for was Jimmy Connors, who played every point of every match with a passion that bordered at times on madness. Connors flung his entire body into his strokes as if he wanted to disintegrate the ball. As Lloyd's losing streak dragged on, Evert came to believe that he couldn't cope with the pressure of being married to her and was taking it out on her.

"I don't care if you lose every match, but why do you humiliate yourself out there? You've got no guts," Evert angrily told Lloyd after the match. "It doesn't matter to me what you do—paint walls if you like—but put your heart into it."

Evert was rocked again at Wimbledon a few weeks later. First, John's free fall continued. He lost in the first round to Sweden's

Ove Bengston, again in straight sets. This time David Lloyd, John's brother and Davis Cup teammate, chewed out John—in the newspapers.

Then Evert lost to Navratilova for the second consecutive year in the final, 6–4, 6–4. The match wasn't as close as the score appeared. Evert barely held on in many of her service games, and she rarely threatened Navratilova, who played the match with a light heart and extra incentive.

Watching from the friends' box was Navratilova's beaming mother, Jana.

The Duchess of Kent, touched by Navratilova's mention of her absent family a year earlier during the 1978 Wimbledon trophy presentation, had helped reunite Navratilova and her mother for the first time since Martina's defection. At the duchess's request, the All England Club sent Jana an official invitation to the tournament, which Martina's father, Mirek, insisted on hand-delivering to the Prague office of the Czech prime minister, Lubomir Strougal. Three days before Wimbledon began, Navratilova learned that her mother had been granted a temporary visa to travel to England.

By their emotional reunion at Heathrow Airport just seventy-two hours later, the same Monday the 1979 tournament started, they hadn't seen each other in nearly four years. They cried for joy on sight. Jana brought her daughter a tin of cookies she had baked that morning in Revnice. Each of them giggled and exclaimed that the other was even prettier than she remembered.

"Winning here last year was the greatest moment of my career," Martina said the next day, "but yesterday [at the airport] was one of the great moments of my life."

Jana had to return to Czechoslovakia three days after Martina won the Wimbledon title. But they were able to attend the Champions Ball and went on a shopping spree in London before Jana left. By the end of 1979, they received more heart-lifting news: Martina's parents and sister, whose visa applications had been denied every year since Martina left, would be allowed to emigrate to the United States. Navratilova happily prepared for their December 1979 arrival by buying a house for them just three hundred yards down the street from her Dallas home.

Navratilova's personal life seemed to be coming together just as Evert's was in flux. After her negotiation of the coming months, no one could call Evert the Ice Maiden anymore.

When Tracy Austin snapped Evert's 125-match clay-court winning streak at the Italian Open in May and Navratilova upended her at Wimbledon, Evert's contention that marriage had left her no longer "obsessed" with the number one ranking had begun to look like manifest destiny.

Evert was not the same player without her singular sense of purpose. She knew that. After sobbing the first few times she and John had to leave each other to return to the tour after they were married, Evert told herself that her behavior couldn't continue. "To protect myself, I got hardened," she recalls. "I told myself, 'Just stop it' and 'This is just the way it's going to be.' " Evert's solution was to compartmentalize her feelings. "If I was playing tennis, my reality was my life on the tour, and when I came home, my life was with John," she says. "But it was hard. It was always all or nothing. We were on our separate tours. We were always like strangers for a few days when we got back home. And I always kept something in reserve after that because I didn't want to get so emotional again."

John was still struggling to recapture his game. Only nineteen months had passed since his advance to the 1977 Australian Open final, and a career that had been climbing toward the top twenty before his romance with Evert had now dramatically hit the skids. If Lloyd—a genial man who enjoyed celebrity—had any pretensions that he and Chris would preside as the sort of glamour couple that she and Jimmy Connors were, he fell miserably short.

"I think John had started believing he had to compete with Connors, be a big name, and if he didn't, he was a failure," says their coach Dennis Ralston. "That was just not true. Not everyone can be number two, three, four in the world. John was an accomplished player, but not in that top echelon. He was good, but at a level below the very best. And Chrissie did everything she could for a while, but it wasn't enough. It was hard—hard on John, hard on Chrissie."

Evert's disgust with John's tanking was an open secret on tour. People began to titter that Lloyd was a wonderful fellow, a fantastically supportive husband who got along beautifully with Evert's family and friends, but he couldn't handle being Mr. Chris Evert. He couldn't operate in the heat that Evert's celebrity and success threw off.

The English press was especially hard on Lloyd.

When it comes to self-mockery or artful dissection of one's own sportsmen, the English are unparalleled; they've made eating their children a highly stylized parlor game. They excel at self-flagellation and deep contemplations on Big Themes such as what English tennis players (or soccer stars, or cricketers . . .) reveal about the national character. A tepid adjective is never used when a hyperbolic one will do. Losses aren't just disappointing—they're disastrous, mortifying, unconscionable! The English press is unsurpassed too at putting new psychic wounds into historical or literary contexts that stretch back hundreds of years. And all of it is spurred along by one of the few things that the English will actually brag that they're good at: losing.

The British had been pining for one of their countrymen to come along and win Wimbledon since Fred Perry last had in 1936. Building up each new tennis hopeful and then bemoaning their annual failures at the All England Club was a well-entrenched pattern by the time Lloyd came along, igniting hope anew. As Sue Mott of London's *Daily Telegraph* wrote years later, "No home-grown tennis player starts with the score at nil–nil. Psychologically, they are one down already. They play in a trench of old bones, sore defeats, and diabolical performances from which it is wretchedly hard to excavate themselves."

Ralston, sighing at the memory of the criticism Lloyd endured, says, "They expected more from John than he had."

At first, Evert and Lloyd's individual stumbles and Evert's psychodrama with Austin were written off to the distraction of being newlyweds. But while Evert was constantly churning inside, loathing each loss, asking herself how she could balance both marriage and her career, John said he saw a bright side to his early tournament exits: he could hop the next plane and be together again with his wife that much sooner. In time, he became awestruck at what he called "the absolute fire" that Evert had and he did not.

"Certain things about her drive were just incomprehensible to me," Lloyd recalls. "If I had lost the singles final at Wimbledon, I would probably go have a few nights out, probably drown my sorrows. Then I'd probably lie on the beach a couple weeks. But when I said to Chrissie on the plane home once after she had lost Wimbledon, 'What do you want to do? Do you want to take some rest?' she said, 'No. I want to practice as soon as we get into Florida.' I said, 'You've got to be kidding. It's about 110 degrees, 100 percent humidity. We've just flown eight hours.' And she looked at me and said, 'I don't want to lose a match like that again.' When we landed, she did work out."

At moments like that Lloyd would think, "Now I understand why you're as great as you are."

By the 1979 U.S. Open, Austin was no longer just Evert's problem. She became Navratilova's obstacle too. Playing with a total lack of self-consciousness or fear, Austin edged Navratilova, 7–5, 7–5, in a breathtakingly tense semifinal match. Then Austin denied Evert her fourth straight Open title in the final with a dominating 6–4, 6–3 win. Evert says, "I was shattered." Journalist Steve Flink, who was sitting next to Chris's mother, Colette, in the friends' box that day, says, "When Chris was down one set and fell behind 5–2, she looked over at us, and I never saw a more disconsolate look on her face. She just shook her head like, 'Forget it. It's hopeless.' "

With the victory, Austin became the youngest U.S. Open champion in history at sixteen years and nine months. Evert says, "Of all my losses to Tracy, the U.S. Open was the worst, because, honestly, that was the first time I doubted myself and whether I could ever beat her. I thought Tracy would dominate the next ten years. I thought she was that good."

After Austin trounced Evert three more times indoors in a ten-day span in early 1980, Evert was struggling to keep playing, period. Following the last defeat, a 6–2, 6–1 rout in Cincinnati, Austin says, "I saw Chris crying so hard in the training room, it really shook me up. I was looking at a person who was crumbling. I got out of there as fast as I could."

Evert asked Lloyd to join her immediately at a Chicago tournament. "I need you—I feel like I'm having a breakdown," she said. John quickly flew in. Evert tried to soldier on to the next few tour stops, but it was no use. She lost badly in a final again—this time to Navratilova—and she turned on John during their car ride back to their hotel with Ingrid Bentzer.

John gently told Chris, "Listen love, it's just one loss, it's not the whole world," only to have Evert wheel toward him and say through gritted teeth, "That's not the point. I don't care if I win or lose, I care about doing my best and I didn't do my best. I *couldn't* produce my best. *That's* the whole point."

Bentzer says that the edge in Evert's voice gave her chills.

"Tracy was tough: 'little punk, goddamn pinafore'—that's what you thought as she was beating you," Bentzer says. "And Chrissie just got to the point with her life and with tennis where she said, 'I cannot hit another ball.' It was like being in a hamster wheel and the wheel just rolls faster and faster and faster."

Evert announced a few weeks later that she was "burned out" and would be taking an indefinite leave from the tour to "assess my future." She had never lost five straight matches to anyone in her career as she had against Austin.

When Evert looked at Austin, she thought, "This girl is more eager. She's younger, she's faster, she moves better than I do. She hits the ball harder. She does everything better than I do." Evert likened the fearless—almost feral—look in Austin's eyes to what Jimmy Connors saw across the net when he first played young John McEnroe. Austin wore pigtails and that pinafore; McEnroe, hailed as a boy genius when he became the youngest man in one hundred years to roll to the Wimbledon semifinals in 1977 as an eighteen-year-old qualifier, used to bring a paper bag lunch onto the court with him like some schoolboy, just in case he became embroiled in a long match.

Exceptional as Austin was, not everyone agreed with Evert's assessment. The greater consensus was something Lansdorp voiced: "Tracy had crawled inside the Ice Maiden's head."

In addition to her problems with Austin, Evert was 2–5 against Navratilova in 1979—her first losing year against her. John Lloyd says, "It had literally gotten to the point where Chrissie was scared to play anyone."

The February morning that Evert decided to leave the tour, she vomited in her hotel room in Seattle. It was the first time in her career that she had done that before a match. She was preparing to play a final against Virginia Wade, and John told her, "Chrissie, this is just not worth it." This time, Evert agreed. She called the tournament office and defaulted. Then she and John caught a flight to their condominium in Palm Springs.

Evert wasn't sure when she left the tour if she would ever return to tennis. But no one who knew her believed that for a minute. Her pride was too great. Her desire too unquenchable.

"When Chrissie did come back," Bentzer says, "she was chewing iron and spitting nails."

The toll that tennis had taken on Evert, the anxiety attacks and psychological torment she experienced as her losses to Austin mounted, are not uncommon at the world-class level of the sport. Bullfighting and boxing are the only other sports in which as many athletes report going out for their battles feeling so absolutely vulnerable, naked, so utterly alone.

Harold Solomon, who played the men's tour for fifteen seasons before he turned to coaching, says, "I've seen plenty of players puke from the pressure. I've seen people's hands go cold as if there's no blood in them. I've seen people cramping before they walk on the court. I've seen them have panic attacks, hyperventilate, cry, go crazy. Regular people don't know what it's like. Some players get nervous to the point where they can hardly speak before they go on the court."

"And it's not just the women," says IMG agent Barbara Perry, who coordinated the Legends Tours that many of the retired stars played during the 1990s. "We had a round-robin tournament at McNichols Arena in Denver one year. It was your usual exhibition— in one day, out of town the next. Well, John McEnroe lost to Jimmy Connors, and later I found John crying in the boiler room at the arena. That's how badly he still wanted to win."

McEnroe, after three years of being number one, said, "If I'm the greatest ever, then why do I feel so empty inside?"

Something vital snapped in Bjorn Borg, perhaps the most driven champion of all, when McEnroe defeated him in the 1981 U.S. Open final and took away his number one ranking. Borg didn't even bother to stay for the on-court award presentation. He walked directly off the court and climbed into a car, drove to the airport, and boarded a flight. Three months later, he retired at age twenty-six.

Driven as Evert was, even she never approximated Borg's off-court ablutions or ascetic lifestyle. As Tim Adams detailed in his book *Being John McEnroe*, Borg's rituals for Wimbledon, which he won five consecutive times from 1976 to 1980, reflected a fanatical, "almost pathological" focus:

> Each night he set the air conditioner to 12 degrees [celcius] and slept naked with no blankets for 10 hours. His pulse rate on waking was never above 50 beats a minute. He maintained his body weight for the duration of the tournament at exactly 73 kilos. Anything else, he felt, altered his balance and took the edge off his reflexes. Two days before the tournament began he had a two-hour massage with his coach, the giant former Swedish Davis Cup captain Lennart Bergelin. . . . Lennart's strong fingers don't spare a single

square inch of Bjorn's body, but Bjorn takes it all in silence as if it were an initiation rite.

The night before his opening game, Borg and Bergelin, as they always did, took his fifty highly strung Donnay rackets and, for a couple hours, tested the tension of each by gently hitting them together and listening to the sound they made. Each racket was laid on the floor according to its relative musical pitch, an arrangement not disturbed for a fortnight, save to remove, in order, the six rackets he would use in each match.

Like Borg, Evert had just been overtaken for number one when Austin drove her off the tour in 1980. Evert sent Borg an understanding note when he quit. She had long ago gotten used to the nausea she always felt before she played. Some nights before a match Evert wouldn't think she was particularly nervous. "Then I would be watching TV in my hotel room, and I would look down and notice both of my fists were clenched," she says. "The pressure was just there. Every day that I woke up, it was there."

During some matches Evert's hands would cramp from squeezing her racket grip so tightly. As she waited once to do an on-court TV interview with Mary Carillo immediately after a U.S. Open match, Evert asked Carillo, "Can you help me?"

"She wanted me to pry her fingers off her racket handle, because she couldn't," Carillo recalls.

The public knew none of this. Evert was still seen as the imperturbable champion, the goddess atop the pedestal, the woman with the perfect husband and perfect life. Privately, however, Evert had deep misgivings about the effect tennis was taking on her marriage and her life.

"My self-image depended on my tennis, my moods depended on whether I won or lost," Evert says. "You just get so involved. I was totally selfish and thought about myself and nobody else, because if you let up for one minute, someone was going to come along and beat you. So I really wouldn't let anyone, or any slice of happiness, enter. I won, but most of the time I didn't enjoy it. I would think, 'I have to win this match. I'm supposed to win this match.' "

Still, it didn't take much downtime to convince Evert that quitting wasn't the answer. Her second week in Palm Springs, Evert accompanied John to the practice court one day and hit with him a little bit. The next time out, she played for nearly an hour. Soon it became two hours again. Within a month, Evert was driving herself to make a comeback.

Ultimately, Evert decided that instead of quitting tennis completely, she needed to overhaul her approach. She needed to better balance her enormous will to win against her impulse to regard every defeat as a disaster. "Otherwise, it'll kill you," she said.

Given the opposite trajectories their careers were taking, there was no argument about whether her career or John's would come first. "John decided, 'Okay, I'm going to be with you, I'm going to coach you for a while,' " Evert says. "But he wasn't happy."

Evert ended her break after two months. She vowed that she wasn't going to worry about how Austin or Navratilova were playing. If she could just get her own hunger back, Evert told herself, she still had enough game at age twenty-six to beat anybody.

Then she set out to prove it, with Austin and Navratilova fixed squarely in her crosshairs again.

Even as Evert realized that she wasn't built for a life of domesticity just yet, Navratilova's new home life with her parents was descending into difficulties just a few months after their reunion. Her parents' initial amazement at routine features of American life, things as commonplace as the well-stocked supermarkets near their Dallas home, faded quickly, replaced by a sense of displacement that Mirek, especially, found acute.

Navratilova's parents depended on her heavily whether she was at home or on the road. Before they arrived they had had no idea of how often Martina had to travel to play the tour. Mirek was a traditional Czech man with traditional values. He was fifty years old and he still wanted to work. But work at what? He had been an economist at a trolley factory in Czechoslovakia, but his English was rudimentary. He began to miss his friends, his card games, and village life back home.

"The way Martina put it to me was, she had become the parent," Bud Collins says.

Navratilova had not told her parents that she was gay. But when she mentioned to them a few months after they arrived that she was considering buying a second home with Rita Mae Brown in Charlottesville, Virginia, Mirek confronted her. He said he believed that she and Brown were living as "man and wife."

"I didn't want to lie to him," Navratilova said. "So I told him he was right."

Mirek was upset. He told Martina she had a "sickness." He urged her to see a doctor. He said, "I'd rather you were an alcoholic or a hooker who slept with a different man every night." Then their argument escalated.

Navratilova and Brown went through with the house purchase. But when Mirek and Jana made their first trip to Charlottesville a few months later, Mirek became so uncomfortable at the sight of Rita Mae and Martina together, he and Martina again fell into a roaring argument when Brown was out. This time, Martina's mother, Jana, joined in. During the heated back-and-forth, there were more insults by her parents, and more rejoinders from Martina.

Finally Navratilova's mother blurted out that she was afraid Martina was going to end up just like her biological father.

"What does that mean?" Martina shot back. And everyone stopped.

For the first time, Navratilova learned why her natural father's visits had abruptly ended when she was ten. He had committed suicide seven years after he and Jana were divorced. He was distraught that another woman had left him, and he killed himself while he was in the hospital for a treatable stomach problem. Martina had been told he died in surgery.

"You're just like him—you're going to be just like your father," Navratilova's mother now cried.

Martina was crushed.

"Some of the things that were said to her, she didn't get over—she probably never has, and never will," George Vecsey says. "Martina's parents later came around and accepted her sexuality. But I don't think Martina had the forces or the background back then to interpret what her parents said about her father's suicide, except to think, 'Oh my God, what if I do turn out like him?'

"You have to understand, these are not psychological people," adds Vecsey. "Martina is more psychologically oriented now than she was twenty years ago. [But coming from] Eastern Europe, from Communism, the people there, to them a tree is a tree, a man is a man, a river is a river, and what's all this symbolism stuff? To suddenly be told, 'This is how your father died' and 'You remind me a lot of him'—I think that was a real concern for her for a long time. I don't know that she ever said, 'I have found myself feeling suicidal.' But I think she said, 'I have found myself worrying that I could someday be feeling that way.' And, I mean, that's obviously reasonable. It's just one notch removed."

Navratilova loved her parents. She believed that her parents loved her. But in July of 1980, just eight months into their stay in the United States, her parents returned to Czechoslovakia with Martina's sister, at Mirek's insistence.

They were freely choosing to return to life behind the iron curtain, to a place where they would no longer be able to travel freely or see their oldest daughter. And she would again be unable to visit them.

The decision was achingly sad for everyone.

"We had our chance to be together back in 1980," Martina told Vecsey, "but we let it get away."

After her parents' return to Czechoslovakia, Navratilova began living with Rita Mae Brown in the twenty-room stone mansion they bought just outside Charlottesville. The sprawling house, which sat on nine acres and was built in the mid-1800s, had six baths and a five-car garage that was nearly big enough to handle the seven cars Navratilova had acquired. The fleet included a Mercedes convertible, a BMW, a Pontiac J-car, a Jeep, a Porsche 928, and two Rolls-Royces, one a Corniche and the other a Silver Cloud with Virgil's phrase *Amor Vincit Omnia*—or "Love Conquers All"—painted on the side.

The University of Virginia was nearby, and Navratilova, for the first time, experienced life in a college town. But Brown quickly grew tired of Navratilova's schedule and quit joining her on the road by their second year together. Brown decided to concentrate instead on finishing her latest novel. She thought Navratilova should consider what to do next with her life too. Navratilova would later admit that she listened to Brown's advice to concentrate less on tennis more than she should have. She started to drift.

While Evert was tuning up her game for a comeback under Ralston's keen eye, Navratilova was losing in 1980 to lesser players whom she rarely, if ever, lost to before. While Evert ratcheted up her training and became fitter and leaner, Martina decided to skip the 1980 French Open altogether. Then Evert beat her in the 1980 semifinals of Wimbledon, snapping Navratilova's nineteen-match winning streak there and her two-year reign as Wimbledon champion.

When eighteen-year-old Hana Mandlikova upset Navratilova in the fourth round of the U.S. Open—Navratilova's worst finish at a major since her tearful 1976 loss to Janet Newberry—even Navratilova conceded that she was starting to look like the previous decade's wunderkind. Her absence from the U.S. Open was quickly forgotten.

Evert and Austin were advancing toward a hotly anticipated semifinal showdown on the other side of the draw. When the day of the match arrived, Evert told John Lloyd during their car ride to the stadium, "I've never wanted a win more in my life."

The buzz that filled cavernous Louis Armstrong Stadium at the start of the match was quickly replaced by anxious murmuring when Austin galloped off to a quick 4–0 lead. Evert looked tight and Austin was outslugging her from the baseline and running down Evert's replies, same as their other encounters before.

Had Evert panicked right then, Austin might have overwhelmed her for a sixth straight match. Instead, Evert thought back to a conversation she had had the day before with Pam Shriver's coach, Don Candy.

Evert and Candy were sitting around the tennis center at Flushing Meadow, and Evert asked him, "What do I have to do to beat Tracy tomorrow?" Without hesitation, Candy replied, "The only way you can beat Tracy is if you're the aggressor."

Candy stressed that if Evert tried to be steady or cautious against Austin, she would surely lose.

"So when I fell behind 0–4, that thought stayed in my mind and I started to try things," Evert says. "I drop-shotted Tracy. I got up to the net. I lobbed. I hit short balls to make her come in. I was the one that went for the first winner. And even though I lost that first set, 6–4, I had come back. And I remember thinking as I came off during the changeover, 'Okay, I think I can win this . . . I think I know now what I need to do!' "

Evert bulldozed Austin in the next two sets, 6–1, 6–1. By the last set, Evert felt so perfectly in tune, it was as if she merely had to think of the shot she wanted to hit and the ball would go there with precisely the right spin and placement and pace. Austin couldn't adjust to the way the pattern of the match had changed. Evert became unpredictable, and Austin's errors began to come in bunches. Before the tournament Austin had been bothered by hamstring injuries. Now she hit a wall of fatigue.

On match point, Austin hit one last backhand that died in the net and Evert felt the stadium shake from the explosive cheer for her. After she embraced John and her mother in a hallway beneath the grandstands, she hurried off to telephone her father in Fort Lauderdale.

"Dad, I won!" Chris exclaimed.

She heard her father's voice crack.

"Chrissie, that's great!" he said.

About a half hour later—still overcome with disbelief—Jimmy Evert rose from his chair, walked back to the telephone, and called the stadium in New York just to make sure he had heard Chris correctly.

"Yes, I did do that," Jimmy says, laughing sheepishly, "but Chrissie hadn't beaten Tracy in such a very long time."

From that day forward, Austin's spell over Evert was broken. With the victory, Evert reclaimed the number one ranking. She reestablished her hunger to be a champion. At Chris's urging, Jimmy flew to New York and watched Chris defeat Hana Mandlikova in the U.S. Open final—the first major title he saw Chris win in person. Within a year, Austin would begin a sad, fitful slide into a series of debilitating back, shoulder, foot, and hamstring injuries. She drove herself to return each time. Perhaps too hard. She was forced to retire in 1984 at the age of twenty-one, having won just two majors.

Instead of being preempted by Austin, Navratilova and Evert's rivalry continued to develop into the stuff of legend. And Austin nods sadly and softly finishes the sentence when told it's almost as if those years that she seemed ready to eclipse Evert and Navratilova . . .

". . . never really happened at all," Austin says.

The winning streak and U.S. Open title that Evert strung together and her postcomeback win over Austin were a reaffirmation of her belief in herself. She made the finals of the first five tournaments she played and won four of them. She felt that she was playing the best tennis of her life. Evert's marriage, like her engagement to Jimmy Connors, had sharpened her realization of what tennis meant to her. What she chose to do in response revealed something profound about her, something she still isn't completely proud of—but there it was.

"When it came down to it," Evert says, "I was married to my tennis. Tennis was how I identified myself. With Jimmy, we both had goals and I didn't want to quit yet to follow him around and have kids. And I didn't have much energy left over after tennis for my relationship with John. Maybe my priorities were wrong, but I'd always fit things into my tennis, not the other way around."

Lloyd's bad losses had continued. Because his ranking had plummeted from a high of number 23 in the world to number 356, he had to endure the added embarrassment of playing in qualifiers just to get into the main draw of most tournaments. At the 1980 U.S. Open, Lloyd didn't make it. He squandered an early lead and then quit against American college student Leif Shiras. "I virtually just started slamming balls into the fence and looked at Chris, who was getting more and more upset," Lloyd said. "I could see she was in tears."

Again, Chris angrily told him that he had played "gutless tennis." She told him that she wasn't coming to his matches anymore unless he promised to try, and Lloyd vowed that he would. But a few months later another embarrassment was heaped atop the rest.

World Tennis magazine published an article called "Best in a Supporting Role." Pictured along with Bjorn Borg's wife, Mariana, Jimmy Connors's wife, Patti, and Rosie Casals's dog Midnight, there was John Lloyd.

As Evert and Austin were locked in their drama, Navratilova, now twenty-four, was dogged by talk that she was a promise unfulfilled. By the end of 1980, Evert still enjoyed a 27–13 edge in their rivalry. The few breakthroughs Navratilova had made, such as her 1978 and 1979 Wimbledon wins, were increasingly offset by her inconsistency and persistent reputation for blowing matches. Evert was hailed as the reborn champ. She had resumed winning tournaments with metronomic consistency. But Ted Tinling's astringent assessment of Navratilova remained true: she really did swing from arrogance to panic with nothing in between.

"She sees vultures that no one else can see," Tinling sighed.

Navratilova's relationship with Rita Mae Brown was growing strained. Her parents' return to Czechoslovakia remained a source of sadness. When Navratilova ran against Evert for president of the WTA players' union in 1980, Navratilova found—to her surprise—that her sexuality was an issue again.

"In our little speeches to the board of directors," Navratilova said, "I told them, 'Look, I'm with Rita Mae Brown. I'm in a relationship. If the press asks me, I'm not going to lie about it. So I don't want you guys to be surprised if this comes out.' And Chris got the presidency for whatever reason. I was told later that [the relationship with Brown] was the biggest reason."

Navratilova tried to make sense of why the vote went against her, but she couldn't.

"I really felt America was the land of opportunity, the land of dreams, the land where you can be who you are and not have to make any apologies," she said.

"In her wildest imaginings," said Rita Mae Brown, "Martina couldn't believe that people would mistreat her because she was a lesbian. That was un-American in her mind."

By 1981, her eighth season on the tour, Navratilova had a dream about Evert, still her uncatchable nemesis: she was playing Evert from a deep valley, and she kept having to scramble uphill, hit a shot, then chase Evert's return down into the abyss again.

CHAPTER EIGHT

"KILL CHRIS"

Navratilova never stopped believing that she could win more Grand Slams or reclaim the number one world ranking. But by the time she and Evert arrived at Amelia Island, Florida, for a tournament on clay in March of 1981, the talk of her potential had grown stale and tiresome. Evert had won eleven major titles and Navratilova, now twenty-four, remained stalled at just two. Many tennis insiders, even Navratilova's past supporters such as Billie Jean King, had begun to voice doubts that Navratilova would ever summon the discipline or temperament to be a legendary champion. Navratilova didn't exactly refute that assessment the day she met Nancy Lieberman.

Unlike Evert—who once knocked over a linesman's abandoned chair in dogged pursuit of a ball, then didn't remember the collision at all when the concerned official asked, "Are you all right?"—Navratilova tended to let her concentration waver during a match. It wasn't that Navratilova was oblivious to her surroundings. If anything, her senses were hyperacute. It was as if the same mental hardwiring or fast-twitch fibers that allowed her to pounce on volleys or make her catlike leaps at the net made it nigh impossible for her to reduce the world to just the ball, the court, and her opponent. Over the years it was not uncommon for Navratilova to spot Bud Collins in the stands and comment on his latest pair of loud trousers as she began swaying from side to side, awaiting a serve on Court Two at Wimbledon. She'd sometimes sing out a hello on changeovers to surprised friends who weren't even aware that she had seen them slip into the stadium during her match.

At Amelia Island, Navratilova was playing a match against Kathy Rinaldi when, sports junkie that she was, she recognized Nancy Lieberman sitting in the players' box. Lieberman's red hair caught Navratilova's eye.

At the time, Lieberman was the best-known female basketball player in America. She was raised in Far Rockaway in Queens, and she had become very famous very young for being an anomaly—a white Jewish girl who played a flashy "black" game honed against men during pickup games on the famously ruthless playgrounds of New York. Though her nickname was "Lady Magic," a nod to NBA star Magic Johnson, Lieberman was actually more like a kosher Larry Bird—flinty, intense, cocksure. Lieberman was so obsessive about basketball, even as a child, that her mother used to puncture her balls with a screwdriver to keep her from dribbling in the house.

By the age of fifteen, Lieberman was taking the A train to Harlem at night to find better competition, navigating the occasional hazing she got from subway patrons or disapproving male players by staring right back at them or, she jokes, trying to act crazier than they did. In 1976, at seventeen, Lieberman became the youngest player ever to make the U.S. Olympic Women's basketball team. More than a hundred college coaches patted their fluttering hearts and plied her with scholarship offers.

Once at Old Dominion University, the low-profile school in Norfolk, Virginia, that Lieberman chose because she wanted to "build something somewhere," she won back-to-back national championships with help from six-foot-five Inge Nissen, a chain-smoking Swede, and six-foot-eight center Anne Donovan. They were so colorful, writers from *Sports Illustrated* and *Rolling Stone* made pilgrimages to Norfolk to do stories on them. And Lieberman was full of quintessential New York swagger and comical, blurted observations. Her first impression of Norfolk? "Hey! Where's all the concrete? The sirens?"

The Dallas Diamonds made Lieberman the number one pick in the 1980 Women's Basketball League draft and gave her the unheard of $100,000 contract that she demanded. She promptly led the Diamonds to the 1980–81 championship as a rookie. Shortly thereafter, however, the young league suspended operations and Lieberman was heartbroken. It was as if a trapdoor had opened beneath her. She was twenty-two years old, at the apex of her sport and her ability, and yet she no longer had a domestic league to play in. She had come to Amelia Island at the invitation of Anne Smith, a tennis player whom she had met after moving to Dallas. But Lieberman made the trip more for the warm weather than the lure of watching any tennis.

"Honestly, I thought tennis was a little bit of a sissy sport—I mean, nobody was even getting hit," Lieberman says with a faint smile. "I really didn't know anything about tennis at that time. I didn't even really like it."

Navratilova and Lieberman liked each other from their first introduction in the tournament press tent after Navratilova's match. They found each other amusing. Lieberman told Navratilova with a straight face that Chris Evert had always been her favorite tennis player. Navratilova, smirking back, said Carol Blazejowski had always been her favorite basketball player. And their banter went from there.

Navratilova asked Lieberman to wait for her while she changed into street clothes. They took a seat in the empty bleachers by one of the courts and talked about sports, Dallas, their lives. Hours rolled by. A day later, Navratilova and Lieberman sat next to each other at the tournament's Saturday night banquet and talked throughout dinner too. When the banquet broke up, they went back to Navratilova's suite and stayed up until six a.m., though Navratilova had a final to play at noon. Against Evert. Who had won 174 of her last 175 matches on clay.

The score—6–0, 6–0—was the worst defeat of Navratilova's career. Navratilova was so hapless, she handed her racket to a ball girl at one point and suggested that the girl could play better. On the two or three occasions that Navratilova did manage to scratch out a game point, Evert was merciless. She wouldn't give Navratilova even one face-saving game. "She just kept going at it, 6–0, 4–0 . . ." Navratilova said. "I was upset with her." The debacle was over in a mere fifty-four minutes, and Navratilova felt so bad, she apologized to the crowd in her on-court address during the award ceremony.

In time, legend had it that Navratilova's humiliating loss at Amelia Island was the spark that convinced her that she needed to reinvent herself to salvage her career. But that's only half true.

"Let's just say that that [night before] was when my relationship with Nancy Lieberman started, so that was not the optimal way of getting ready for a match," Navratilova said.

Navratilova had lost yet another encounter with Evert. But the moment was epochal in another sense. In Lieberman, Navratilova had found the person who was going to change her career, forever.

Evert's too.

Rita Mae Brown, looking back on the 1981 Amelia Island tournament where Martina and Nancy first met, sardonically said that Navratilova came from the "Mario Andretti school of departure: put the pedal to the metal and get the hell out of Dodge."

Brown was hardly the first—or last—armchair psychiatrist to note Navratilova's career-long penchant for abrupt change. In a way, Navratilova's defection became a template for how she handled conflict in the rest of her life. She had a pattern of picking up and leaving and starting anew. She always seemed to be searching for something better just over the next ridge. Whether her habit was driven by her hunt for excellence, her craving for self-expression, her robust idealism, or her quest to reduce the loneliness in her life, the result of Navratilova's restiveness was easier to pinpoint: she went through a steady stream of coaches, gurus, girlfriends, homes, reincarnations, and allegiances to various causes in her unrelenting effort to get—what?—better, stronger, faster, fitter, happier, freer, more content? More beloved?

People close to Navratilova found that she was both vulnerable and daring, highly intelligent and yet malleable, apt to say anything on principle and yet so admittedly adverse to conflict that she'd avoid important conversations for weeks. Navratilova could be incredibly engaged in whatever adventure or topic interested her at a given moment—from coauthoring three mystery novels to adopting her fourth stray dog to donating half her winner's check to the Ethiopian famine relief effort, all of which she has done. "Martina has always had that wonderful big soppy heart," says Ingrid Bentzer.

But Navratilova was also intensely uninterested in the mundane aspects of life, such as monitoring her finances or preventing people from taking advantage of her. Navratilova had other people for that. She was the eternal wide-eyed kid. "Be free, play tennis, make money—YAY!" Billie Jean King says with a laugh.

Navratilova frustrated her closest friends to no end at times. And yet the same friends, loving Navratilova's spirit, knowing all she had been through, found it hard to stay irritated at her for long, even when she fell into the thrall of the latest new guru or lover who had arrived in her life.

All of which is to say, Navratilova is complicated.

Navratilova sold both of her houses in Dallas when her parents returned to Czechoslovakia and began living with Brown in their rambling mansion in Virginia. In the weeks after her humiliation by Evert in Amelia Island, Navratilova's contact with her new friend Lieberman had increased to the point that Rita Mae Brown began to question Navratilova's claims that she and Lieberman were just friends.

Brown didn't know that Navratilova had already invited Lieberman to accompany her to the French Open and Wimbledon. Shortly before Navratilova was scheduled to leave for Europe,

Brown again confronted her about Lieberman because she had come upon Navratilova engrossed in yet another long phone conversation with the basketball player. This time, Brown asked Navratilova point-blank if she and Lieberman were lovers. Navratilova said it was none of Brown's business. Lieberman described what happened next in her 1992 autobiography.

Soon Navratilova and Brown were storming from room to room and then floor to floor in their rambling house. Navratilova—hoping to avoid a fight—told Brown that she didn't want to discuss Lieberman anymore. Brown grabbed a fistful of Navratilova's shirt as Navratilova tried to leave the kitchen, insisting, "We're going to talk about it right now."

Again Navratilova refused and went upstairs. Brown followed. But this time Brown went into the bathroom, grabbed a gun that was sitting on the windowsill, and told Navratilova, "You're not going anywhere. We're going to talk about you and Nancy right now."

Navratilova pushed Brown out of the way and bolted down the stairs. She sprinted out to the front driveway and jumped into her BMW, frantically turned the key, and slammed the car into gear—only to have the engine stall.

Brown, still carrying the gun, was upon Navratilova by now. She flung open the back door of the car just as Navratilova restarted the engine and again slammed down the gas pedal. The gun went off. The bullet traveled through the passenger side headrest and out the bottom left corner of the windshield. The glass shattered, cutting Navratilova's face as she tore out of the driveway.

When Navratilova got to a nearby friend's house she telephoned Lieberman in Dallas and cried, "Nancy, Rita Mae shot me! Rita Mae shot me!"

Brown has never publicly confirmed or denied Lieberman's retelling of the story.

But when Judy Nelson, who was Navratilova's partner for nearly eight years before she also had a two-year relationship with Brown, is asked if Brown meant to shoot at Navratilova that day, Nelson scoffs as if the question is ludicrous. She hoots, "Oh, yeaahhhh."

"But knowing Rita Mae," Nelson adds in her Texas drawl, "I think she'd also say, 'If I'da really meant to shoot her, I wouldn't have missed.' "

Lieberman has said that she believed her relationship with Navratilova was cemented the night of Navratilova's confrontation with Brown. Yet as Lieberman flew to the French Open to join Navratilova in late May, she felt a ripple of uncertainty. Lieberman kept reminding herself that she hardly knew Navratilova. Lieberman also had no comprehension of Navratilova's fame or wealth or work habits. She was about to undergo a crash course in professional tennis in particular, and the lifestyle of rich, world-class athletes in general.

Once in Paris, Navratilova asked Lieberman if she wanted to come to practice with her.

"Well, we got to these courts," Lieberman remembers, "and Martina takes the warm-up jacket off, hits a few balls. She talks to Betsy Nagelsen, talks to Billie Jean, hits a few lobs. Says hi to Pam Shriver. And then we leave."

On their drive back to the hotel, Lieberman uncertainly said, "Uh, Martina? When are you going to practice?"

"I just did," Martina replied.

"That was *practice*?" Lieberman boomed. "That *sucked!* That was *terrible*. So . . . what? You win the weeks you feel good, and the weeks you don't feel good, hey, who knows what happens?"

Navratilova was stunned.

She couldn't believe that Lieberman was being so blunt. And Lieberman couldn't fathom how Navratilova could be a world-class athlete without training like one.

"At that point I would have given my right arm to play in another pro league," Lieberman says, "and I just couldn't understand how somebody could be like Martina, given the position she was in and all the wealth there was in tennis. I couldn't imagine putting myself in front of the whole world and practically setting [myself] up to fail. Her workouts were uninspiring. There was no quality. Martina is a remarkable person, one of the nicest people I've ever met. But she wasn't training to be a champion. She was just training to play tennis.

"I could see that Chris Evert wanted to win and Martina just wanted to play. Chris saw Martina as her rival. Martina saw her as her friend. Martina wanted to be 'nice.' Winning was important to her but it wasn't the end all. And I advocated Chris's philosophy at that time. I admired how Chris approached the game. As I got to know Martina, I saw I was mentally tougher than her. I was basketball's Chris Evert."

It was hard for Lieberman to avoid making comparisons between tennis and her own sport. The two- or three-hour workouts she drove herself through for basketball were lung-searing, leg-burning descents into hell meant to be so challenging that whatever she encountered in games felt easier. Lieberman slammed weights, ran sprints, practiced shots, took hits, threw elbows, collected floor burns, and played with an intensity so white hot, she rubbed people the wrong way. Not that Lieberman cared.

Her sports idols as a girl in New York City were larger-than-life athletes like Muhammad Ali and Knicks stars Walt Frazier and Willis Reed—people given to the heroic gesture, the flamboyant riposte. But above all, they were winners. Their stated desire to make an all-time mark in their sports resonated with Lieberman too. *That* was the sort of athlete Lieberman wanted to be.

When Navratilova suffered a thudding loss in the 1981 French Open quarterfinals to Sylvia Hanika, Lieberman was astonished again when Navratilova dealt with her early exit by going on a $15,000 shopping spree in Paris that netted a Piaget watch and an expensive bracelet Lieberman had commented on. "Do you want it?" Navratilova asked her.

"No," Lieberman said.

Navratilova bought it for her anyway.

"Martina, you don't have to buy me something for me to like you," Lieberman told her. "Why don't you save rewarding yourself for when you win?"

At Wimbledon a few weeks later, Navratilova suffered another

After two years of humiliating losses to Martina and much soul-searching, Chris's dedication to revamping her game finally paid off when she defeated Navratilova for the 1985 French Open title, 3–6, 7–6, 7–5. Evert still regards it as her greatest win. GERARD RANCINAN/*SPORTS ILLUSTRATED*

Martina visits with her parents, Mirek and Jana, at their home in Revnice for the first time since her defection eleven years earlier. Martina, by now an American citizen, was able to return to Communist Czechoslovakia because she was playing for the U.S. team in the 1986 Federation Cup in Prague.
AP/WIDE WORLD PHOTOS

Chris gazes across the net during her last appearance at Wimbledon, in 1989. She was two points from defeat in her quarterfinal match against Laura Golarsa when she looked up and was surprised to see Martina in the stands, cheering for her to make a comeback—which she did.

SIMON BRUTY/GETTY IMAGES

Martina (*in sunglasses*) steps out with partner Judy Nelson and Nelson's parents, Frances and Sargent Hill (*left*). Nelson encouraged Martina to repair the damage her friendship with Evert had suffered during the Nancy Lieberman years. ART SEITZ

Martina lifts the champion's plate in 1990 after accomplishing her dream of winning her ninth Wimbledon singles title, a record for men and women. Navratilova later tied Billie Jean King for the most singles and doubles titles at Wimbledon (twenty). GETTY IMAGES

Martina bade farewell to the Centre Court crowd after losing the Wimbledon final to Conchita Martinez in 1994. Martina plucked a few blades of grass from the hallowed court to take with her, and retired from singles play later that year. BOB MARTIN/GETTY IMAGES

Chris watches play on Wimbledon's Centre Court in 1995 with her husband, Andy Mill, and Alex, the oldest of their three sons. Both Chris and Andy say becoming parents was the happiest day of their lives. CLIVE BRUNSKILL/GETTY IMAGES

Chris and Martina share a laugh on their return to Wimbledon in 1997 for the ceremonial opening of the new Court One stadium. Three years later, Navratilova would come out of retirement and make a doubles comeback. AP PHOTO/DAVE CAULKIN

Martina and Chris reprised their rivalry with an arm-wrestling bout at *Sports Illustrated*'s 1999 celebration of the greatest athletes of the twentieth century. Late in their careers, Navratilova joked, "After all this time, we're still trying to prove something to each other." REUTERS/CORBIS

RIGHT Chris, happy in
retirement as a wife,
mother, and charity
fund-raiser, visited the U.S.
Open in 2002. Evert says
that the first few years after
she quit tennis, she would
wake up and think, "You
mean I can do anything
today? Anything?" ART SEITZ

BOTTOM Chris and Martina
clown around at the 2002
International Tennis Hall
of Fame Gala at the
Waldorf-Astoria in New
York. "I was the tough
one," Evert often said.
ART SEITZ

TOP Martina, 47, serves during a women's doubles match in Sydney in January 2004. After setting new standards of fitness, she has spent the second act of her career revising ideas about female athletes' longevity.

DAVID HANCOCK/GETTY IMAGES

LEFT Martina, snaring a volley, used to wonder why she had so few imitators—until fellow Tennis Hall of Famer Robert Kelleher told her that there's a reason others don't play like her. "They can't," Kelleher said.

AP/PHOTO/SANDY HUFFAKER

Evert and husband Andy Mill, a former Olympic skier, at the dirt bike track near their home in Florida with their sons (*left to right*) Colton, Nicholas, and Alex. ART SEITZ

galling loss, this one to fellow Czech Hana Mandlikova in the semifinals. Afterward, Lieberman peppered Navratilova with more pointed observations. She said that Martina she was wasting her talent. She had no sense of urgency.

"I told her, 'You should be the greatest player ever,' " Lieberman says. "I was trying to fill her dreams with mine. To me, when I said 'greatest ever' to Martina, I didn't make that phrase up. That was Muhammad Ali. He was my hero. He wanted to be"—here Lieberman drops into the same hushed voice Ali used to use—"*the greatest of all-l-l-llll time. Because he whupped Joe Frazier and he whupped George Foreman and he beat Sonny Liston in 1964 and 'They didn't believe me! The odds were against me!'* You know? '*Rumble, young man, rumble.*' "

Lieberman smiles.

"Those were the things that filled my childhood, those words," she says. "And here I am, looking at Martina and going, '*Rumble, young girl, rumble.*' Or at least *wanna* rumble."

After tumbling out of Wimbledon, Navratilova was finally ready to listen.

Evert, who had just moved into a new flat with Lloyd that sat ten minutes from the All England Club, enjoyed unprecedented support from the British crowds as she dispatched Mandlikova in just sixty-one minutes in the Wimbledon final, 6–2, 6–2. Afterward, Navratilova sent Evert a bottle of champagne. And Evert invited Navratilova to celebrate the victory with her and Lloyd.

Exactly two years had passed since Navratilova's last Grand Slam singles title.

Lieberman and Navratilova decided that when Martina returned to the States, she would move to Dallas to live and train with Lieberman.

"I needed someone at that time to kick me in the butt," Navratilova said.

The 1981 U.S. Open was seven weeks away.

"My understanding," says Evert, "is Nancy told her, 'You're my project now.' "

———

Within a year of Navratilova's relationship with Lieberman, Evert had come up with a derisive term for the in-your-face approach Lieberman brought. Evert called it "Kill Chris."

"What bothered me," Evert says, "was Nancy made it personal, not just about tennis. She thought that Martina would play better if she hated me."

Evert was still ensconced at number one, but Navratilova had slipped behind Tracy Austin to number three in the pack of challengers nipping at Evert's heels. Austin, still a daunting threat when healthy, missed the first five months of the 1981 season while recuperating from her first serious bout of sciatica. Austin was just eighteen. Other teenagers like Mandlikova, Andrea Jaeger, and Pam Shriver were making noise. But Evert knew that Navratilova was the ticking time bomb, the one player who, if she ever pulled herself together, possessed athletic ability that Evert couldn't begin to approximate.

Lieberman had now decided that bringing those talents out of Navratilova was her job.

The first week Lieberman and Navratilova trained together in Dallas, Lieberman took Navratilova to the track at Southern Methodist University. From the start they were in near perfect sync. "I was discovering true pain in my body for the first time in my life, and Nancy was discovering that I did not like pain," Navratilova joked.

Lieberman would bark out instructions to Navratilova, ordering her to do one sprint, then another, then another. They did sets of forty-yard dashes, hundred-yard sprints, quarter-mile runs around the track. It wasn't long before Navratilova crumpled to the ground. And she was crying.

"Get up!" Lieberman screamed, standing over her.

"I can't get up," Navratilova claimed.

Lieberman was aware that other people on the track were staring.

"Okay, Martina, look, we can't be doing this," she said. "I know it's going to hurt. I live it too, okay? It's who I am. It's who you're going to be. Mentally, it's scary because it's unknown. Physically, it's going to take some time, some work. But it would be a shame to have that body, those genes, and not max it out . . . You're wasting your talent."

Navratilova got up.

She began to run again, still cursing and complaining.

It was a start.

For a twenty-two-year-old woman just one year removed from college, Lieberman had an extraordinary grasp of what makes a great athlete great. Her astute take on who Navratilova was and what it would take for her to challenge Evert seems even more remarkable in hindsight, given the heights Navratilova would reach.

Once they began fitness training, Lieberman resorted to the same basic approach that is used at army boot camps and 12-step programs, not just the high-level basketball training camps she was familiar with. Lieberman was consciously trying to break Navratilova down and then build her back up. "You're physically, mentally, emotionally trying to push someone where they don't know they can go, but you know they can go," Lieberman explains. "Mentally, Martina didn't know what she could do physically."

Caustic as Lieberman could be, it meant something to Navratilova that she was there beside her, doing every sprint or workout drill she drove her through. Navratilova did as she was told because she began to see results. She and Lieberman worked hard, and they talked at length about the training. Navratilova thought Lieberman's reasoning made sense.

Lieberman said that the most successful athletes look for separation from their competitors, and that gaining that edge is especially crucial at the highest level of sport. "Your body, your athleticism, is your separation," Lieberman told Navratilova.

Lieberman urged Martina to think ahead to a day when she had done all the work the other tennis players hadn't, and the psychological effect it would have—on her and on them. "If I walk in the gym and I'm in okay shape, people look and are like, 'Uh, whatever,' "

Lieberman said. "But if I walk in the gym and I'm ripped, I had to *do* something to get a body like that, right? So have I not influenced you? Without saying a word?"

Lieberman urged Navratilova to imagine how confident she would be if she knew she'd been in the weight room five days a week, she'd been on the track three days a week, she'd played basketball for footwork and hit tennis balls three hours a day. "Now you show up at the U.S. Open or in Philadelphia for an indoor tournament," Lieberman said, "and you're ready. You've done the work. Even on your worst day, when you're not feeling good, when things are not going great at home, the stars are not aligned in the right place—on your *worst* day—you should still be able to beat that opponent. That's what you should be striving for. You *know* you're going to win."

Evert, who had always understood that transference between fitness and confidence, success and intimidation, says, "Say what you like about her, Nancy was very effective. Nancy had the power. I think Nancy made Martina feel like, 'Okay, you're nothing right now, but in six months I'm going to have you in shape and you're going to beat Chris.' Psychologically, she let it be known to Martina that she was a wimp and that she was going to toughen her up. And it worked."

For all the attention Navratilova's physical makeover received, the psychological overhaul she began with Lieberman's help was just as amazing. Like most great basketball players, Lieberman had a tremendous feel for the psychological ebbs and spikes in a game. She talked to Navratilova about manipulating the emotional tide of a match to *her* advantage for a change.

"In basketball," Lieberman told Navratilova, "when [you go] in for a layup, it's my job to knock you on your ass, to send a message. And I'll find out next time if you're willing to come down the lane again." Relating that now to tennis, Lieberman urged Navratilova to play intimidating points, to show off her athleticism. "It's not just about winning—it's about *how* you win," Lieberman said. "You should be emphatic. You put all this work in. So let them know. *You* set the standards for excellence. *You* become the measuring stick."

That Lieberman had never played tennis didn't matter. A significant part of her approach was culled from the proving grounds of those city basketball courts where she grew up. Lieberman's philosophy about what Navratilova needed to do to overtake Evert was shot through with the reductive reasoning of a streetball player who swaggers onto a court asking, "Who's got next?"

If Evert was number one, and number one was indeed all that mattered, then—in Lieberman's mind—Navratilova had to go one-on-one with Evert to bring her down.

" 'Chris wants what you want and you've got to take it away from her'—that was Nancy's famous line," *World Tennis* writer Steve Flink says.

"I don't know if Martina actually thought like that, but I certainly did," Lieberman admits. "Chris was in my head. Chris was number one. I always had blinders on for being number one, and Martina was kind enough or trusting enough to take on that personality. I didn't want her to be satisfied with mediocrity, even if mediocrity in tennis could mean two million dollars a year and a bunch of tournament titles. To me, there's only one thing. And that's to be a champion. That's all that mattered.

"I just didn't know another way, to be quite honest."

Navratilova bought into it. Nearly all of it. The more Lieberman laid out scenarios, the more Navratilova started to connect the dots and have epiphanies of her own. Some of the traits Lieberman highlighted about her did sound right. Navratilova did feel empathy for opponents she was beating. Evert did not. Navratilova had always wanted to be liked; Lieberman had no such ambition. And Navratilova admired that.

Lieberman says, "I can remember maybe trying to be a little bit of Martina's conscience at that time. It's like there was the good conscience with the little guy dressed in all white sitting on Martina's shoulder saying, 'Oh, come on. Just play' versus the one dressed in black sitting on her other shoulder saying, 'Just kick the shit out of her. Just win this!'

"I was the second guy," Lieberman says.

CHAPTER NINE

THE TRUTH COMES OUT

As Navratilova's training regimen with Lieberman proceeded, several off-court events shadowed the couple throughout the summer of 1981. And all of them were still percolating by the mid-August start of the U.S. Open.

In May, Lieberman had accompanied Navratilova to Los Angeles for her final hearing regarding her U.S. citizenship application. Navratilova had long been warned that among the standard questions she might face, there could be one about her sexual orientation. She had always been fearful that if she told the truth her citizenship application would be denied.

In 1967, the U.S. Supreme Court had ruled that homosexual aliens could be deported as persons "afflicted with a psychopathic personality." That characterization was eventually refuted by the American Psychiatric Association, which in 1973 reversed its hundred-year-old policy and voted to no longer classify homosexuality as a mental disorder.

By the time Navratilova defected just two years later, her lawyers

had been concerned enough about the issue and any lingering preju-
dices to apply for Navratilova's citizenship in the more liberal state
of California, though Texas had become her adopted home.

Once in Los Angeles for her citizenship hearing, Navratilova
sweated through her private interview with the Immigration and
Naturalization Service agent, which was conducted under oath. The
agent did ask her about her sexual preference.

"Bisexual," Navratilova answered.

The agent never glanced up. She proceeded to the next question
and Navratilova felt enormously relieved.

Within five weeks Navratilova received the news that her citizenship had been approved. She returned to Los Angeles for the
swearing-in ceremony on July 20, 1981, a day she regarded as one
of the most precious in her life.

Being an American has always meant something dear to Navratilova. She has always spoken passionately about how she never
took the freedoms Americans enjoy for granted. After so many years
of having to write "stateless" on her visa applications and being
treated as a nonperson back in Czechoslovakia, it was profoundly
important to Navratilova to feel she belonged somewhere. At the
U.S. Open years after she became a citizen, Navratilova was so genuinely moved by a reporter who began his question to her with "As
a fellow American . . . ," she interrupted him.

"Thank you, *thank you* for calling me that," she said.

At her swearing-in ceremony in Los Angeles, Navratilova finally felt
she had a home. "I felt like cheering and clapping and giving high fives,"
she later said, "but the other people were filing quietly out of the room."

Back in Charlottesville, Rita Mae Brown was not yet ready to
joke wryly about Navratilova's enrollment in the Mario Andretti
School of Departure. Brown felt jilted. As she and Navratilova
discussed their breakup and division of their property, Brown
threatened to go to the press and cause an even bigger scandal for
Navratilova than the one that was currently rocking the tennis
world. That scandal involved Billie Jean King.

———————

On May 5, 1981, King had returned to her hotel room after losing a first-round match at a tournament in Orlando, Florida. She found a pink message slip asking her to call a reporter from the *Los Angeles Times* to talk about "the lawsuit." That's how a panicked King found out she was being sued for palimony (or "galimony") by Marilyn Barnett, a former hairstylist who had been her traveling secretary for several years in the early 1970s. King, who had never gotten divorced from her husband, Larry, though they had been living separate lives for years, says, "I went into shock. I screamed."

When a stricken Billie Jean held a press conference a few days later with Larry and her parents at her side, her somber admission that she and Barnett had had a lesbian affair caused a sensation.

In 1981, hardly anyone was publicly "out" or candid about being gay. Barnett's suit against King came four years before Rock Hudson's 1985 admission that he was homosexual and dying of AIDS. In 1983, Cher was called "brave" when she agreed to play Meryl Streep's lesbian friend in the movie *Silkwood*. At the time that King was outed, there were no daytime talk shows that frankly discussed gay life, no prime-time sitcoms with gay characters. It was inconceivable. Few Americans could have dreamed that by 2003 there would be a lighthearted reality show with fashion-impaired straight guys being tutored by self-proclaimed "queers" who could confidently tell them whether to buy a merino wool or cashmere sweater.

Being gay or lesbian was still treated as a slur, a stain, and even a crime in some states. There were no hate crime laws yet. The U.S. Supreme Court had, in recent years, refused to hear the case of a Washington teacher who was fired for being gay, and in 1978 the Court voted 7–2 not to interfere with states' rights to pass and enforce antisodomy laws after a North Carolina gay man was sentenced to nearly a year in prison for a consensual sexual encounter.

"You have to remember," says George Vecsey, "in 1981, '82, '83, '84, it was still a pretty serious thing for anybody on any occasion to be out. It just wasn't much done yet. It wasn't even talked about."

In the wake of King's admission, there was runaway speculation that the women's tour might be catastrophically damaged. King says she was told directly by the Women's Tennis Association's top executives, "If you decide to come out, we won't have a tour."

Avon, the circuit's chief sponsor, denied it would pull out. But Avon was gone within a year.

King conservatively estimated she lost more than $1.5 million in endorsements over the next three years alone. Several companies, including NBC, stayed with her. But within a year King was the only major tennis player in the world without a clothing endorsement. After a brief retirement, King returned to the tour and played on her bad knees until past her thirty-ninth birthday because she was concerned about her earning potential once she quit. She feared that she wouldn't have any.

Evert—the same woman whom *Playboy* magazine had trumpeted as "the most famous conservative girl in America"—was so appalled at Barnett's decision to sue King and out her that she took a stand. Evert wrote an editorial for the July 1981 edition of *World Tennis* called "In Defense of Billie Jean." In it, Evert cited King's selflessness, her life's work, and asked, "Who are we to knock it if someone is gay? . . . We're in no position to judge right and wrong in someone else's life."

Barnett's suit against King made Evert furious.

"I thought it was a betrayal," Evert says. "I also thought whether Billie was straight or gay was a nonissue, something that people were using to tarnish Billie. I just kept coming back to the same thought: 'Why should we be judgmental?' Billie had always, always been there for me. To me, speaking up about it was nothing to be 'admired.' "

Still, a persuasive case could be made that Evert's impeccable image and replacement of King by then as the face of the women's tennis helped insulate the tour from more damage. And Evert's refusal to distance herself from her friends King and Navratilova after they acknowledged being lesbians helped humanize them to the public in ways that they, by themselves, could not have.

When Barnett's suit finally moved through the California courts seven months later, the presiding judge, Julius M. Title, dismissed the case outright, stating that Barnett had displayed "unconscionable conduct," especially by threatening to make public personal letters that King had sent her during their relationship unless King paid her more than $125,000. "If that isn't attempted extortion, it certainly comes close to it," Title said.

Despite the ruling, King was left in a no-win situation. To those who found homosexuality offensive, she was a pariah. To many gays, she was no hero either. King had spoken frankly to the media about the mortifying shame she felt when Barnett's suit was filed. King said she actually hid for the first few days because, "I didn't want to be anywhere where people could look at me." Her ashen, shaken demeanor when she finally did hold her press conference was appallingly contrite. "I hate being called a homosexual," King told *People* magazine at the time. "I don't feel homosexual."

To this day, King deeply regrets those remarks. She remembers feeling "completely overwhelmed." She felt bad for her husband, Larry. Her parents were devastated. She was tormented by fears that all she had worked for would be destroyed, that her female friends would be presumed gay by association, and that other women athletes would be harmed too. "We're all supposed to be gay anyway, right?" King wrote in the autobiography she quickly published with Frank Deford to defuse the issue.

Nor were King's fears unfounded. "A lot of people who are straight are scared," admitted Nancy Lopez, the most popular golfer on the LPGA Tour. And Lopez was married. Other tennis players—Navratilova among them—spoke of a "gay witch hunt" that King's admission sparked. Supermarket tabloids were offering $25,000 for salacious stories about other lesbian athletes.

Press coverage and fan reaction to King's revelation varied

wildly. A significant number of writers stood up for King, criticizing her only for having had an extramarital affair. On the other end of the spectrum, a *New York Post* story claimed that lesbianism was so widespread on the tennis tour, the terrified parents of some of the younger girls—Tracy Austin's mother, Jeanne, among them—posted "shower guards" to protect their daughters from predatory lesbians. Austin's mother denied the report. Evert denounced the story.

Navratilova was drawn into the roiling mess in August of 1981 when Steve Goldstein, a sports reporter for the New York *Daily News*, reached her in Monte Carlo, where she was playing.

Goldstein told her that he wanted to use some comments she had made to him in a formal interview conducted months earlier. In that conversation, Navratilova had told Goldstein about her breakup with Rita Mae Brown and talked at length about her fears that her sexuality would be used against her. Navratilova knew Goldstein was taping their talk and taking notes throughout. But at the end of the interview, she implored Goldstein not to use the remarks after all. She cited her concerns about getting her citizenship. After much discussion, they reached a compromise: Goldstein agreed not to publish the information until Navratilova was ready to go public. Then he would write the story. He honored the bargain even after Barnett outed King.

By late July, however, about a week after Navratilova received her citizenship, Goldstein got a tip that Avon was indeed likely not to renew its $16 million support of the tour, and that Navratilova's name—in addition to King's—had come up during internal discussions. When he called Navratilova in Monte Carlo, he suggested that it was time for her to go public. Again, Navratilova balked, this time saying the Billie Jean story was too hot. Goldstein, by now under pressure from his editors to use the interview, felt he had to print the story; to Navratilova, Goldstein's decision was a betrayal of trust.

On July 30, 1981, in a *Daily News* copyrighted story by Goldstein headlined "Martina Fears Avon's Call if She Talks," Navratilova was quoted for the first time about her broken-off relationship with Brown. She also said, "If I come out and start talking, women's tennis is going to be hurt. I have heard if I come out—if one more top player talks about this—then Avon will pull out as a sponsor."

Navratilova added, "I feel I can be a good example for other people. But not now [given the reaction to King]."

Now Navratilova was in a bind too.

Professionally, Navratilova felt a responsibility to protect the tour. Personally, she saw nothing wrong with being a lesbian and wasn't opposed to telling the truth. But Lieberman emphatically did not want to be outed. Navratilova, like King before her, came to regret some of her reactions to Goldstein's story, calling that time "a low point. But I did it to protect Nancy . . . who was in the closet in a big way."

Navratilova and Lieberman went into damage-control mode immediately after the *Daily News* story ran. They gave an interview to a friendly Dallas newspaper columnist and insisted they were just friends. Navratilova reiterated that she was bisexual, but Nancy was straight, and that no assumptions should be made about their live-in relationship. Lieberman even said she was going to try to lead Navratilova back to men.

"In this," Rita Mae Brown drolly noted, "[Lieberman] failed spectacularly."

Writing much later about those histrionic-filled days, Brown gave Navratilova high marks for refusing to subscribe to the tour marketers' preference for ultrafeminine "retro-women" and for refusing to appear on court "with so much green eye shadow that she resembled a shrimp gone bad." Brown added: "Imagine living day in and day out in an environment where the mere mention of lesbianism enshrouds everyone in a cloud of ornate gloom."

Brown's contention that the rest of society was far more liberal than the tennis tour seemed to be borne out when Navratilova arrived at the 1981 U.S. Open a month after the *Daily News* story ran and advanced to the championship match for the first time.

"The reason that Martina today has been transformed," Brown said, "is because once and for all she has said who she is, period. There's no point in the powers that be pretending otherwise."

Navratilova's career-long ability to play through turmoil has often been characterized as extraordinary. But the trait is hardly unique to her. Many athletes find sanctuary in the games they play when the rest of their lives are troubled, including Evert.

What was unique to Navratilova was the type of tempests swirling around her. She defected and couldn't go home. She and her family were reunited, and then her family left. She won tournaments, but never quite enough for the detractors who kept harping that her emotional fragility offset her lavish physical gifts. She loved America but it never seemed to love her back quite as much. Now she was an admitted lesbian who had just been outed a few weeks earlier, and rather than shrink from inviting any more scrutiny, she happily accepted an offer from Renee Richards, a six-foot-two transsexual, to be her coach, starting with the 1981 U.S. Open. Richards, then forty-seven, had been eliminated in the first round of the U.S. Open and decided to retire. Navratilova hadn't had a tennis coach after leaving Czechoslovakia and Vera Sukova.

Jeanie Brinkman vividly remembers the first time she heard about Richards. "I got a call from a reporter saying, 'Do you know there's a man playing the women's tour?' " Brinkman says, laughing. "I was like, 'Are you nuts?' "

The player in question was, of course, Richards. Before undergoing a sex-change operation in 1975, she had been known as Richard Raskind, a former captain of the Yale men's tennis team who served in the navy, later played one match at Forest Hills in 1960, and built a career as one of New York's leading ophthalmologic surgeons. After her sex-change surgery, Richards relocated to California to start a new life with a new identity.

One of the first people who recognized Richards in California was Bobby Riggs, an old friend from their amateur tennis days.

Riggs noticed a rather tall woman playing at the John Wayne Tennis Club in Newport Beach one day, swore he recognized her distinctive backhand, and ambled over for a closer look. "Oh, it's you! You're out here now," Riggs exclaimed. He hadn't seen Richards since before the sex-change surgery, but he had heard rumors.

Before long—Riggs being Riggs—he had lined up a hustle for them at a San Diego club forty-five minutes down the road, a doubles match with a couple of "pigeons" who, Richards says, "looked like mob guys from Vegas."

Riggs walked across the court when they arrived to lay out the terms of the bet—"A thousand dollars a corner, or four thousand among the four of us," Riggs suggested—and came shambling back, loudly telling Richards, "They wanna see you hit some first, sweetie"—then, under his breath to her—"but not too good."

After Richards and Riggs won, Riggs went back toward the men to collect, but not before whispering, "Get in the car" to Richards so they could make a quick getaway.

When Brinkman got the reporter's call about Richards, it was because Richards had entered and won a local tournament in Connecticut that qualified her to play on the Avon satellite circuit, a competition level one notch below the women's main professional tour. When Richards was told she would be prohibited from future events unless she could pass a chromosome test, she began a controversial legal battle for the right to play. In August of 1977, she won a favorable decision in the New York State Supreme Court. She was then forty-three years old and, after years of hormone therapy, no threat to dominate the women's tour.

Still, some players boycotted the first few pro tournaments Richards entered, and alarmists cried that allowing Richards to play would only encourage more men to have sex-change operations and stream into women's sports—an argument Navratilova, among many others, found patently ridiculous.

After meeting Richards for the first time in 1977 in São Paulo, Brazil, and defeating her in straight sets, Navratilova had told her, "Stick with it, Renee. You'll make it"—a kindness Richards never forgot. Billie Jean King and Ilie Nastase were also early, unwavering supporters who asked Richards to play doubles with them. "I don't know what the other girls are so upset about," Nastase impishly told reporters. "She's old enough to be their mother."

King also tried to defuse the controversy with humor. During a 1977 match that Richards and King played together in Port Washington, New York, King grew so weary of Richards's incessant whining about having to play through a bad case of the flu, King finally turned to the crowd and screamed, "This is the last time I'm ever playing with a Jewish American princess!"

Richards laughed. They won.

Brinkman says that once people moved past what Richards blithely calls "my being a notorious world figure, or whatever," what they typically found was "Renee is a lovely person." Her tennis acumen was unquestioned, her intelligence acute. She had hundreds of friends inside and outside the tennis world, and a raconteur's gift for telling a good story. Deep down, Richards also had some of the same blunt New York sensibilities as Lieberman, a fellow native of Queens. Neither was Richards above poking fun at herself. After the news broke that she was a transsexual, more than a hundred reporters flocked to cover a match she played in Orange, New Jersey. Richards made a grand entrance, having accepted her friend Gene Scott's offer to arrive in his Rolls-Royce.

"She wanted to be a girl and she is what she is, she'd done what she'd done, so what more was there to say?" Brinkman says.

Navratilova had gotten to know Richards better in the years after they first met, and she didn't worry about how hiring Richards to coach her would look. Navratilova felt Richards could improve her game, period. When she looked around, she saw that Evert had Dennis Ralston and John Lloyd helping her, Bjorn Borg had Lennart Bergelin, Tracy Austin was working with Marty Riessen, and Pam Shriver, Navratilova's doubles partner, relied on Don Candy. So why not hire Richards? And why not start right away? The U.S. Open had been the scene of so many of Navratilova's worst losses, not just to Janet Newberry in 1976, but to Wendy Turnbull in 1977, Shriver in 1978, and Austin in 1979.

Richards, like Lieberman, was initially dumbstruck.

"I couldn't believe how little Martina knew about playing tennis and how faulty her strokes were," Richards says. "At times, I used to go berserk. Things like strategy were second nature to me. I would have thought somebody like Martina, who was a Wimbledon champion, would know what to do. But she's just Martina. She's very intelligent, but she's not an abstract thinker, per se. She was playing on talent and instinct."

Navratilova admitted that Richards's approach of thinking out a match before she played was a "revelation" to her. Richards took meticulous notes and prepared game plans that she and Navratilova reviewed the night before and morning of each match. Richards highlighted tendencies and weakness in opponents that Navratilova had never noticed.

Knowing Navratilova was almost sure to encounter Evert in the semifinals, Richards spent almost the entire two weeks of the 1981 U.S. Open preparing Martina for Chris.

When the showdown arrived, Navratilova felt ready.

The Open semifinal was Navratilova and Evert's first meeting since Evert embarrassed Navratilova 6–0, 6–0 at Amelia Island six months earlier. Evert noticed immediately that Navratilova's body had changed during her weeks of training with Lieberman. "She was leaner and yet stronger," Evert says.

By the time Evert and Navratilova played, the press had been steadily harping on the theme that Navratilova, like Bjorn Borg on the men's side of the draw, had never won the U.S. Open. Asked about her litany of troubles at the event, Navratilova renewed her usual gripes about the gusting winds, the stifling late-summer humidity, the dirty courts, and the screeching jets from nearby LaGuardia Airport.

Once on the court against Evert, Navratilova seemed unbothered. She prevailed in a magnificently played first set, 7–5. And Evert's play, as usual, became fiercer, even more urgent in response. Before long it was obvious Evert and Navratilova had put aside any thought of winning whole games; they had winnowed their focus down to arm-wrestling for each point—then the next one, and the one after that. In the fourth game of the second set they seemed so lost in what they were doing, it was almost as if they had forgotten that they were playing in a stadium full of 18,000 people. They both blinked and stole a look around as if they were startled by the loud, partial standing ovation they got after one breathtakingly long rally featuring almost every conceivable shot: ground stroke bullets and wickedly angled slices, a couple of rat-a-tat volleys, an exchange of dinks. Both of them had scrambled in toward the net and then back to the baseline twice before Evert finally won the point with a drop shot that a sprinting Navratilova couldn't . . . quite . . . lift over the net after a long, determined run.

Evert eked out the second set, 6–4, to even the match and push Navratilova to the third set—the territory that had spelled doom for Navratilova so many times before. But Navratilova later said, "I don't think I have ever been that pumped up since the last Wimbledon I won." When Evert got a service break to go ahead 4–2 in the final set, Navratilova broke right back. During each of the next two changeovers, Navratilova and Evert had to wait as a scuffle among three men high in the stands delayed the match. Still, Navratilova was unaffected. She pulled even with Evert with her most emphatic game of the match, breaking Evert's serve at love by snapping off four straight winners. Then, in a game that would haunt Evert, Navratilova escaped three break points in the ninth game, starting her climb back from a 15–40 hole by blasting an ace.

Instead of serving for the match, Evert was down 4–5 instead. Navratilova was so close to victory she grew even more animated, more aggressive. She pushed Evert to match point and let out a shriek when Evert's final shot—a long lob—floated out of bounds.

Navratilova won, 7–5, 4–6, 6–4. She had washed away her

shutout loss to Evert at Amelia Island by winning in a place that mattered more. She had finally made her first U.S. Open championship match after eight years of trying.

"I just kept believing in myself," Navratilova said.

Navratilova had spoken touchingly throughout the two-week U.S. Open about how much winning America's tennis championship as an American citizen would mean to her. So when she wilted in the final against Tracy Austin and lost in the third set again—this time by committing a slew of errors, then double-faulting on match point to help Austin escape with a 1–6, 7–6, 7–6 win—Navratilova said she wanted to "crawl in a hole." She had just committed what is still regarded as the worst choke of her career. On four or five occasions in the last two sets—then again in the decisive tiebreaker—Navratilova was so eager to put points away, so anxious to get the match won, she missed three, then four, then five routine forehand volleys. The crowd shrieked each time in disbelief. "I'll never forget the tiebreaker, how I wanted to crush the ball, get the monkey off my back," Navratilova said.

Navratilova had strained and sweated and even argued line calls with passion; she had shrugged off each agonizing error and hunkered down again, refusing to give in to Austin. It was obvious how badly she ached to win. Needing to seize a service break in the last game of the third set just to stay in the match, Navratilova had stirringly done so, fighting off three spellbinding match points for Austin just to force that winner-take-all tiebreaker that she lost so cruelly on that haunting, horrible double fault.

So when Navratilova was called back on the court to accept the runner-up award, she couldn't believe her eyes when the New York crowd rose and gave her a warm, loud, steadily crescendoing standing ovation that lasted nearly two minutes. At first Navratilova just bit her lip and tried to speak. She couldn't. She had never been paid such homage anywhere. Soon tears were streaming down her face. For once, she was crying for joy.

As Navratilova later explained, "They weren't cheering Martina the Complainer, Martina the Czech, Martina the Loser, Martina the Bisexual Defector. They were cheering *me*.

"I had never felt anything like it in my life. Acceptance, respect, maybe even love."

Gratified as Navratilova was by the ovation, the events of the previous weeks and months had taken a toll. Evert, knowing the tumult that Navratilova was going through, was quoted in the *Daily News* story that outed Navratilova, saying, "Her tennis isn't going to get straightened out until she straightens out her life."

Rather than feel angry that Evert had delivered such a message through the press, Navratilova regarded the remarks as a sincere show of concern, telling herself, "Chris is right."

Evert had her own distractions at the U.S. Open. Lloyd, by now despondent about his career, had hoped to slip into the tournament unnoticed and win a match or two. Instead he drew Jimmy Connors in the first round. In a match that only rubbed more gravel into Lloyd's wounded confidence, Connors seemed to take relish in routing him off the court, 6–0, 6–0, 6–2.

"That's it," John told Chris. "I don't ever want to play in front of a crowd again." Again Evert talked Lloyd out of retiring. But the strain on their marriage continued to build.

After Navratilova's loss in the U.S. Open final to Austin, Lieberman had privately begun to mark the time—six months and counting—until Navratilova won the first title of their partnership.

"I was starting to wonder, 'Is it me?' " Lieberman admits.

Until Navratilova won something major, there was still rampant suspicion that the latest Martina was just a restyled version of the past models that couldn't sustain success.

The first three majors of 1981 had been divided among Hana Mandlikova, Evert, and Austin.

Navratilova's Grand Slam title drought, meanwhile, had extended to twenty-eight months.

Yet as Navratilova and Evert walked out onto the court at
Kooyong Stadium in Melbourne for the 1981 Australian Open final,
Evert felt that "Martina had the momentum"—an odd remark con-
sidering that Evert hadn't dropped a set. But Evert noticed that
Navratilova had begun to display a fiercer edge, a more resilient con-
fidence during her tournament run.

At times Evert felt sure she had struck unreachable shots—
"Against anyone else they would've been winners," Evert said—only
to see Martina somehow run down the ball or snare it at full stretch
and crack back a volley winner. "She would be on top of the net so
quickly I would have to hit a perfect passing shot," Evert said.

Evert was magnificently up to the challenge. In the brilliantly
played first set, Evert and Navratilova were even at 5–5, then 6–6,
then 4-all in the tiebreaker before Evert captured three straight
points to win it. Evert inched away to a 4–3 lead in the second set
too. But Navratilova produced her best game of the match to hold
at 4-all. Then Navratilova allowed Evert only two points in the next
two games, and the seesawing match was level at a set apiece.

Navratilova, seemingly exhilarated by her comeback, bolted off
to a 5–1 lead in the final set, only to see something stir in Evert
that was beyond fear and closer to self-loathing. It was that same
stomach-turning thought that often drove Evert: the galling idea of
having to make nice at the net with her overjoyed opponent after a
loss. In that instant, the details faded and Evert quit thinking about
how Navratilova's net-smothering play had demanded almost impossible precision from her. Like Navratilova, Evert began playing
on raw emotion now. "At that point you are so mad, you just find
yourself going for your shots more stubbornly," Evert said. "My
shots were hitting the lines. I was connecting with the ball as well as
I could have."

For the next six or seven games, she and Navratilova were like
two fighters deep into a fifteen-round bout, weary but willing. Evert
stormed back to 5-all. The tension was thick. Each rally had now be-

come a test of nerve. Yet again, Evert didn't feel safe. When Evert searched Navratilova's body language or eyes right then for any familiar hint of tightness, none was there.

In this, their forty-fourth confrontation, Navratilova was suddenly an opponent Evert did not quite know.

"Martina didn't panic," Evert said.

Evert was serving now at 5–5. With the score knotted at 30-all, Evert blasted a forehand long to give Navratilova a potentially decisive break point. Hoping to surprise Navratilova, Evert rushed the net first—only to end up in an eyeball-to-eyeball exchange of volleys that Navratilova won.

For the third time now, Navratilova began a new game serving for the match. Evert struck one last passing shot—long—and her shoulders sagged.

Navratilova had won the Australian Open, 6–7, 6–4, 7–5.

Her career total of major titles had finally ticked up to three.

At the season-ending Colgate Championships in East Rutherford, New Jersey, two weeks later, the year-end number one ranking was at stake between Evert, Navratilova, and Austin. But the shaky version of Navratilova returned. Austin roared back from 0–2 down in the final set to beat Navratilova again.

With Navratilova's loss, the pecking order in women's tennis snapped back to the usual: Evert was voted the year-end number one for the seventh time in eight years. Austin was second. And Navratilova, despite ten titles won in 1981, slid back to number three in the world.

Though the crowd at the Toyota Championships applauded Navratilova's losing effort against Austin almost as stirringly as the U.S. Open crowd had three months earlier, this time she wasn't gratified by the loser's ovation.

"I was mad," she said, "not sad."

And the rest of tennis was about to pay.

With Lieberman, her black-hearted conscience, still whispering in her ear and Richards on board to sharpen her strategy and strokes, Navratilova was about embark on the sort of run no one in tennis had ever seen before, a streak that would forever lift and transform her rivalry against Evert from a one-sided affair into the most epic, compelling, longest-running saga in the sport.

Between 1982 and 1986, Navratilova posted annual records of 90–3, 86–1, 78–2, 84–5, and 89–3. She won twelve Grand Slam singles titles in that span and—even more incredibly—seventy of eighty-four tournaments she entered. When Evert was asked along the way if she saw anyone in tennis with a realistic chance of beating Navratilova besides her, she said, "I'm sorry. I don't."

More than ever, Navratilova and Evert's matches would become can't-miss occasions that, Lieberman says, "brought out celebrities, brought out the media, brought out casual fans, brought out men, not just women. It was soap opera. It was drama."

It was a rivalry that was about to hit unprecedented heights.

CHAPTER TEN

TEAM NAVRATILOVA

When Navratilova first joined the professional tour, she would look at the big-name players and imagine herself eclipsing them one by one. She was now twenty-five years old, and her ambition was about to become a reality. The arrival of Richards and Lieberman marked the start of Team Navratilova, the continually evolving coterie of gurus and partners, friends and training specialists, that Navratilova would enlist to help her reach the top and stay there. But reaction to Navratilova's ascension and eventual domination of Evert was decidedly mixed.

The backlash wasn't just because Evert was a wildly popular champion. Few areas of society—let alone women's sports, or the still tinier subset of women's tennis—had ever seen anything quite like Navratilova or her convention-flaunting, openly gay, sometimes gender-bending entourage. Her girlfriends didn't hide. They sat in the friends' boxes at tournaments, forcing television commentators to euphemistically identify each one as Martina's "close friend" or "longtime companion." (After Evert retired in 1989, she worked as an NBC-TV commentator in 1990, the year Navratilova won her record ninth singles title at Wimbledon and went climbing up through the Centre Court stands, clambering from pillar to post, all just to give her partner, Judy Nelson, a hug. "If you guys had held onto each other any longer, I didn't know *what* I was going to say," Evert needled them later.)

Whereas Billie Jean King had been deeply, visibly rattled when forced to admit she was a lesbian, Navratilova's attitude was "Yeah. So?"

The technical and strategic changes Richards made in Navratilova's game reduced her unforced errors and shored up her ground stroke game, which was never Navratilova's strength. Richards took the pronounced swing out of Navratilova's erratic forehand volley—the shot that cost her the 1981 U.S. Open title against Tracy Austin. The topspin backhand that Richards added to Navratilova's slice backhand finally gave Navratilova a passing shot down the line, an added weapon that especially improved her prospects on clay. She now had a better chance to prevail in baseline rallies.

Under Lieberman's guidance, Navratilova's workouts increased from one hour a day to three. Their regime underwent constant tweaking. For a while, Navratilova did weight training four to five times a week with Lynn Conkwright, a former championship bodybuilder. Navratilova hired Rick Elstein of the Syosset Health Club on Long Island to help her with her footwork and hand-eye coordination. Elstein called their drills "tennis kinetics" and equated them to those used by hockey goalies to improve their reaction time.

Navratilova became an acolyte of Robert Haas, a Miami-based nutrition specialist and part-time computer wonk who seemed determined to make good on his boast that Navratilova would be "the first bionic tennis player." Haas wrote the diet best seller *Eat to Win*, which advocated a low-fat, high-carbohydrate diet. He claimed that he performed tests on daily drawn samples of Navratilova's blood for thirty-nine variables and then planned her meals accordingly. He gave her foil-wrapped vitamin packs that he concocted and made special shakes for her to drink. He sometimes sat courtside with a laptop computer too, the better to chart Martina's strokes and Evert's responses in the matches they played. "Chrissie was the only player we did the computer analysis with," Haas says.

Haas was often ridiculed for his computer habit, as well as other touches like nicknaming his analysis program "Smartina," and setting up his laptop to read, "May the Force Be with You" when he logged off. Richards says she never consulted Haas's match printouts once. (Her nickname for Haas then was "the nitwit nutritionist"; to this day, Haas still refers to Richards as "he," not "she.") But Navratilova was initially enamored of Haas's match analysis, insisting that it did reveal some of Evert's tendencies.

By the end of 1981, Navratilova was easily the fittest, fleetest, strongest player on tour. She was also the most experimental in her training. From month to month and tournament to tournament, Navratilova also employed a revolving group of massage therapists, specialists, osteopaths, acupuncturists, and alternative-medicine practitioners. Over the years her diet evolved from eating meat to forgoing red meat to eating no meat or chicken at all, then no dairy products. By 2003, when Navratilova was still winning doubles titles at age forty-six, she was entertaining a switch to a total raw foods diet. During her heyday, she once employed a shamanic woman who claimed she could take Navratilova back to the womb through meditative massage and waved a device called an "activator" over Navratilova's body, supposedly to flush out her aches and pains.

Haas says, "I used to tell her, 'Martina, that's snake oil. An activator is a chiropractic gimmick. That's total nonsense.' She'd say, 'No, no, Robert. It works. This woman told me one of my legs is longer than the other.' And I'd shrug and say, 'Okay, if you think it works for you . . .'

"Let's face it," Haas continues, "athletes are the most neurotic people on the planet. If they think something works, it works. Even if it doesn't work and it helps them psychologically, that's no less important. Over the years, Martina has gone through scores and scores of people. There were a lot of peripheral, shadowy figures who would come and go. All of a sudden she'd have a whole new set of advisers and they'd convince her of things. But Martina was entitled to do that. It happens in sports all the time. All athletes are ready to jump on any new thing that can help them. Or jettison something."

When Richards resigned after the French Open in 1983 because of friction with Lieberman and returned full-time to her ophthalmologic practice, Navratilova's new coach was Mike Estep, a former World Team Tennis teammate who urged Navratilova to commit to a more aggressive style of constant pressure serve-and-volley tennis.

"Too many women's tennis players play it safe," Estep told Navratilova. "You're going to go for it. Just go for it. You're not trying to be number one. Your goals are beyond that."

Their goal was to make history.

When Estep asked Navratilova in his first interview what she hoped to achieve by hiring him, Navratilova said, "I want to win the Grand Slam and be the greatest player who ever lived."

If the results were stunning, so was the uneven reception Navratilova received.

Given that Navratilova had always provoked strong feelings, it was often hard to determine exactly what accounted for her uneven treatment by the press and the increasingly cool reception she evoked from fans as she began to dominate tennis and defeat Evert regularly.

Many Americans now regard Navratilova with misty affection—Martina the Unsinkable, or, more recently, the Inspirational Active Geezer, as Grace Lichtenstein jokes. But that migration and warming of popular opinion came late in Navratilova's career, long after her transformative period in the first half of the 1980s, the contentious time when she became a tennis legend.

As Navratilova and Evert marched inexorably toward one title showdown after another, they evoked increasingly polarized reactions when they played. Lichtenstein says, "I have friends who were tomboys or jocks when they were kids, and whether they're gay or straight, to this day they will tell you that they never liked what Chris Evert 'stood for,' because she was adored because she was feminine and not because she was a champion."

George Vecsey regularly encountered people who volunteered, "I never liked that Martina."

"I think Martina disturbed people on a psychological level even more than she did on a physical level," Vecsey says. "For years, some people still treated her like the Commie defector. Other times, it was as if there was this fear she was going to seduce everyone's little girls, that Mrs. Austin's daughter might somehow not be safe from her."

Truman Capote's droll observation of how gays are truly thought of—"Everyone knows a faggot—a faggot is the gay gentleman who has just left the room"—did not apply to Navratilova. Because she was out and a public figure, people often felt free to express a full range of sexist or homophobic tropes to her face. She was derided as unnatural, freakish, something less than a woman. "A monster," she sadly said. For years, Navratilova shouldered the burden of being the only lesbian many people thought they knew. And Navratilova admits that it was often a lonely existence. But she remained forthright, unapologetic, unbowed.

Many gays and lesbians looked at Navratilova and felt that their honor had been defended as human beings.

A still larger group of people seemed to wish Navratilova would just shut the hell up and go away. Many of them regarded Evert as their avenging angel.

"It was as if Martina became the bully to some people, and I was the person who could silence the bully," Evert says. "To me, that had to be because of something people thought I symbolized. They couldn't have liked what I stood for, because I never opened my mouth or showed the 'real' me until late in my career.

"People didn't even know us, people had no idea," Evert continues, "and yet, if I met somebody then, it was often like, 'Oh, I never liked that Martina. She's so tough.' I'd say, 'You know what? She's a kitten. She really is. I'm the hard one. I was ruthless.' And they'd always say, 'No, no, not you—you're so frail and feminine. We always felt sorry for you.' It was like Martina was the villain. And I was the fragile lamb, the little slaughtered lamb. I'd finally just throw up my hands."

During one of Navratilova's matches against Evert at the U.S. Open, a female heckler seated next to George Vecsey shouted, "C'mon, Chris, I want a real woman to win!" As Navratilova began to overtake Evert, Evert began to receive mail with exhortations such as "*Please* beat Martina."

Pam Shriver remembers playing a doubles match with Navratilova at a tournament in Houston during which Navratilova suddenly wheeled around when a point ended and shouted at a cat-caller, "Doesn't hard work count for something?"

"What I gathered had happened," Shriver says, "was the guy had yelled out some accusation that Martina was on steroids."

The 1980s were the last, fitful decade of the cold war. Clashes between East and West were still treated like morality plays and sports outcomes such as the 1980 U.S. hockey team's "Miracle on Ice" victory over the Soviet Union at the Lake Placid Winter Olympics were hailed as triumphs of good over evil. Female athletes from the Eastern Bloc countries were frequently accused of being juiced up on steroids. The fall of the Berlin Wall brought evidence of systematic state doping programs in the old East Germany: in 1998 five coaches and doctors confessed to having administered performance-enhancing drugs to swimmers during the 1970s and 1980s.

Robert Haas and Billie Jean King were constantly approached by people who would sidle up to them, nod toward Navratilova, and conspiratorially say: "Come on, you can tell me . . . She's on steroids, right?"

King says, "I used to hear that so much. I was like, 'Are you *kidding*? This woman? She wouldn't go near a steroid. Ever.'"

Haas says, "I'd tell people, 'Believe me, steroids have never been within a hundred feet of this woman.' They'd say, 'But look at her vascular structure. Look at her body.' I'd say, 'Nope.' Doctors would come up to me and say, 'Look, we've looked at such things. We know . . .' And I said, 'No, no, no, no, no. You're wrong. It's just her. It's hard work.' "

As Navratilova began piecing together winning streaks of forty- and fifty-plus matches for a second consecutive year in 1983, it was suggested—once, in jest, by Evert herself—that Navratilova should just go join the men's tour and "leave us alone."

Hana Mandlikova reacted to a disappointing three-set loss to Navratilova at the 1984 French Open by bitterly telling her parents and coach, Betty Stove, that she intended to walk into her post-match press conference and disparage Navratilova. Stove, one of the Women's Tennis Association founders, urged Mandlikova not to do it. But Mandlikova pounced on the first question that gave her an opening.

"What did you think of the way Martina played today?" a reporter asked.

"It's hard playing against a man—I mean, Martina," Mandlikova said. "She comes to the net and scares you with those big muscles. She is very big and difficult to pass."

Mandlikova knew she had just made headlines. To make matters more uncomfortable, she had to play Navratilova and Shriver the next day in a doubles match. Mandlikova kept the insults up—aping at Martina across the net and flexing both arms like a body-builder, pointing at her biceps and gawking at Navratilova again. Navratilova was appalled. Just a few years earlier at a tournament in Mahwah, New Jersey, after Mandlikova upset her, Navratilova had sent Mandlikova an encouraging note, urging her to go on and win the tournament.

After the incidents at the French Open, Navratilova didn't speak to Mandlikova for more than a year.

"I did a horrible thing," Hana says, "and it took me a long time to apologize. But Martina was nice enough to forgive me."

At Wimbledon one month after Mandlikova's French Open remarks, other players crowded around the television set in the women's locker room and cheered wildly for Evert as Evert routed Mandlikova in their semifinal match. Mandlikova had made the mistake of insulting Evert a few days earlier, saying she had no cause to fear either her or Martina.

"Hana must've been feeling pretty good—she [did] beat me three years ago," Evert said.

Lieberman had read the press's depictions of Navratilova for years. When she actually met her in 1981, she was surprised by how small she actually was. Though Navratilova was often described in print as a muscle-bound Goliath, in reality some differences between her and Evert were not as great as portrayed. At five foot seven, Navratilova stood only one inch taller than Evert, and she weighed 145 pounds at the height of her career—laughably puny compared to later ball-crushing champions such as the Williams sisters or six-foot-three Lindsay Davenport.

The sports media of Navratilova and Evert's time—which was just inching toward coed—often depicted Navratilova in extremis anyway. Navratilova was portrayed as both emotionally fragile *and* some fearsome ogress. The contrast between her and Evert, who was still many people's standard of femininity and grace, never seemed starker or more cause for comment than when Navratilova began trouncing her.

While Evert was an unabashed pressroom darling (sometimes charming male reporters with a wink and a sly "I'll never tell" if asked what she did the night before a match), Navratilova was sometimes challenged with baiting questions.

"Are you still gay?" a male reporter once asked.

"Are you still the alternative?" Navratilova shot back.

In a particularly perverse piece for the *St. Paul Pioneer Press* that columnist Tom Powers wrote about Evert's retirement, Powers lamented that with Evert gone, "Today's youngsters . . . will grow up thinking all women tennis players have thighs like Schwarzenegger and last names that end in the letters o-v-a. But those of us who grew up with Chrissie know better . . . [We could] flip on the tube and see Chris volleying demurely from the baseline. Her opponent, often a European with serious facial hair, would be lunging and twisting and grunting after the ball."

Powers claimed that Evert would never charge the net "like some disgusting buffalo." He concluded by pointing out that Evert reigned between Billie Jean King, who "was involved in a palimony suit with another woman. . . . Nice p.r. for the sport, eh?" and Navratilova, "a walking mixed doubles team."

Navratilova was always acutely aware of the paradox her late-coming transformation created. "My attitude seems to turn off a lot of people," she told the *New York Times*'s Neil Amdur. "When I didn't care or wasn't motivated, my attitude wasn't right. Now I turn people off by being too confident, too good?"

Her decision to assemble Team Navratilova and her willingness to consider anything that might help her performance catapulted her to greatness. But her unorthodox methods—many of which were ahead of their time—also made her vulnerable to various interpretations.

She was celebrated for revolutionizing training for female athletes and broadening ideas of what was possible. Unlike plenty of female athletes before her, she was not conflicted about looking strong or acting powerful. Navratilova believed strong *was* beautiful.

But Navratilova's reliance on her team was treated as a sign of weakness. She was often cast as a fragile woman in need of intense support or an incorrigible spendthrift who was pursuing her latest over-the-top extravagance. (At Wimbledon one year, she had to rent two houses to accommodate everyone who was traveling with her.) It was said Navratilova was determined to assemble what amounted to a surrogate family in her new country even if that required putting everyone on the payroll.

"Why is it that when other people travel with people, they're just considered their friends?" a stung Navratilova said after one news account referred to Lieberman as her *aide de go-fer* and called a businesswoman friend a glorified dog walker. "It's degrading," Navratilova said.

Evert often traveled with people too—first her mother, Colette, and later her coach, her husband, her best friends, or sisters Jeanne or Clare. Unlike Navratilova, Evert loathed looking to the stands for support. "For me it felt like a form of weakness," Evert says. "I didn't understand why people look up after every point. I didn't need a team for support or motivation. All of that was inside me."

Navratilova would sometimes look at her supporters so beseechingly at a lost point or game that tears seemed a possibility. Diana Nyad, who sat in the friends' box during one Evert-Navratilova match at Wimbledon, says, "Martina looked so strong out there, and yet you just knew she could turn into this crumpling, withering ball of insecurities and start barking at the linesmen, or looking at her entourage like, 'I don't *deserve* this . . . I'm a good person . . . It's not *fair*!"

Navratilova never denied that she hated to be alone or that she was at her happiest when she had someone to share her victories with. She once told a young girl during a question-and-answer session at a tennis clinic that the reason she loved playing doubles was that after a doubles match "you always have someone to hug."

In addition to her assorted friends, Navratilova often traveled with a changing menagerie of dogs and cats, many of them strays she took in. For years, Navratilova used to hide her beloved Chihuahua K.D. (short for "Killer Dog") inside her shirt or coat and smuggle the teeny dog into restaurants, onto planes, almost everywhere she went. Navratilova's personal record for most pets on the road is believed to be six—the four dogs and two cats that she and Judy Nelson traveled with on the European circuit one summer. Nelson's brother drove the animals in a rented van from tournament to tournament, starting in Rome, and even the best hotels allowed the pets in. "Celebrity has its privileges," Nelson says with a laugh.

"It was a lot like the circus coming to town," a former player says, chuckling. "You didn't know what or whom you'd see next."

"I love Martina," says Pam Shriver, her record-setting doubles partner, "but let's face it. By the time she was seeing Judy Nelson [beginning in 1984], some of the jobs that people on Team Navratilova had were just absurd."

Navratilova's defensiveness about the characterizations of her and her friends was understandable. And she was right: in a perfectly inclusive big-tent, nonjudgmental world, having a traveling caravan that at various times included a best-selling lesbian novelist, a six-foot-two transsexual ophthalmologist, a sharp-tongued personal trainer who was called "Agent Orange" behind her back, and another girlfriend (Nelson) whom the tabloids unfailingly referred to as a "blond Texas beauty queen and mother of two" should not automatically be cause for censure.

But behaving as if such a collection of people was an everyday occurrence was absurd.

"What does it say," Renee Richards once cracked to a friend, "that I'm the most normal one in this group?"

Time has vindicated Navratilova. Her idea then—that having a support team of experts might be the future of sports—proved true. As Robert Haas says, "Even though other people weren't doing it, our thing was, sports science will be huge one day—it's not now, but it will be. Having your own trainer, nutritionist, using computers for analysis and teaching, will be very big one day—it isn't now, but it will be. I think Martina was able to establish a [new] model for athletes.

"People were, of course, skeptical, and they laughed at us. But what are you going to do? As it turned out, we were right."

One of Mike Estep's first impressions when he began to coach Navratilova in 1983 was how defensive she could be. "We used to have some long talks about it," he says. "She did get a raw deal from the press. But I also thought—and she agreed—that sometimes she made things even harder on herself because she felt so antagonized. She would be in a press conference, a reporter would ask her something about her match, and sometimes, right off the bat, she'd shoot back, 'Didn't you see the match? Where were you?' She'd challenge people."

And still . . .

Navratilova evolved into a legendary athlete and symbol of freedom because of the very same traits that earned her so much rebuke: her refusal to temper what she said and her defiance, her impetuous, almost utopian world vision that colored everything from her faraway view of America as a young girl to just about every love affair she's had. "When Martina is in love, it's like storybook love," her publicist Linda Dozoretz often said. "Nothing can ever be wrong."

Reasonable people can debate Navratilova's personal politics or the choices she made. But there is no disputing her bravery. By refusing to act as if being called gay were an insult, by rejecting generations of thought about female athletes or homosexuality—the so-called love that dare not speak its name—Navratilova did more than refuse to conform to social conventions. She was important because she resituated the argument and illuminated something else: how gay people are constantly required to forgive heterosexuals for their bigotry and ignorance.

When most people speak of "tolerance" between straights and gays, they never think of it flowing in both directions.

Navratilova made them.

So much of what she accomplished was as the Outsider. But because of that footing, she often became a prism that refracted what America promises versus what Navratilova thought America should deliver, especially regarding basic human rights.

"I left one country because I couldn't be who I was," Navratilova said, "and then I come to the United States and now this country is telling me I can't be who I am. I don't feel as American as I would like because I'm not *allowed* to feel like an American. I can't fight for the country. I can't deduct a child [on a tax return]. They can throw me out of [teaching] school, they can throw me out of work, because I'm a lesbian. It's pretty frightening."

At Wimbledon one year a reporter at one of Navratilova's post-match press conferences snidely asked her about the meaning of the pink triangle on a T-shirt she happened to be wearing. Navratilova calmly and without condescension proceeded to give him a two-minute tutorial about how the Nazis ordered pink triangles stitched on the clothing of homosexuals they sent to the concentration camps during World War II.

By the end of her answer—not the usual fodder of your average sports press conference—the other reporters were listening raptly to Navratilova and the smirk had fallen off her interrogator's face. The man looked as if he wanted to slide to the floor and crawl on his belly from the room.

But no matter how much Navratilova sloughed off the treatment that she or Team Navratilova received, privately she was deeply wounded.

"Scarred," she once said.

That Chris Evert—arguably the most popular American female athlete of the twentieth century—could not ultimately beat back Navratilova's challenge after years of prevailing in her other rivalries against Billie Jean King, Evonne Goolagong, and Tracy Austin did nothing to warm the public's regard for Navratilova.

If Navratilova's 1981 Australian Open win over Evert suggested that she was finally capable of ending Evert's long stay at number one, Navratilova's results in the first six months of 1982 absolutely confirmed it.

Unlike other years, Navratilova didn't regress. She stormed into Paris for the French Open in late May having won thirty-four of the thirty-five matches she played in 1982. Even her only loss—a thudding three-set fold against Sylvia Hanika at the Avon Championships in New York, which was filed away as another Navratilova choke job—was perversely encouraging to her.

"I realized the only person beating me consistently was myself," Navratilova said. "And those days were about to stop."

Navratilova's new, resilient optimism was a significant marker of just how much her psychological underpinnings had changed. By the spring of 1982, the anniversary of her first meeting with Lieberman, Navratilova pronounced herself happier and more settled than she'd ever been. By summertime she had decided to lighten her hair from brown to blond and began pulling it back into a ponytail wrapped in a ribbon. She told people she was beginning to actually like the way she looked for the first time in her life. She said she felt "prettier, more feminine."

She even thought she knew what caused her mind-set change. It was something Lieberman had predicted would happen.

"So much of my attitude is the product of working hard," Navratilova told *Tennis* magazine's Peter Bodo. "I respected myself because I'd given it my best shot and realized when you do that, things work out okay. Knowing that I like myself made me better at handling all kinds of situations."

Navratilova and Richards had set a goal of catching Evert on the 1982 weekly computer rankings by late May and the end of the clay court season.

"And I did it," Navratilova said, beaming.

Navratilova's rapidly accumulating successes did nothing to mellow Lieberman. She could still be as hard-driving and acid-tongued as ever. "Martina, why don't you just get off the court. That stinks!" she would yell. Sometimes Navratilova would toss a racket or shout back. Sometimes she would storm off. "But I'm telling you, I was working with Martina on an instructional book at the time, and there was a lot of good energy there too," sports commentator Mary Carillo says. "Martina knew at that time she needed what Nancy brought. I think she liked that here was somebody finally talking to her in a real way. And Nancy made Martina laugh. She'd make fun of Martina's nose or something, and Martina would make fun of Nancy's and her mother's accents. Martina would be doing this New

York Jewish accent in her Czech accent, and Martina didn't know how funny *that* was. Nancy would just say, 'Look at her. She thinks she's hilarious.' "

Lieberman's mother, Renee, never got used to Navratilova walking around the house naked when Martina and Nancy stayed at her Far Rockaway, New York, home. When Martina, not thinking, opened the front door one day without any clothes on to let out her dogs, Renee trilled, "You should like it if I went to the door without a stitch?"

Effective as Lieberman was at goading Navratilova to transform her career, her success in working with other members of Team Navratilova was more uneven. Lieberman never denied that she could be a "control freak" and hard-driving. In addition to feuding with Richards over coaching strategy, Lieberman clashed with Mike Estep, Richards's successor. She prodded Navratilova's longtime agent Peter Johnson about Navratilova's lack of endorsements and irked him by asking to see his marketing plan for her. Some friends of Navratilova's often objected to the way Lieberman spoke to her.

Yet Lieberman's sway over Navratilova remained great despite the tensions, in large part because nearly every prophecy Lieberman made seemed to come true. It was as if Navratilova's rise had been spoken into existence.

Lieberman had promised that Navratilova would dominate tennis. And it was happening.

One of the reasons the year-end Virginia Slims Championships went to a best-of-five-set final instead of the usual two-of-three format was that Navratilova was defeating even the best players in the game in under an hour.

"Nancy's whole attitude was 'Look how much harder you're working, look how much more you can bench press, look how much faster you can run—these other women don't deserve to be on the court with you,' " Carillo recalls. "Nancy would actually tell

Martina, 'This better not take more than an hour' or 'You should be able to beat Chris in this final in about forty minutes.' And that's when Martina started having forty-minute finals.

"Martina went from somebody who got nervous and thought, 'I can be up a set and a break and still lose' to someone who thought, 'This shouldn't take more than forty-five minutes.' That's an *incredible* mind change. Martina would look over at Nancy during a match and Nancy would look at her like, 'What are you doing? Why the hell is this match taking so long?' And then Martina would get on with it. It was something to see. It really was."

Navratilova had always had a bit of an on-court strut, even as a teenager. Once Navratilova began winning everything, some opponents came to regard her antics or body language as an extra, unwanted aggravation. Some fans found her more off-putting as well. Wasn't it enough for Navratilova that she was trouncing everyone 6–2, 6–2?

"At times I thought she was arrogant on the court," Evert admits. "Sometimes when I'd hit a passing shot by her she would actually laugh out loud, like, 'How can anybody hit a passing shot by *me*?' That bugged me. But I also felt she used her body language to her advantage. When you look your opponent in the eye even when you're down 4–2, you let them know that you're still in this match. So I learned from her also. Like it or not, she was smart to do that. The way she carried herself created an advantage."

Not everyone could rationalize Navratilova's behavior like Evert could. At the 1982 French Open, Andrea Jaeger upset a curiously flat Evert in the semifinals, 6–3, 6–1. But Navratilova bulldozed to a 7–6, 6–1 victory over Jaeger in the final.

The title was Navratilova's first at the French Open, and what it suggested was ominous and new. Navratilova was no longer just the greatest serve-and-volleyer or the most athletic player in the women's game. She had proven that she could win even the biggest tournaments on any type of surface, and by playing any way she needed to, from the baseline or at the net.

But Navratilova's joy over her win quickly curdled. She was told in her post-match press conference that Jaeger had churlishly suggested that Navratilova's romp was aided by coaching signals from Richards and Lieberman in the stands. Even if it had been true—and it wasn't—such signals weren't against the rules.

Jaeger's father, Roland, a pugnacious former boxer, was suspected of persuading sixteen-year-old Andrea to make the complaint. But an incensed Navratilova refused to forgive either of them.

"Jesus Christ, I win this great title finally and I have to hear this?" Navratilova told Curry Kirkpatrick of *Sports Illustrated*. "Thank you, Andrea. I could decide in my sleep what to do. Players know I'm as fair as they come . . . If she can't be a gracious loser, that's tough. And if she is getting this stuff from her father, Mr. Jaeger is a louse."

By the time Navratilova arrived at Wimbledon three weeks later, still having lost only once in the first six months of 1982, sportswriters were tracking the swath she was cutting across the tour as if she were some coalescing storm front capable of uprooting trees and overturning cars.

Navratilova had now captured eight of her last nine tournaments, and forty-two of her last forty-three matches. After just eleven months of training with Lieberman and eight months of strategizing with Richards, Navratilova had already won two Grand Slam titles—equaling her total for the first seven years of her career.

A third Wimbledon title for Navratilova was considered a fait accompli. With the victory, Navratilova would be halfway to a calendar-year sweep of the Grand Slams, a feat that only two other women, Maureen Connolly and Margaret Court, had achieved. Navratilova could also reap an extra $500,000 bonus from a promotion called the Playtex Challenge if she won Wimbledon. (She had already won the challenge's first two designated tournaments, the U.S. Indoor Championships and the Family Circle Cup.)

Lieberman was so sure that Navratilova was going to win Wimbledon, she had carried with her for three weeks of travels the magnum of champagne that Martina received for winning the French Open. "And that bottle was big, like a torpedo," Lieberman says.

Lieberman's confidence did not dim even when Evert advanced to the Wimbledon final opposite Navratilova. The day before the match, Lieberman stole off to London with three friends, Barbara Wood, Nancy Nichols, and Debby Jennings, to buy Navratilova a gown for the traditional Wimbledon Champions Ball as an unsuspecting Navratilova practiced with Richards for the final.

"Martina had told me before we left the States that it was bad luck to buy the dress before you won the title," Lieberman says. "But I was like, 'You guys, you *know* she's gonna win.' We were all excited, thinking it would be such a great surprise for her. So we take off and get to the store and I don't know exactly what size Martina is. So I said, 'Okay, okay, Barbara—we'll measure you for the length. And Nick, we'll measure you for the hips. Me for the arms.' Then I was looking around the store and saying, 'Oh my gosh, I guess I need two of those, four of those, some stockings, and hey—give me one of those hats. And give me that thing too, whatever that is.' Then the saleslady says, 'You've got to have the parasol to go with that.' And I said, 'Well . . . it is Wimbledon. And it is raining . . . Okay! We'll get that too!'

"We were so stupid," Lieberman says.

Once the match began, Lieberman's confidence was eventually tested. Navratilova needed just twenty-two minutes to seize the first set from Evert, 6–1, scoring as often from the backcourt as the net, nailing winners on the run. Evert, meanwhile, was so scattershot, she said later she was hoping only "not to be humiliated." But Evert rallied to take the second set, 6–3, and it was Navratilova who was discombobulated. She rushed a few approach shots and plowed the ball into the net. And Evert began finding her range. In the final set, Navratilova barely won her first service game, but Evert broke her the next time to go up 2–1—Evert's first lead of the match.

Thinking back now to Navratilova's past chokes against Sylvia Hanika and Tracy Austin, Evert later admitted: "I thought maybe

Martina would crack under pressure." But Navratilova immediately broke Evert's serve right back for 2-all in the final set.

Then, with a suddenness that was astounding, Navratilova ended the match in seven minutes. It was as if a sonic boom had hit.

Navratilova began carving volleys out of air and covered the court like a dervish, making the spots where Evert could safely hit the ball seem fleeting and small. Serves cracked off Navratilova's racket. Evert struggled just to win a point here and there. Forget an entire game. In the final game of the match, Navratilova broke Evert's serve at love.

In the friends' box, Team Navratilova rejoiced.

"We're rich! We're rich!" Lieberman yelled, thinking now of the $500,000 Playtex bonus.

"Uh . . . you already were rich," one of her friends whispered back.

"Oh," Lieberman blinked.

When Navratilova returned to their rented house just a few blocks away from Wimbledon, she was happily surprised to find the gown for the Champions Ball laid out on her bed. She had just finished filling her bathtub for a long post-match soak when Lieberman and the others burst in, whooping and hollering and spraying her with that well-traveled magnum of champagne. Navratilova laughed and screamed and tightly shut her eyes as the champagne began to sting.

When Navratilova tried on the ball gown, Lieberman had to laugh. "The waist was too big, the dress was too long, the arms were too loose, and the shoes we got her—they were too small," Lieberman says. "The only thing that actually worked was the parasol. It opened."

Navratilova wore the dress anyway, pinning it in here and there to make it fit, and she carried the parasol to the microphone with her at the Champions Ball and opened it as she began her victory speech.

"The weather has been so bad this fortnight, I just didn't want to take any chances," Navratilova joked. And the audience laughed warmly.

Navratilova had now stared down Evert in their last two major finals, both of them high-pressure, three-set fights. Since the autumn of 1981, Navratilova had advanced to nineteen straight tournaments finals and won fourteen of them. Her rivalry against Evert now stood at 29–17. But Navratilova had won six of their last nine meetings.

If she defeated Evert again in eight weeks at the 1982 U.S. Open—the event that had always been Navratilova's personal chamber of horrors, and a tournament Evert had won four of the previous six times—Navratilova could rightfully claim she had exorcised her last ghost.

Navratilova was asked after Wimbledon where a fabled Grand Slam sweep of the four majors might place her in tennis history, and she said among the sport's all-time greats—a comment that Evert quietly took note of, and stewed.

CHAPTER ELEVEN

THE INVINCIBLE
YEARS

If Evert had one middling gripe about the way in which she was re-garded, it was her belief that her career-long consistency became undervalued, even forgotten, as Navratilova began winning. "I've had seven great years, Martina's had two," Evert reminded reporters in 1983 when she began to feel prematurely written off. Evert knew she didn't have the gasp-inducing athleticism or shot-making flair that Navratilova did, but she was proud—fiercely proud—of how she had won with the skills she had. Evert knew the whitecapping confidence that Navratilova was beginning to feel now, knowing her advance to every tournament final seemed inevitable. Navratilova's increasing audacity was familiar to Evert too.

"You have to have an arrogance to maintain a high level of con-fidence, and most of the time I kept it inside," Evert said. "But boy, it was there. You know you're better than the other players because there are so many times you're down 5–3 in the third set and you don't get worried. You still know you're going to win. That's true ar-rogance."

Recognizable as the arc of Navratilova's transformation was to Evert, it was still going to take more than an eight- or ten-month hot streak to convince her that Navratilova was better, let alone about to forever shove her aside.

Unlike for many subsequent tennis champions—none more than the Williams sisters, Venus and Serena, who were candid about their reluctance to play often enough to maintain the number one world ranking—being number one was enormously important to Evert and Navratilova and their contemporaries such as Jimmy Connors, Bjorn Borg, and John McEnroe. Being number one is what goaded Connors through the spectacular four-hour comeback wins he was known for, playing as if he were demonically possessed. "I left DNA out there," he once growled, nodding toward the stadium court at the U.S. Open. A yearning to be the indisputable best player in the world drove McEnroe to such irrational angst, he once complained, "I don't want to sound paranoid, but that Cyclops [line-calling] machine knows who I am."

Evert was no different.

"Being number one is an ego thing—I mean, you've got to be frank about it," Evert says. "It's a power thing. You're the woman of the hour. You get used to it. And then, all of a sudden, when you're on top and somebody starts taking it away, it's difficult. The press wants to talk to somebody else. You're not the first priority. And that's when you realize too, 'Gee, that tournament promoter who's always coming up to me and chatting, I really thought he liked *me*. I really thought I was special. But now all of a sudden he's chatting up Martina. He wants her to play his tournament and he hasn't even talked to me.' It happens to everyone in every profession. When you get older and have more of a balanced life, you can fall back on that. But when all you have is your tennis, it's your entire life, you know?"

And so it was no coincidence that Evert seemed to be lying in wait at her first press conference at the 1982 U.S. Open when Navratilova's name came up. Evert admitted she was "a little insulted" that Navratilova had tried to turn one great year into instant immortality. "I don't think one year merits that," Evert said.

A reporter asked, "Will you go to Australia [in December] to break up a Grand Slam sweep by Navratilova?"

"Hopefully, it will already be broken," Evert said, leveling the man with a look. And the temperature in the room seemed to plummet twenty degrees.

Evert, who since 1974 had never gone a calendar year without winning at least one major title, was sending Navratilova a message that she was not conceding the U.S. Open. And Navratilova threw more kindling on the fire when she proclaimed that her game had ascended to a new plane: "I don't have to play my best to win. If I'm on, nobody can beat me. If I'm off, I beat myself."

Impudent as it sounded, nothing contradicted Navratilova's boast until the second Wednesday of the tournament.

Evert was napping in her hotel room when John Lloyd called her from the Manhattan showroom of Ellesse, the clothing company they endorsed. He reported some shocking news: Navratilova had just lost her quarterfinal match to Pam Shriver. And Navratilova's novel post-match explanation had caused a sensation. Navratilova was just two points from victory—leading 6–1, 5–4, 30–15—when she began to unravel.

As Curry Kirkpatrick of *Sports Illustrated* would later write:

Somewhere between the time Navratilova belted one photographer with a towel and ransacked another one's film— free-lancer Art Seitz swears he's hiring Marvin Mitchelson to sue for damages—she got around to explaining how she had recently contracted acute toxoplasmosis, a viral condition sometimes transmitted by cats that weakens the muscles. Navratilova didn't say how weak she felt in the 17-minute first set or when she was serving for the match in the second, but Seitz verified that her muscles didn't seem weak when he encountered her. In that fray she was aided by her strawberry-blonde henchperson, Nancy Lieberman—a/k/a Agent Orange—who elbowed Seitz in the back.

What was more perplexing was that nobody seemed to know whether Navratilova had lost to Shriver, her good friend and doubles partner, or to a cat who had nibbled from her bowl of nuts. *Wild Kingdom*. Film at 11.

Kirkpatrick was a regular on the men's and women's tennis tours and often covered them as if they were camp soap operas. Though he and Navratilova clashed over the years at some of his snide descriptions—later in her career he called her a "braying old mare"—the truth was, Kirkpatrick was an equal-opportunity strafer. In his gossipy, wise-guy stories, Tracy Austin was a "squeaking wonder" and Evert was depicted as an overly cautious woman who deserved to be sent up—"Chris! No!"—for her conservativism. Kirkpatrick's "bowl of nuts" reference was a guffaw at Navratilova's post-match guess that she might have contracted toxoplasmosis on a recent visit to see Rita Mae Brown, her ex-girlfriend. Navratilova ventured that she had eaten from a dish of nuts that she later noticed one of Brown's cats tiptoeing through.

"The Grand Slam gone on tiny cats' paws," Kirkpatrick wrote.

The day after Navratilova's loss, Dr. Gary Wadler, a Long Island–based physician, confirmed Navratilova's illness to reporters, saying he had diagnosed her with toxoplasmosis before the U.S. Open began. Shriver sarcastically replied, "If she was *that* diseased, I can't believe I lost a game."

Evert won the U.S. Open title, thrashing Hana Mandlikova, 6–3, 6–1, in the final. And Navratilova's fear that the press would say she couldn't "win the big one in New York" came true. Kirkpatrick wasn't the only writer to lampoon Navratilova's excuse for losing. She ruefully told Lieberman, "No one believes I was sick." As if to raise the boil on her rivalry with Navratilova a few more degrees,

Evert said that she wished she had been the one to defeat Navratilova, not Shriver.

"If determination is any factor," Evert said, "I would have won this tournament anyway."

Navratilova took a few weeks off, then started another winning streak that carried her all the way to the 1982 Australian Open, which was still held at that time in late November. But the renewed suggestions that she was a choker continued to trail her like a kite tail. Once in Melbourne, Evert defeated Navratilova in the Australian Open final, 6–3, 2–6, 6–3. What began as a potentially historic year for Navratilova had ended limply. One of Navratilova's friends said the long flight home felt like 250 hours, not 25. With the win, Evert had earned a split of the year's four Grand Slam championships.

She also gave no clue that she was playing the tournament under duress. Her marriage to John Lloyd had been drifting, but now it had reached a crisis point.

Lloyd had declared 1982 his make-or-break season. But over the last six months of the year, his pattern of early tournament defeats continued. During the weeks he was home from the tour, Lloyd was sometimes so despondent he would watch television for hours each day and deep into the night, often eating his meals in front of the TV too. At first Evert told herself that it was just Lloyd's way of escaping his bad results. Her attitude started to change as weeks dragged on and Lloyd couldn't seem to rouse himself. "Respect is very important in a marriage," Evert said. "And I started losing respect for John."

Not even some unexpected, career-best success in mixed doubles—a run to the 1982 French Open title in his first tournament with Wendy Turnbull, then an advance to the Wimbledon final—inspired Lloyd's singles play. Wimbledon organizers had spared Lloyd the indignity of having to qualify for the singles tournament by giving him a wild card entry into the main draw. After leaping to a two-set, 2–0 lead against Russell Simpson of New Zealand, Lloyd caved in and lost his first-round match. At the Australian Open, Lloyd spiraled out in the first round again, this time to an unknown American named Joe Meyers.

Evert had to leave Melbourne immediately after winning the 1982 Australian title to prepare for the season-ending Toyota Championships in East Rutherford, New Jersey, which would determine the number one ranking for the year. Lloyd had decided to remain in Australia for an extra month of training. He and Chris both cried at the airport when they said goodbye.

Evert's relationship with a mutual friend, forty-two-year-old Adam Faith, a sometime actor and 1960s-era British pop star, had become an issue. John had befriended Faith a couple years earlier when they met on a cross-country flight. By the end of the trip, Lloyd had offered Faith tickets to see him and Chris play. Soon the favors became a regular occurrence. Before long, Faith was a conspicuous presence at Chris's tournaments around the world.

Though married, Faith had a long and much-publicized history of extramarital affairs in Britain. Neither Evert nor Faith would confirm they were involved—which is not the same thing as denying it outright. (Evert later said that she and Lloyd "made a pact" not to discuss any liaisons with other people during this period.) But Evert and Lloyd were, even then, already discussing whether to separate or divorce.

They decided to spend the December 1982 holidays apart—Lloyd with his parents in Palm Springs and Chris in Florida with her disapproving parents, who kept urging her to fly back to California to see John and work on their troubled marriage. Just before New Year's, Chris finally did. But she and Lloyd suddenly found being together again awkward.

"We were like strangers forcing our marriage to work," Evert said.

Evert was grateful when she arrived at the year-ending 1982 Toyota Championships to have her tennis to preoccupy her. Evert's two-year hold on the number one ranking was at stake, and the sniping between her and Navratilova and Lieberman was sizzling now.

Lieberman had never stopped believing that Navratilova had to forget her friendship with Evert to play her absolute best against her. Lieberman continued urging Navratilova to reject the buddy-buddy culture of the women's tour. The closer Navratilova came to overtaking Evert, the more Lieberman ratcheted up what Lieberman called "My Act."

She stopped saying hello to Evert when they crossed paths at tournaments, though Martina still did. But such gestures were hardly enough to prevent Navratilova and Evert's friendship from sliding into what Evert calls "the lowest depths. The worst."

While Lieberman regarded Navratilova as guileless, she saw Evert as a master of mind games, a shrewd manipulator of a news media that tended to fawn over her. "That bothered me," Lieberman says. Evert came to feel that Lieberman was "brainwashing" Martina to hate her.

"I don't know if I'd say I felt betrayed by Martina," Evert reflects. "It was more like hurt, and then anger that Martina would be influenced like that. That she couldn't stand up for herself. I felt like, 'Don't you have enough guts to stand up to your girlfriend?' Some of the things that went on were like high school stuff."

Evert sometimes found Navratilova and Lieberman staring at her across the practice court. Then they'd say something and burst out laughing. "It was as if they were trying to humiliate me," Evert says.

Word got to Evert that Lieberman had told Navratilova to stop revealing any details about their fitness regime to the press or other players. "We don't give away our secrets," Lieberman said.

Lieberman did volunteer that she had begun to save press clippings of Evert's remarks about Navratilova, the better to "motivate" Martina.

"I would ask Martina, 'If Chris is such a good friend, how could she say these things about you?' " Lieberman recalls. "But Martina still didn't want to believe Chris was saying negative things about her. So finally I said, 'Enough.' I would cut Chris's comments out of the paper and put them up on the bathroom mirror for Martina, where she couldn't miss them. Then I could say, 'Hey, *I* didn't say it—she said it. Your friend. Not me.' "

Lieberman admits, "Most of Chris's comments were just little, biting things. Chris might say, 'I don't think Martina plays the big points well' or 'In tight moments, Martina hits tight shots.' And sure enough, in the third set, Martina would do what Chris said she would. To me, it was just part of trying to help Martina with the process of competing. And understanding if you're going to war, you have to know your enemy, know your strengths and weaknesses. It was all psychological at that point."

Early in the year, Navratilova had complained when Evert again skipped the dreary 1982 winter indoor season. Evert retorted: "Tell Martina not to worry. She'll have nine months to play me." Navratilova dominated the first half of 1982, but after Wimbledon Evert was clearly the better player, winning forty-two of her last forty-three matches and narrowing Navratilova's 1982 head-to-head record against her to 2–1 by defeating Navratilova at the Australian Open.

When asked at the Toyota Championships if she was still in the running for the year-end number one ranking, Evert said, "If I beat Martina here, I feel I am."

"[There's] not one statistic in Chris's favor—not one," Lieberman protested.

Lieberman telephoned Evert's friend Steve Flink, a senior editor at *World Tennis*, the magazine that issued the most respected year-end rankings, and accused him of leading a whisper campaign to promote Evert for the top spot. But Flink, who had long abstained from writing about Evert because of their friendship, told Lieberman, "Nothing could be more untrue."

Navratilova, remembering that Evert had been voted the year-end number one in 1978 when she thought she deserved it, turned snappish when people suggested Evert could spirit away the 1982 ranking too. "I believe I'm number one no matter what happens here," Navratilova argued, pointing to her 89–3 record versus Evert's 76–5 won-lost mark, and her fourteen tournament titles to Evert's ten. Navratilova had already won a tour record $1,386,055 in prize money. Her single-season winning percentage of 96.8 was the highest since the Women's Tennis Association began tracking the statistic in 1973.

"That ought to be good enough no matter what happens here," Navratilova said. "All of a sudden this has become a big tournament, but it wasn't last year. When it was me, Chris, and Tracy, it was all decided [beforehand]."

Implicit in Navratilova's complaint was an unspoken question: *Why are the ground rules different for me?*

As it turned out, Navratilova rendered the hand grenade tossing moot. Playing with a resourcefulness and calm that was stunning, Navratilova defeated Evert, 4–6, 6–1, 6–2. Over the last two sets, especially, Navratilova put on a virtuoso performance, pulling Evert in to the net with expertly struck drop shots, then feathering topspin lobs over her head. Navratilova mixed in her power game to keep Evert off-balance, and she forced Evert to cover the entire court. Renee Richards called it the most intelligent match she'd ever seen Navratilova play.

"Now there should be no question who is number one," Navratilova proclaimed.

Evert agreed.

"I concede—but not next year," Evert said.

It was impossible for Navratilova and Evert to know it at the time, but Navratilova's win at the December 1982 Toyota Championships would become a significant benchmark in their rivalry. Navratilova's victory was the start of a thirteen-match winning streak over Evert that lasted more than two years and left Evert so disconsolate, she would sometimes think to herself, "Who in the world is ever going to beat this girl?"

Navratilova and Evert were ranked number one and two in the world and meeting only on Sundays now, for titles. The gap between them and the rest of the tour had become so pronounced, even Pam Shriver, a perennial top five player, spoke with poignant resignation about the "hopeless feeling of chasing two opponents you never, ever draw any closer to."

"That's what Chris and Martina do to the rest of us, those of us who never fulfill expectations and who begin to doubt that we ever will," Shriver said. "I try to defend myself, uphold women's tennis and say that the other players aren't that far behind, when, in fact— at least at the majors—we're light-years behind. No one likes to admit she doesn't have a serious chance."

Evert was about to find out what that despair felt like.

By the summer of 1983, the results between her and Navratilova had taken on a numbing sameness. Only the datelines changed from week to week:

DALLAS, March 7—Martina Navratilova defeated archrival Chris Evert on Sunday in the final of the $150,000 Virginia Slims of Dallas, 6–4, 6–0.

"I don't think she's ever played better," Evert said.

NEW YORK, March 23—At the Virginia Slims Championships in New York City last week, Martina Navratilova demonstrated a talent as well rounded as it is splendid. She bludgeoned opponents with her serve, outdueled them from the baseline and teased them with drop shots and lobs. Even Chris Evert could do little to slow down Navratilova. . . . The look in Evert's eyes [before the match] seemed to say, "If I don't make it back, tell Mom and Dad I love them." Little more than an hour later, Navratilova had swept 10 straight games en route to a 6–2, 6–0 win.

The loss was Evert's most lopsided in 950 singles matches on tour, spanning 13 years. Since the start of 1982, Navratilova has won 114 of 117 matches.

"She really cleaned my clock today," said Evert. "That was one of her better matches, I hope."

LOS ANGELES, Aug. 7—Martina Navratilova captured her seventh win in her last eight matches against Chris Evert yesterday with a 6–1, 6–3 rout in the finals of the Virginia Slims of Los Angeles.

"We've played three times this year," Evert said, "and I haven't won a set."

Navratilova, true to her boast, had ascended to the point where she lost only if she beat herself. She seemed invincible. And Evert was the only player given even a remote chance of derailing her. But some strange occurrences conspired to ruin their hotly anticipated showdowns at the first two majors of the year.

At the 1983 French Open, in a flop that still ranks as one of the most shocking upsets in tennis history, Navratilova was bounced in the fourth round by seventeen-year-old American Kathy Horvath, 6–4, 0–6, 6–3.

Renee Richards, who was still helping to coach Navratilova, had arrived in Paris the morning of the match. She resigned immediately afterward and left without even bothering to unpack a bag because of yet another dispute with Lieberman, this one coming *during* Navratilova's loss to Horvath, after Lieberman learned Richards had instructed Navratilova to follow a conservative game plan.

Navratilova had blitzed her first three opponents by attacking. Lieberman was so livid that the late-arriving Richards had changed the strategy, she left the friends' box to cheer for Navratilova from another spot in the stadium, which Navratilova distractedly noticed. She angrily confronted them both about it after the match. As bad as the defeat felt at the time, it was even more galling in hindsight. Navratilova finished the year 86–1. She was that close to authoring professional tennis's first perfect season.

Evert had been returning from playing a doubles match and paused in the runway beneath the stadium court when the crowd's sudden roar signaled that Horvath's staggering upset of Navratilova had ended. "Damn. I wish I had been the one to beat her," Evert muttered to herself.

Later, speaking to reporters, Evert said: "I wanted Martina on my surface."

Told that it now looked like her tournament to win with Navratilova gone, Evert bristled and said, "You mean it wasn't my tournament before?"

Evert won the 1983 French Open, routing Mimi Jausovec of Yugoslavia, 6–1, 6–2, in the final. For all the talk about Navratilova's indomitability and newfound knack for playing through turmoil, it was Evert—with her own marriage in shambles, and she and John often spending most of their time apart—who had won the last three majors.

When they arrived at Wimbledon three weeks later, Evert this time encountered the unexpected. A nasty case of the flu kept her up all night vomiting before her third-round match. Looking noticeably wan, she weaved and tottered through a 6–1, 7–6 loss to twenty-three-year-old Kathy Jordan, a feisty American serve-and-volleyer who had never taken a set from Evert in five previous meetings.

"I wouldn't have walked on the court if I hadn't thought I was fit," Evert insisted, convincing no one. Jordan had so much respect for Evert, she barely celebrated when she took match point.

The result was profoundly dislocating for everyone involved.

Evert's loss ended one of the most amazing streaks in sports. Starting with her sensational 1971 U.S. Open debut as a sixteen-year-old, Evert had never failed to reach the semifinals of the first thirty-four Grand Slam tournaments she had played—a peerless run that stretched back twelve years.

When the streak was over, the praise rolled in.

"An unbelievable feat," Navratilova marveled.

"One of the greatest achievements in any sport," Rosie Casals enthused.

"A miracle," Billie Jean King agreed. "It was sad to see it end."

A dazed Evert told *Sports Illustrated*'s Curry Kirkpatrick that it felt "strange" to watch the tournament go on without her. "Now I have to sit around drinking tea and watching the girls play singles while I wonder what the hell happened," she said.

Evert and Lloyd's relationship had warmed to the point that they decided to spend Wimbledon together at their home ten minutes from the tournament grounds. In a cruel coincidence—almost as if fate wouldn't allow them both to enjoy success in the same tournament— Evert suffered her earliest major tournament loss in the same event that Lloyd fulfilled a lifelong dream. He and Wendy Turnbull won the Wimbledon mixed doubles title in a dramatic final over Billie Jean King and Steve Denton. With the win, Lloyd became the first British man to win any sort of Wimbledon title since Fred Perry forty-seven years earlier. During the joyous victory party that John and Chris threw back at their house, they put the tape of the match in the VCR and hit the rewind button again and again as John beamed.

With Evert gone, Navratilova cruised to her second consecutive Wimbledon title. She demolished Andrea Jaeger, 6–0, 6–3 in the final. The press, seeking some new way to quantify Navratilova's dominance, began noting the elapsed time of her wins. All told, Navratilova thrashed her seven Wimbledon victims in an average of just forty-seven minutes per match. Jaeger was so conscious of the statistic, she actually considered stalling on changeovers when she noticed the scoreboard clock showing that Navratilova had taken just seventeen minutes while shutting her out in the first set.

Navratilova's resounding Wimbledon victory was a reassurance that Richards's resignation would not be catastrophic. What was more troubling was that Navratilova's relationship with Lieberman had begun to fray as well.

A few days after Richards quit, Navratilova hired Mike Estep, her former World Team Tennis teammate in Boston, as her coach and hitting partner. But Lieberman admitted that she wasn't initially receptive to Estep's walking in "full of ideas and opinions." Lieberman still maintained a tense relationship with Martina's agent, Peter Johnson. In the previous months, Navratilova's friends and fellow players had become aware of some explosive fights between Navratilova and Lieberman. When Lieberman arrived at Wimbledon late in the first week—a delay the London tabloids quickly noted—she and Navratilova were bickering daily.

The rancor climaxed the night before Navratilova's final against Jaeger in what Navratilova and Lieberman both characterized as a "knockdown, drag-out physical fight" that raged on past two a.m. Lieberman screamed at one point that Navratilova would be "nothing" without her. She said she hoped Jaeger beat Navratilova the next day. Navratilova, not for the first time, told Lieberman she should start getting on with her own life and stop living her thwarted athletic dreams through her. Navratilova said she was tired of being controlled and smothered.

Pam Shriver, who won the Wimbledon doubles title with Navratilova after her defeat of Jaeger, says, "How Martina played so amazingly well, I'll never know. By then her relationship with Nancy was a passionate . . . roiling . . . mess."

Amazingly, Navratilova said she felt "at peace" that day on the court against Jaeger. Once on the court, nothing could bother her. Looking back on that 1983 Wimbledon victory, which reasserted her place ahead of Evert, Navratilova said, "I felt I had willed away all the problems of the past."

All but one.

By the late-August start of the 1983 U.S. Open, Navratilova had won all five of her 1983 encounters with Evert, and eight of their last nine matches overall. The U.S. Open still loomed as the last major title Navratilova had never won despite ten previous tries. If

Navratilova was going to finally win the tournament, it seemed only fitting that she found herself having to go through Evert for the championship. As the two of them padded around the otherwise deserted dressing room the day of their final, staking out their own corners and quietly preparing themselves to play, they both knew they were at a crossroads.

Navratilova and Evert were about to play the thirty-ninth final of their decade-long rivalry, and their record now stood at perfect equipoise: a 19–19 deadlock in championship matches. After so many years spent chasing Evert, Navratilova would finally, inarguably nudge ahead with a win. It would be the last accomplishment Navratilova needed to signify that she had finally conquered herself as well as Evert.

As Navratilova waited to take the court, her legs began to shake. Her hands were trembling. She told Mike Estep, "The time is now. It's now or never."

Navratilova took the first set from Evert so quickly, a skywriting plane that was droning high over the stadium was unable to finish writing "Good Luck Chrissie" until three games were already gone in the second set.

Nothing hindered Navratilova—not the 93-degree heat, not her pre-match nerves, not her awful history at the Open. She overwhelmed Evert, 6–1, 6–3, in just sixty-three minutes. She celebrated match point as if a jolt went through her body. She flung both arms in the air. Her eyelids snapped up like two window blinds that had been tugged down and let go. Her mouth opened wide and she screamed.

"If I don't win another tournament in my life," a giddy Navratilova said, "at least I can say I did it all."

Navratilova's performance was so complete, there was little Evert could do beyond affectionately tap Navratilova on the head with her racket and smile when they shook hands at the net, same as she had done the first time Navratilova finally won Wimbledon five years earlier. After shaking the chair umpire's hand, Navratilova ran to the friends' box, which was on field level at the U.S. Open, to high-five Lieberman, Estep, and the rest of her friends.

Navratilova had just administered Evert's worst pounding ever in a Grand Slam match. Navratilova had again torn through another major tournament like a buzz saw, averaging a mere fifty-two minutes per win.

Though most of the next-day headlines would proclaim that the torch had officially passed from Evert to Navratilova, Navratilova was nonetheless bothered by the tenor of her post-match press conference.

Rather than dwell on her happiness or how she had finally erased any doubt about her eminence after a decade of pursuing Evert, writers were again asking whether Navratilova thought it was "unfair" that she had won by such a margin—that old theme again. Finally, an exasperated Navratilova said, "Look. The other women can do everything I do, all the line drills, the quarter-mile runs on the track, the full-court basketball games. If they want to, they can do it. I've put in the *work*. I'm a size eight, same as Chris. The only thing that's big about me are my feet. So how is it unfair?

"*How?*" she demanded to know.

Navratilova indisputably ruled tennis, all right. But the insinuation at her press conference was that some people didn't like where she had taken the sport. Navratilova left the room feeling she'd never be totally accepted.

"If I lost, I was a choker," Navratilova said. "If I won big, I was 'unfair' to women's tennis."

Even in defeat, Evert was determined to plant a seed.

"She's human," Evert said. "We'll see how long her domination lasts."

Navratilova finished 1983 with an 86–1 singles mark and the number one ranking—this time by acclaim.

Evert, though already in Tokyo for a mid-November tournament, scratched from the Australian Open in Melbourne the following week because of plantar fasciitis.

A few days later Evert received a phone call from Navratilova, who was in Melbourne. Navratilova indignantly told her, "The press here is hounding me, saying you're getting divorced, how you're separated from John and seeing some other man who's British, some ex-rocker. But don't worry, I told them, 'What are you talking about? She'd *never* do that. You guys have no right to say that. It's not true.' "

"Thank you for sticking up for me," Evert told Navratilova, "but actually, they do have a right to ask. It's true. The story is true.' "

Rather than join Lloyd in Melbourne, Evert had flown to London to see Adam Faith.

On January 28, 1984, Lloyd and Evert issued a press release saying that they had agreed to a trial separation.

"While there's still very much a chance that we will get back together," their statement read, "at the present time we need time to be by ourselves."

By April of 1984, Navratilova and Lieberman had split too, ending the three-year relationship that had forever transformed Navratilova and her career. Lieberman, who was still only twenty-five years old when they parted, talks with both fondness and regret about those years. "I can see now," she admits, "that some things got out of hand."

Not long after Lieberman and Navratilova split, Evert received a surprising telephone call. It was from Lieberman, asking if Evert would be interested in hiring her as a personal trainer to help her overtake Navratilova—which Evert was not.

CHAPTER TWELVE

CLIMBING BACK

Surprising as Lieberman's overture to jump to Evert's camp was, Evert and her coach Dennis Ralston had already concluded that Evert needed to change her training regime to better compete with Navratilova's speed and power. All of Evert's early-career reservations about not wanting to be seen as a jock—"Lift weights? Chrissie? Heaven forbid," says Rosie Casals—were gone. Evert and Navratilova had together passed from teenagers to women, unknowns to world-famous figures, friends who used to warm up together before matches to cutthroat adversaries who barely spoke during the Lieberman years. Now it was as if a giant wheel had turned. Their places had switched. Evert was stalking Navratilova as Navratilova once chased her.

But there was one enormous difference.

While some approximation of Evert's mental toughness was theoretically attainable by Navratilova, how in the world could Evert hope to equal the extraordinary athleticism with which Navratilova had been born?

The same entrenched contrasts in style and strengths that had made their rivalry such great theater seemed to portend doom for Evert now that Navratilova had finally dedicated herself to tennis completely. Evert was twenty-nine going on thirty. Conventional wisdom said that she could no more completely overhaul her game than a river could suddenly reverse the direction it flows. Chris Evert was a baseliner. That was her game.

Even people whom Evert respected were beginning to suggest that her days at the top were over.

"Martina is so head and shoulders above everybody, a baseliner can't beat her anymore," Billie Jean King said. "Chris is going to have to change her style, and it's kind of late for her to do that."

As Navratilova would underscore years later by winning Grand Slam doubles titles into her mid-forties, she really was a genetic marvel as well as a product of discipline and hard work. Navratilova was among the young girls identified as future sports stars when Communist officials visited her elementary school armed with their calipers and measuring tapes and actuarial charts. Every tennis coach Navratilova ever had was amazed that they could teach her a new serve, a different stroke, and she'd be using it in a match within days. "She took teaching like no one I ever saw," Mike Estep says. Diana Nyad, the long-distance swimmer and sports commentator, remembers the first time she met Navratilova during preparations for a 1976 *Superstars* competition. Bowling was one of the events the athletes practiced before the competition started. Navratilova, who hadn't been in the United States very long, asked, "How do you throw this ball?"

"So we showed her," Nyad says. "Pretty soon she was hurling strikes with her right hand *and* her left hand. BANG! Strike! BANG! Pins were flying everywhere. I think she scored something like 140 her first try."

Richard O'Connor, a six-foot-five All-American basketball player who later became a writer for *Sport* magazine, told of playing a one-on-one basketball game with Navratilova after interviewing her for a 1979 story. O'Connor was stunned on game point when Navratilova—who said she was just learning the game—deked to his right, drove by him to the left, and dunked with two hands on the eight-foot-high rim at the junior high school where they were playing.

"I think Martina could have been world class at whatever sport she chose," Evert says. "For a while, I truly didn't have an answer for her."

To Evert, the gap between her athleticism and Navratilova's was obvious. But she refused to accept that it had to be damning. Evert still had great footwork, superior concentration, and the purest strokes in women's tennis. "Chrissie hit bombs, and don't let anyone say otherwise, don't let anyone think she played patty-cake," Renee Richards says. Evert's hand-eye coordination—her ability to connect cleanly with the ball match after match—was incredible. Evert was quick, too, if not as quick as Navratilova. But Evert also got to balls because everything she did was so economical. She rarely took a false step. Every shot she hit was purposeful.

"Everybody would go right to the mental part with me and say, 'Well, she's tough as nails' and 'She plays well under pressure,' " Evert once told writer Peter Bodo. "But as Billie Jean pointed out one time, you have to be a good athlete to be number one in the world. I just wasn't physically exceptional and some others were. Martina and Billie Jean and Evonne Goolagong, they had mobility, they were exceptional athletes. But I kept winning and I told myself, 'Wow, I'm not the strongest, I'm not the quickest, I don't hit the ball the hardest, I don't have a great volley, I don't have the greatest serve. But I am still winning.' "

Evert clung to that conviction no matter how bleak things looked.

Some of the animosity began leaking from Evert and Navratilova's rivalry almost immediately after Lieberman departed in early 1984. But the match results remained unchanged. At one point Evert lost an unfathomable fifteen consecutive sets to Navratilova. Navratilova's winning streak over Evert climbed up toward ten matches.

"And she wasn't just beating me," Evert admits, "she was killing me."

While Navratilova had now become the focus of much of the private work Evert did, nutritionist Robert Haas says that by the time he departed Team Navratilova in early 1984, "there wasn't any real consternation in the Navratilova camp day to day about Chris. There was not even a lot of discussion. Chris was a given, known quality, still the one to beat. But the feeling was, it was the end of Chris's reign."

Navratilova, twenty-seven, seemed entrenched at the top of tennis for as long as she remained interested. At the start of 1984, with her team temporarily whittled down to just her and Estep and his wife, Barbara, a television newscaster who often traveled with them, Martina set out to prove that she could continue to win without an entourage.

She set her sights on a Grand Slam sweep of all four 1984 major tournaments.

Tennis is given to extended, uninterrupted runs of individual dominance. Renee Richards thinks she can explain why. Richards maintains that a tennis match will almost always be won by the better player because in tennis, victory cannot be achieved with a single blow, one dramatic gesture—there is no tennis equivalent to the lucky knockout punch in boxing, the last-second Hail Mary pass in football, the game-winning baseball home run with two out in the bottom of the ninth.

A tennis victory is an accumulation of blows. A tennis match is a war of attrition that's won only after hundreds of points are fought over and a thousand shots have been struck.

"The scoring system in tennis is very much in favor of the slightly better player," Richards says. "In tennis you can make mistakes and still win a game. You can lose a set and you can still win the match. It's very forgiving. That's why the top players win most of the championships most of the time. And that's true in women's tennis, especially, because the serve is not as determinative.

"The better player is going to win almost all the time."

The better player and the inferior opponent across the net know it, too. In almost any other sport, Navratilova's boast "I only lose if I beat myself" would sound like tiresome self-delusion. Not in tennis. One of the reasons tennis players don't regard choking with the same contempt as tanking is that at least when you choke, it's because you care *so* much. "But tanking—tanking is like, 'You quit. You *dog*,' " Mary Carillo hisses. The tennis player's code of valor requires players to ignore the substantial proof of their own limitations and dutifully run after every ball, hopeless as it may seem.

When Evert was at her dominant best in the 1970s, Navratilova noticed that when Evert's opponents staggered back into the locker room, they weren't asked who won. They were asked, "How many games did you get today from Chris?" The outcome was a foregone conclusion.

Now, the same air of predestination perfumed Navratilova's path through tournament draws. Her burgeoning aura, the psychic burden she inflicted on opponents, left many of them beaten before a ball was struck. Including Evert.

"There was a stretch," Evert admits, "when I lost to her before I even took the court. I was intimidated."

Others could tell.

"It's really strange what Martina's play has done to the women's tour," Billie Jean King told the *Washington Post* in 1984. "Everyone seems so paranoid to walk on the court with her. I don't think most of the top ten players have the attitude they need to win. People tend to forget so quickly. People used to say it was boring that Chris won all the time. Now listen to them. They think Martina will never lose again."

Part of the joy and wonder of watching Navratilova at her net-charging best was that she didn't just hit shots—she seemed to invent them on the spot, often while performing some arabesque in midair. Navratilova could be tearing to the net at top speed and suddenly pop up off both feet, twist, and, while still airborne, somehow lift a perfect volley over the net for a winner—all in a split second, before Evert could even take a couple steps in from the baseline. It didn't matter that the ball came screaming back at Navratilova at a hundred miles per hour. She would lunge left or right at the net to snare passing shots as if guided to the ball by some awesome sense of premonition.

Bud Collins broadcast a match at Amelia Island once at which he actually called out how much ground Navratilova covered in a successful sprint after a ball. "Two, three, four, *five-six-seven-EIGHT*! Eight yards! Who can beat her with *that*?" Collins exclaimed.

It wasn't until late in her career that Navratilova, who always yearned to be loved and adored, accepted why she had so few imitators. Robert Kelleher, a fellow member of the Tennis Hall of Fame, told her there was a simple reason that other people didn't play like her. "They can't," Kelleher said.

"I don't think Martina ever realized how special she is," said Wendy Turnbull. "Most people aren't athletic enough to play the way Martina did, and they don't have her imagination."

Navratilova always had an incredible aptitude for math and numbers. Fred Barman, the Beverly Hills business manager who helped Navratilova defect, said he would sometimes sit the nineteen-year-old down across his desk to give her an update on her finances. "Before I could even go down the column, she would have already read the numbers upside down and added them up in her head," Barman says.

Mary Carillo says, "There's something amazing about Martina's mind that way. She'll remember a phone number you gave her three years ago, like, 'Oh, is your number still . . . ?' She remembers her matches point by point. One of the reasons it always looked like Martina could anticipate where to go was she understood the geometry of the court—the cause and effect of 'If I drag someone off the court with this shot, there's no way they can get to that shot and do anything else but this.' "

And so, though Renee Richards was utterly astonished that

Navratilova couldn't *talk* much about tennis strategy when they first met, Navratilova was nonetheless able to articulate some strategy in her game, if only instinctively.

It was when Navratilova put everything together—the conscious focus on tactics along with fitness and natural ability—that she became nearly invincible.

"Martina is one of those people that have that great jock mind," Carillo says, "and hyperanalyzing is the opposite of what a true jock does. What true jocks know is just some sort of organic, almost animal instinct. With true jocks, things get edited. Things get simplified. In a fraction of a second they know what has to happen, what doesn't, what to add, where to make an adjustment. They can process data in a fraction of a second and make it look seamless, really. It's almost like playing with a cat. They're making moves, anticipating, doing things that most other people have to reason out first."

For all the good work that Mike Estep did in improving Navratilova's strokes and serve, perhaps the most important contribution Estep made as Navratilova's coach was his conviction that she should attack in all her matches, all the time. He told her to forget how many times she got passed or what volleys she missed. Push the pace. Storm the net. Keep up the pressure. "There's no one in this game who can stay with you," Estep told her. "Trust me."

The result was breathtaking.

"Mike has made me play the kind of tennis I never knew I could play," Navratilova raved. "I'm not making many errors. Chris is the one now who has to hit the great shots and the winners."

Estep's aggressive, swashbuckling philosophy also appealed to Navratilova's sense of self-drama. "I like to think I play tennis the way it's supposed to be played," she often said proudly. She repeated Estep's central exhortation like a mantra: "A good attacking player will beat a good baseliner almost all the time."

Evert's prospects never looked bleaker than in 1984, when Navratilova strung together an eleven-month-long, seventy-four-match winning streak, a record that still ranks as one of the most amazing achievements in sport—on par with Joe DiMaggio's fifty-six-game hitting streak in baseball.

Estep, reflecting on that run, says, "Martina made the game very simple for anybody who played her. You either come to the net and attack Martina or you lose. But you won't necessarily win even if you do come in—in fact, you'll still almost surely lose. But it's your only hope. What Chris did against Martina was phenomenally difficult: just go out there and never miss a ball for hours and have the nerves to know you have to pass your opponent every time she comes in."

Had Evert been a differently constructed person, she might have walked away from tennis when Navratilova overtook her, the same as Bjorn Borg did at age twenty-six when John McEnroe eclipsed him. As Borg later explained to his bewildered archrival, "When you're number two or three, you might as well be nobody." Evert could have ceded to the growing impatience of her husband, John, for her to quit tennis and have children. But as 1983 turned to 1984, Evert lit out after Navratilova instead. She rejected taking a sabbatical as she had done twice earlier in her career. Like Navratilova before her, Evert vowed to reinvent herself.

Ingrained in Evert's subconscious, if not her conscious mind, was a mantra of her own. It was the ethos that her father, Jimmy, had instilled in her long ago on those furnacelike days spent at Holiday Park: *"Who are you? How hard will you fight? How will you put your values as a human being into the game?*

"You're going to get out on that big green rectangle and decide."

When Evert returned to the tour in January of 1984, she had begun to lift weights for the first time in her career. She adopted new training techniques to improve her footwork and stamina. Ralston booked her with left-handed hitting partners, the better to approximate Navratilova's game. Evert had started playing with a new midsize graphite racket too, the better to match Navratilova's power. (Before tour players made their wholesale switches to metal rackets in the early 1980s, Navratilova was already serving with a wooden racket at faster than ninety miles per hour, the fastest serve in the women's game. Luckily for Evert, she had the best service return.)

Evert being Evert, the first personal trainer she hired was Kathy Smith, a Los Angeles aerobics video queen who later appeared in an instructional photo spread for *Tennis* magazine wearing a leotard and leg warmers. By all outward appearances, Smith was the Anti-Lieberman—except that Smith soon had Evert taking seven-mile jogs and working out at the track at UCLA and running stadium steps to build her endurance.

At John's suggestion, Chris worked for a while too with Australian trainer Stan Nicholes, the man who drove Margaret Court through dozens of double knee jumps and lunges, jump rope sessions, and two-hundred-yard sprints until Court was the fittest, strongest player of her era. Nicholes sounded as if he expected a diva to arrive in his Melbourne gym and a pit bull walked through the door instead. He marveled that if he asked Evert to do an exercise five times, she would do ten or twelve reps, unbidden.

"Chrissie was the most dedicated professional I ever coached, man or woman," Dennis Ralston says. "I don't think people ever realized what it took for her to try to climb back. I mean, it would've been easy for her to do a Borg, just pack it in."

"I would've felt like a quitter," Evert says with a shrug.

Evert wasn't the only player who was humbled by Navratilova. She just had the farthest to fall. By 1984, other players spoke in the same ways that Evert did about the unique and daunting experience of playing Navratilova.

"With Chris, you could at least feel like you got into the points because there would be these long rallies," says Pam Shriver. "But with Martina, the points were so short, there was this unrelenting sense of constantly being physically overwhelmed."

"Overpowering," Tracy Austin agrees. "On certain days against

Martina I just felt I was backing up, backing up. There was the barrage of the fast serves and then—*boom!*—you might get the ball back, but then the volley goes in the corner over there. You get the next ball back and then—*boom!*—she hits it over there. You hit a second serve and she's chipping and charging in at you, she's constantly coming at you, at you, at you. So it's just a different barrage.

"Chris was a more mental match," Austin continues, "and Martina was the more physical match. Can you get a hold of her big serve? Can you return it? Can you stay away from that forehand? Can you return balls deep enough so that she can't come into the net? Can you thread the needle and pass her? Can you get the lob over her head just enough? It's not going to be a long or tiring match. It's going to be when you get that rare break point or two, can you come up with the goods? When you were out there you'd think, 'Don't miss this return,' because against Martina, you didn't get break points very often. You knew if you missed against Chris you were going to get another one."

Evert never had a great serve. Just a functional one. As *Tennis* magazine writer Peter Bodo observed, Evert shared an interesting quality with other great champions: she had a formidable ability to blank out any consciousness of her own weaknesses. As Bodo noted, "Jimmy Connors never acknowledged that he had real trouble lifting a forehand approach shot from the forecourt over the net. Stefan Edberg pushed his forehand with a bizarre and reluctant shoveling motion. Tracy Austin's overhead always looked like an adventure . . . So it was with the studied serve of Evert. The stroke never really crumbled under pressure because Evert did not dote on its vulnerability or try to do too much with it."

Navratilova's career was littered with matches in which she double faulted at calamitous moments. But her game was different: there is significant pressure on a serve-and-volleyer to strike a good first serve to set up the rest of the game. "And when you lose your nerve, you lose your serve," Mary Carillo says.

One of the reasons Navratilova began dominating Evert was that Mike Estep urged Martina to devour Evert's serves by going for aggressive returns. Estep exhorted Navratilova to charge the net before Evert could begin controlling the point with her ground stroke game.

"And it eventually got to the point where Martina didn't have to be serving—she was using Chris's [weak] second serve like an approach shot to come in," Dennis Ralston says. "Martina would hit the ball back and just storm right in. Their matches weren't even close.

"There was no way Chrissie could do anything until she changed her whole way of playing her. John and I were telling Chrissie for two years, the only way you're going to win against Martina now is to come to the net, attack. But it was very, very hard for her."

By February of 1984, Navratilova's strafing of Evert and the rest of the women's tour was so complete, the *New York Times* called her rivalry with Chris "anti-climactic in recent years." And that was two months before Evert and Navratilova returned to the WTA Championships in Amelia Island—the scene of Martina's career-worst 6–0, 6–0 embarrassment against Evert three years earlier—to play what NBC was hyping as "The Clash on Clay."

The network had whipped up a split-screen promotional spot for the championship telecast in which Navratilova, pretending to be menacing, looked into the camera and said, "I'm really looking forward to this match" and crushed a tennis ball into a cloud of dust. Then Chris, looking equally tough, took an empty ball can and crushed it too.

Evert had now lost nine straight matches to Navratilova, but in ten years of competing against each other, she had never lost to her on clay. Not ever. Her superiority on the surface was her last fig leaf, her last refuge. Evert's career clay court record was 285–7, and that included a 7–0 record against Navratilova. In those encounters, Navratilova had managed just one set.

By the time Evert and Navratilova advanced to the final at Amelia Island, Evert looked sharp. Her fifth wedding anniversary with John Lloyd, from whom she was still separated, passed during the week with just a quick chat between them on the phone. But Evert didn't seem distracted. She seemed zeroed in. By the championship match on Sunday, what did bother her were the constant questions about whether she could beat Navratilova.

"I want to stop talking about it and just do it," Evert said.

"How?" a reporter pressed her.

"I'll ask Chris Evert how she did it three years ago," Evert snapped.

Once the final began, Evert never threatened Navratilova. Navratilova overwhelmed her, 6–2, 6–0. Evert won a meager total of just 22 points, and only 10 in the last eight games. She snuck only two passing shots by Martina all day. Even when Evert tried taking the net, Navratilova calmly drew back her racket and parachuted lobs over Evert's head, leaving her rooted and helpless in the fore-court.

"She exposed all of my weaknesses," Evert said in her post-match address to the crowd. Then she apologized for the lopsided-ness of the match. "There was such a buildup to today, and it was a letdown to a lot of people, I know. But I feel worse than all of you."

Florida sportswriter Jim Martz remembers fans and reporters fil-ing out of the stadium that day, remarking how touching, even sad, it had been to see Evert humbled that way.

Even Navratilova said, "I started getting a lump in my throat. I know how she feels. I've been there."

When Navratilova blazed by Evert on clay again for the 1984 French Open title, 6–3, 6–1, Evert was spoken about in memoriam once more. Navratilova clobbered Evert in just sixty-three minutes. With the win, Navratilova had achieved a non-calen-dar year Grand Slam sweep of the four majors and, with it, a $1 million bonus from the International Tennis Federation. This time, rather than some show of defiance, Evert confessed awe.

"I couldn't find any weaknesses, I couldn't anticipate the drop shots, I couldn't read her," Evert said. "She came up with angles I've never seen her play before. And such touch. She took advantage of making me run forward, and I wasn't quick enough. Give Martina credit. She is playing the best she has ever played. I don't know how much better she can get."

By Wimbledon, Navratilova seemed like an irresistible force, an untameable whirlwind, and Evert was admittedly "soul-searching."

Publicly, Evert continued to insist, "I still believe I can beat her. If I didn't believe that, I wouldn't still be playing tennis." But Evert was less confident than she let on. "When Martina started to beat me even on clay," Evert recalls, "that's when it really looked hopeless."

A few of Evert's friends actually suggested that Chris should save face and quit. Sportswriters wondered whether Evert's revamped approach to the game and her physical training the past two years was all an admirable waste of time, the last gasp of a prideful legend in denial. But Evert wouldn't hear it. "I know what people are saying, but I don't buy it—and I'm *not* quitting," she said. "I'm not like Borg—cutting all the ties [to the game] when I can't win the big one. I love the game too much. I love putting myself on the line."

Lesser players whom Evert still trounced—the same opponents who once watched what they said publicly about Evert, lest they get a sharp written note of rebuke—now felt emboldened to give Evert unsolicited advice.

Change everything, Carling Bassett suggested.

Don't change! Pam Shriver disagreed.

Navratilova and Evert advanced to the 1984 Wimbledon final despite spending much of the fortnight complaining about their harassment by paparazzi and tabloids. At one point, Navratilova became so incensed, she threatened not to return to England ever again. "It's been horrendous," Evert agreed.

Evert, who traveled to London with her mother, was under siege because the tabloids were trying to gauge the state of her slowly recuperating marriage to Lloyd. When Evert and Lloyd separated at the start of 1984, they had set some private ground rules. They agreed that they would not give interviews about the state of their marriage. They also decided that they could date other people if they liked, but they would be discreet. Evert later told British writer Carol Thatcher that there had been a chance during this time for her relationship with Adam Faith, the British pop singer, to develop into something "more permanent," but it didn't materialize. So they stopped seeing each other.

Lloyd told Thatcher, "When you consider the state our marriage was in, it's hard to feel vindictive." During his separation from Evert, Lloyd dated too.

Navratilova, who had happened to rent a house across the street from Chris and her mother, was being hounded by the tabloids because she had a new partner, Judy Nelson, a married woman and the mother of two boys. Navratilova had met Nelson at a tournament in Dallas, and Nelson, who lived in nearby Fort Worth, began traveling with Navratilova in April of 1984. This was Nelson's first visit to Wimbledon.

Much of the highly sensational coverage was driven by Nelson's striking good looks, her heterosexual past, and later, her Southern belle upbringing. The unspoken subtext of many of the stories was "Who knew lesbians looked like *this*?"

While studying at Texas Christian University in her native Fort Worth, Nelson had been a local model for Neiman Marcus and had won some beauty contest titles, including the 1965 national Maid of Cotton crown and Howdy Week Queen. During her seven-month star turn as the Maid of Cotton, which Nelson recalls with great humor, she traveled the world promoting the cotton industry with twenty-seven suitcases full of designer clothes. "All cotton, of course," Nelson says, laughing. "We needed two cabs everywhere I went—one for me, one for my bags." She also wore a tiara and a sash while on official business. Among the dignitaries who received Nelson in Washington, D.C., was President Lyndon B. Johnson, a fellow Texan.

By her graduation from college, Nelson had married a fraternity president, settled down in Fort Worth, and was running a Bonanza steak house franchise to put her husband through medical school.

Soon they had two sons. With her genteel Southern manners, her country club membership and manicure, Nelson could have been the poster girl for Straight, White, Rich America. But a series of affairs that her husband confessed to, according to Nelson, fractured her seventeen-year-old marriage by the time she met Navratilova. After Nelson left her husband in June of 1984, her youngest son decided to live with her and Martina, and her older son stayed with his father. Over time, Navratilova became close to both boys.

Like Lieberman before her, Nelson had no idea about the world she was entering when she and Navratilova became involved. Nelson says that Navratilova's agent, Peter Johnson, sat her down and gave her what Nelson now dryly calls "The Talk."

"The very first time I ever met him, Peter Johnson called me into a room all by myself," Nelson says, "and it was the one time in my whole relationship with Martina that I was scared. Not when the reporters were flocking around or any of that, but when Peter Johnson said, 'I want to talk to you by yourself.' I was scared to death. And what he basically told me was 'Obviously Martina wants to be with you, and this is the way it's going to be. There have been others before you, you know, and I don't make judgments. But we want Martina to be happy. And your job is to do everything to help her be the best tennis player she can be. All I want her to do is think about hitting that tennis ball—nothing else. So whatever else there is, it's your job to see that that's all she has to think about. Understand?'

"Well, I was stunned," Nelson says. "I had no idea agents became that involved. [But] Peter Johnson made it very clear to me in the beginning that this was my job. I was the good wife. And that's what I did."

Wherever Nelson and Navratilova traveled, Nelson says she made sure to unpack their things and put them in drawers "just so we didn't literally live out of a suitcase." They traveled with a comforter and pillows and remade the bed in each new hotel room, just so it would feel as if they at least slept in the same place they had the night before.

"We had the animals with us, too, running around the places we stayed, and they'd jump up on the bed or whatever," Nelson recalls. "The whole point was to make the road seem as much like home as we could get. [It] was just beginning to look like [Martina's] dominance would last, and Peter Johnson didn't want anything to go wrong. It was like, 'She can win everything out there. We've got to keep the path clear.' "

Once the 1984 Wimbledon final between Evert and Navratilova began, Evert sent a buzz through the crowd by leaping out to a 3–0 lead against Navratilova, only to see Navratilova recover and blaze by her, 7–6, 6–2. But it was a dazzling match. Afterward, Evert was again irked by the press's suggestion that she was a has-been. "If not for Martina, I'd still be dominating," she protested. Rather than gloat, Navratilova spoke sentimentally about how her twelfth straight win over Evert had evened their eleven-year-old rivalry, in which she had once trailed 5–20. Now their record stood at thirty matches apiece.

"Can you imagine, thirty to thirty?" Navratilova said. "I wish we could quit right now and never play each other again, because it's not right for one of us to say we're better."

"Does that mean she's going to retire?" Evert joked.

Despite the loss, Evert left Wimbledon encouraged. She had nearly won the first set. She had battled Navratilova to the finish and forced her to play five match points before she put the title away. The resignation was gone from her voice. "This is the form I've been looking for all year and it hasn't been there, but it's here now," Evert said.

At the U.S. Open six weeks later, playing on a hard-court surface better suited to Evert's game than Wimbledon's grass, Evert lost to Navratilova again in the final, 4–6, 6–4, 6–4. This time, Evert admitted she was "devastated."

When Evert seized the first set from Navratilova, the crowd at Flushing Meadow startled her by erupting into an ear-ringing roar that Evert calls "louder than anything I had ever experienced in my life." In that moment, Evert actually got choked up. "I remember walking off for the changeover, thinking, 'I'm finally going to do it.' And it seemed like everyone else thought so too."

Navratilova hadn't lost a set at the Open in nearly three years.

But the turning point in the match came when Navratilova, who needed the second set to stay alive, was serving at 5–4 but down 15–40. Evert had just conjured up three rousing winners. Had Evert taken that game, she might have been serving to win the match in straight sets. But Evert squandered both break point chances by not daring to come in to the net, though Martina was down to her second serve each time. Then Evert drove a return into the net that allowed Navratilova to pull even at deuce. Given those reprieves, Navratilova narrowly won the second set, and then the match. Evert was once again left to console herself with making progress, coming close.

The thought that Evert found galling months, even years later was that when she searched herself for something more in those last two sets against Navratilova, it wasn't there.

"When it came down to a few big points, I lacked the nerve, and that was uncharacteristic—Chris Evert never choked a match," Evert said a few months later. "I would always come from behind. But I wanted it so badly that I got nervous. My emotions entered into it. And she didn't beat me—I lost that match. [That's why] I was devastated. When it came to the few big points, I lacked the nerve. My whole career, my mental aspect has been the strongest part of my game."

Referring to her thirteen-match losing streak against Navratilova, Evert added, "It inhibited me so badly that when it came to the big points, I was a nervous wreck."

When Evert arrived at the net to shake hands with Navratilova, she couldn't even look her in the eye. She felt transparent, as if Navratilova knew the damning truth as well as she did.

"It was the most devastated I'd ever been over a tennis match," Evert remembers. "All I wanted to do was get off the court."

Evert still told everyone who asked that she was gaining on Navratilova. But privately, she was beginning to question why she was pressing onward. She and John had reconciled shortly before the 1984 U.S. Open. She was approaching her thirtieth birthday that December and thinking more often about retirement.

Even Evert's title win in late November at the Australian Open lost some luster when Navratilova was upset in the semifinals. In a bit of a cosmic twist, Navratilova's seventy-four-match winning streak and her bid for a calendar-year sweep of the Grand Slams were ended by Helena Sukova, the nineteen-year-old daughter of Vera Sukova, the Czech national team coach who had tried to talk Navratilova out of defecting. The enormous upset also ended Navratilova's streak of six consecutive majors.

After defeating Sukova in the final, Evert's mind was still on Navratilova, and the missed chance to measure her game against her.

"At least you won't be the one to beat me," Navratilova told Evert after the Sukova match.

If there was any encouraging news about her chase of Navratilova, it was that Ralston and Lloyd's exhortations that Evert should attack more in her matches were beginning to work. Ralston had prevailed on Evert to play doubles again to improve her volleys, and Evert had. Ralston had less success persuading Evert to come to the net more during her matches. Evert told him she didn't like feeling that vulnerable, marooned, exposed.

Evert was understandably reluctant to alter the baseline style that had made her the champion she was. But she knew Ralston and Lloyd were right: she had to change.

Once Navratilova began taking the net at every opportunity against her, the arithmetic of their matches was altered. The number of passing shots that Evert had to thread by Navratilova at the net had increased exponentially too.

"It became just an impossible way for Chrissie to have to play Martina, having to pass her fifty times to win," Ralston says. "I told Chris her only chance to win was to attack Martina's backhand and on any short ball, come in. Chrissie did get better and better and better. But it was still very, very hard to get her to do it. Chrissie would be winning matches against someone else, 6–0, 4–1, and we'd be saying, 'Chrissie, you've gotta go in now. What does it matter if you beat someone 6–0, 6–0, or 6–4 and 6–2?' "

During an exhibition match against Navratilova that Ralston didn't attend in San Diego, Evert finally made the breakthrough she needed. She called Ralston on the telephone afterward and excitedly said, "I did it! I did what you said. I went to the net and I attacked from start to end and I beat her—I won four and four!"

On January 27, 1985, at the Virginia Slims of Florida in Key Biscayne, Evert knocked off Navratilova again—this time in a match that mattered. Playing just thirty-five miles from her childhood home, in front of a frenzied standing-room-only crowd, Evert prevailed 6–2, 6–4. She snapped Navratilova's winning streak over her at thirteen matches. Again, Evert had attacked. When they met at the net, Navratilova smiled. "It's about time you beat me," she told Evert. And they laughed.

Evert admitted, "I was a little afraid after the first set because I don't think I've ever played that well in my life."

Good as Evert felt about the victory over Navratilova, she wasn't satisfied. And Navratilova was not exactly crushed. One loss to Evert hardly constituted a trend to Navratilova. And one win over her was hardly enough to prompt Evert to declare she had pulled even.

Both she and Navratilova had reached the point in their long careers at which the only shot at total fulfillment came from playing and beating each other—or, better yet, facing each other at the four Grand Slam tournaments, where tennis greatness is measured.

Navratilova and Evert together owned the last thirteen major titles that had been awarded. The idea that the other was out there somewhere, working in private, gathering herself for their next clash, drove them when they were apart. As Navratilova once put it, "Playing against Chris is like battling part of your own nature. You know she will never give up and so you can't either." Evert had just turned thirty, but both she and Navratilova agreed that she was playing the best, most complete tennis of her life.

But playing at a higher level than Navratilova? Good enough to overtake her for number one?

Navratilova had quickly avenged her January loss to Evert at Key Biscayne with straight-set wins at their next two tournaments. Evert, still stuck in the quicksand of her unaccustomed role as the also-ran, put up a brave public face at first, insisting that Navratilova's dominance surely couldn't last forever. She continued to parry back when she felt patronized or underestimated. But as the losses to Navratilova resumed, even Evert's famous defiance had begun to fade, replaced now by some self-deprecating humor.

She had not been ranked number one now in nearly four years.

As spring gave way to summer, Navratilova and Evert looked ahead to the 1985 French Open.

Everything had changed and nothing at all.

As Navratilova and Evert emerged from the shadows of the locker room door into Roland Garros Stadium for the final, they squinted in the blast of brilliant sunlight that hit them as they descended the stairway to the court. Navratilova looked alert, even eager, as she and Evert walked toward their courtside chairs. Evert wore a cryptic little smile. She stole a look around, as if she wanted to remember every detail: the flags snapping on the flagpoles atop the stadium; the tiny funnel clouds of red dust that the gusting winds sent dancing across the court; the smattering of fans who were already standing and applauding before a single shot had been struck, as if they knew that this 1985 French Open final between Evert and Navratilova might be as epic and compelling as so many of their matches had been before.

For the thirteenth time, Evert and Navratilova were about to meet for a Grand Slam tournament title. For all but a brief portion of their rivalry, either Evert or Navratilova had been number one in the world. But as they began unzipping their racket bags to prepare to play, Navratilova remained the prohibitive favorite. Evert had not beaten Navratilova in a major in two and a half years—not even at the French Open, a tournament that Evert once ruled as imperiously as Navratilova now did the grass courts of Wimbledon.

When NBC TV sat down Evert for a pre-match interview before the final, Evert smiled and said she thought she was making progress in her chase of Navratilova. "But I remember sitting here at the French Open last year saying, 'Oh, I have a good chance against Martina.' And I got killed, 6–3, 6–1, so . . ."

So Evert took off the sweater she had been wearing during warm-ups. As she took her spot along the baseline and looked across the net, Navratilova was bouncing on the balls of her feet, kicking one leg out to the side, then the other. Navratilova's arms dangled loosely at her hips. When it was time to begin, a hush fell over the stadium. And Navratilova brazenly danced a good two feet inside the baseline, awaiting Evert's first serve as if she had nothing to fear.

Over the next three hours, everything that their rivalry had ever revealed about Navratilova and Evert as athletes, as people, as friends, was about to be reprised on the floor of Roland Garros. Even on television, their grunts of exertion were audible. So were the sandpapery sounds their sneakers made as they slid into their shots on the clay. When it was through, Navratilova came around to Evert's side of the net to sling an arm around her. And Evert held on to Navratilova's hand just an instant longer when their arm-in-arm walk off the court ended at the umpire's chair, then turned away so Navratilova couldn't see her shoving away a few tears.

The match they played was dazzling—not for its perfection, necessarily, but more for the stomach-gnawing tension, and the stirring determination they displayed. Later, piecing the details back together was hard for both of them. The emotions were what lingered. There had been so many gasp-inducing shots and disasters avoided by each of them, so many narrow escapes and cliffhanger moments in which one of them gouged out a service break or won a couple of games in a row, and then, as if disoriented by the sudden lightness and shedding of pressure, the distracting thought of victory, each of them would give back a game or two. They'd inexplicably plow a make-able shot into the net and stand there, staring, as if to say, "How in the world did I do that?"

And the drama would begin all over again . . .

Navratilova would shriek at her mistakes now and then as if she wanted to shatter every champagne flute on the grounds of Roland Garros. Once or twice Evert directed a burning stare at a linesman whom she suspected of missing a close call. She kicked the ball into the net once when it disobeyed her. Her own errors sent her eyebrows slamming down hard in irritation. Then the right side of her mouth would tick up ever so slightly into a scowl.

Navratilova was, as usual, breathtaking. The way her racket finished high above her shoulder on some strokes, she looked like a musketeer slicing up the air. Evert, as always, seemed lost in concentration, her movements precise, her timing pure, the path of her strokes perfectly grooved. She seized the first set from Navratilova, 6–3. She had Navratilova down 2–4, 15–40 in the second set too, then couldn't apply the sleeper hold. Navratilova slithered free and held serve. Then she broke Evert's serve. Evert served for match at 6–5 in the second, but again Navratilova pulled out the service break she absolutely had to have and forced a tiebreaker, which she also won to stay alive.

And the drama began all over again . . .

No one would've been surprised if Evert had come undone right then. Squandering the chance to close out Navratilova in straight sets was how Evert lost the U.S. Open final eight months earlier. But as Evert so pointedly said of herself then, *Chris Evert never choked away a match.* This time Evert held serve to start the third set. Then, unable to believe a rare stroke of good luck, she broke Navratilova to sneak ahead 2–0. On break point, Evert had bolted in to retrieve a drop shot by Navratilova. But all Evert managed to do was tap back a weak drop shot herself, which Navratilova had anticipated. With the crowd tracing every step she took with a growing roar of "ahhhh," Navratilova reached the ball with a moment to spare—only to slap her reply into the net tape, then drop her racket and clutch her face with both hands in disbelief.

Evert whirled around instantly so Navratilova couldn't see how stunned she was. With great effort, Evert strained ahead now to a 3–1 lead. A flurry of desperate shots later, Navratilova had pulled even at 3-all. In the eighth game of the third set, Evert was stalking a break point to go ahead 5–3. Navratilova slammed a perfect-looking forehand to the deep right corner of the court and charged the net—watching as Evert arrived at the ball on a full run and, with her racket still drawn back, paused just a half beat to scissor her feet into perfect position before she swung and cracked an incomprehensible passing shot winner by Navratilova at the net. The capacity crowd shrieked, and in the television booth, broadcaster Bud Collins reflexively screamed, "*Ohhhhh, that's the forehand of the match!*"

Evert—the Ice Maiden—actually shot a clenched fist into the air.

For the second time in an hour, Evert was serving for the championship. Again, Navratilova conjured up the do-or-die service break she needed. Then she didn't permit Evert a point as she held for 5-all.

The last two games that Navratilova and Evert played were a blur of inspired shots, each more pressure-packed and spine-tingling than the last. Evert held for a 6–5 lead, but only after surviving a 0–40 deficit and four break points in the longest game of the match. By then the crowd had nearly shouted itself hoarse. With Navratilova serving now at 5–6, Evert got to match point and lofted a tantalizing lob over Navratilova's head, and Navratilova turned and gave chase, only to see the ball parachute down just inches long. Navratilova stopped, put both hands on her knees and wagged her head three times in relief. Evert's eyes narrowed, and she dragged her wristband across her face to wipe some sweat away. Navratilova swallowed hard. She caught her breath.

Befitting all that happened in the two hours and forty minutes they had already played, the last point of the match was unforgettable. Navratilova sent a serve sizzling down the center line of the court, and Evert hit a backhand return. Navratilova answered with a forehand reply and Evert tried a crosscourt backhand. Navratilova slammed another forehand down the middle that pushed Evert a perilous six feet deep behind baseline. When Evert hit back a short reply, Navratilova came rushing in to pounce on the ball.

Evert looked doomed—especially when Navratilova smashed a backhand toward the left corner of the court and took the net. But Evert not only made it to the ball; she lunged and jackknifed forward, slid her feet into perfect position one last time, and somehow sent a two-fisted backhand winner from the left corner down the left alley on a low hard line. Navratilova's head snapped around just in time to watch as the ball slammed down just in.

It was the sort of electrifying shot that a tennis player dreams of, and the kind of spellbinding exchange that historians and film librarians bookmark to replay at Hall of Fame induction ceremonies or career retrospectives or any gathering where two rivals' names are mentioned in the same breath. After a shocked pause—as if no one at Roland Garros could quite process what Evert had just done—her match-point passing shot sent a lightning charge through the crowd. Fans bolted to their feet. Evert leaped and her arms shot up in triumph. Her mouth dropped open in wonder. Then, resting her racket on her shoulder, she jogged in toward Navratilova. Both of them were shaking their heads in disbelief.

The final score was 6–3, 6–7, 7–5 for Evert. Navratilova hadn't lost the match. She'd forced Evert to win it.

"We brought out the best in each other," Navratilova said.

CHAPTER THIRTEEN

FULL CIRCLE

Though Evert wouldn't retire for another four years, nothing that came later in the rivalry with Navratilova topped her 1985 French Open win for her. With the victory, Evert recaptured the weekly number one ranking for the first time in three and a half years. One of her lasting memories of her delirious victory party in Paris that night was the sight of her longtime agent, Bob Kain, drinking champagne out of her shoe.

Navratilova immediately reestablished herself after the defeat, winning four of the next five majors she entered. But Evert was playing now to exhaust her love of the game as much as to win major titles. She was thirty, and she had been entertaining retirement questions for nearly two years. For her and Navratilova, the French Open match—the excitement, the nervousness, the torture, the pleasure—underscored how their long careers were inextricably, symbiotically linked. Many of their subsequent showdowns and statements acquired a fond and sentimental tone.

At the Australian Open seven months later, Navratilova found

Evert especially heartbroken in the locker room after defeating her in the final because the 1985 year-end number one ranking had been attainable as well. The tension crackling through the match had been so great, Navratilova—upon seeing Evert—broke down crying too.

What a pair they made.

"I know how you feel, so I can't enjoy this," Martina said, wiping away tears.

"Don't worry about me," Evert sniffled, blowing her nose.

Evert defeated Navratilova again to capture the 1986 French Open, but the victory—the last major of Evert's career—didn't have the same emotion. Evert was moving toward her divorce from John Lloyd later that year when Navratilova and Judy Nelson, knowing Evert was morose, coaxed her to Aspen to spend the 1986 Christmas holidays with them. At a New Year's Eve party at the Hotel Jerome, they introduced Evert to Andy Mill, a former U.S. Olympic downhill skier who accompanied them to the slopes the following morning.

Ten days later, Navratilova was packing to leave for the Australian Open when Evert appeared in the doorway of her bedroom. She asked if Navratilova and Nelson would mind if she remained behind and stayed at their house. And Navratilova smiled.

Mill laughs and says a few mornings later, he woke up with a start. "I looked around and I thought, 'Oh my God, I'm sleeping with Chris Evert—*in Martina Navratilova's bedroom! No one's gonna believe this.'* "

Mill and Evert were married nineteen months later with Navratilova and Nelson in attendance. And Evert felt a tug to stay home once again. "I never *had* a permanent home to go to as an adult before Andy and I settled in Aspen," Evert said.

She and Navratilova still burned to defeat each other whenever they met. Judy Nelson remembers the 1987 Porsche Cup final in Filderstadt, Germany, that began as heatedly as any major title Evert and Navratilova ever played. Navratilova, you see, had promised the Porsche that came with the title to one of Nelson's teenage sons. But Evert had already said she wanted to win the sports car for Mill, who had visited the factory during the tournament and came away enthralled. After a fierce first set, Navratilova pulled away, 7–5, 6–1.

But even Navratilova and Evert's most competitive matches gave way to moments of laughter and genuine affection.

"*You were supposed to go over there!*" Evert shouted at Navratilova during their 1987 Wimbledon semifinal when Navratilova nearly reached a ball that Evert had tapped over the net. Later in the same match, when Navratilova was about to detonate over a serve that was called out, she stopped abruptly when she saw a grin creeping across Evert's face.

At the 1988 U.S. Open, Evert's next-to-last appearance there, she and Navratilova practiced together on a side court before the tournament began, same as they had as teenagers. In 1989, when word raced across the Wimbledon grounds that Evert was about to suffer an unthinkable quarterfinal loss to Laura Golarsa, Evert looked into the stands and saw Navratilova, who had just wrapped up her own victory on another court, shrieking approval for a winner Evert had just struck, and imploring her to make a comeback—which Evert did, forcing a third set after being shoved just two points from defeat.

"No matter how catty we get with each other in private or public," Navratilova said after Evert retired, "I still have a closeness with her that I will never have with another human being because of what we went through together, on and off the court."

Evert agreed. "Maybe the most revealing thing of all about how we feel about each other is that never once, no matter how tough the loss, never once has one of us said to the other, 'I'm sorry, but can you leave me alone?' "

Evert bid farewell to tennis at the 1989 U.S. Open. It had been eighteen years and countless miles and room service meals since her debut on tour. Zina Garrison, who defeated the thirty-four-year-old Evert in the quarterfinals, says, "I was the one crying at the net because Chris was such a great champion. Chris was consoling me."

After 1,454 matches and 157 singles titles, Evert said she was ready to start a family and a new phase of her life. "Boy, was I ready," she says with a laugh. There was even fanciful talk from Navratilova that she might retire and walk off into the sunset with Evert.

"I really am outta here," Evert said. "I want to be a full-time wife."

The last time Evert and Navratilova played was similar to their first encounter in Akron. There was no fanfare, no fuss. On a cold night in Chicago—Jimmy Evert's childhood hometown—Navratilova defeated Evert, 6–2, 6–2, and they shook hands afterward, same as always. The date was November 14, 1988. They had no way of knowing that by the luck of the draw, they'd never oppose each other the entire last year of Evert's career.

The ledger on their rivalry froze at eighty matches, sixty of them finals, with Navratilova leading forty-three victories to Evert's thirty-seven.

"For sixteen years we were left alone on Sundays in that locker room," Evert says. "All in all, I think we handled it pretty damn well."

Navratilova played singles another five years after Evert retired, and enjoyed unprecedented approbation as her career wound down.

In July of 1986, Navratilova returned to Communist Czecho-slovakia for the first time since her defection to play for the U.S. team in the Federation Cup. Navratilova had been a U.S. citizen for five years by then, and a persona non grata in Czechoslovakia for eleven. She hadn't seen her parents or sister for six years. Evert ignored a knee injury to accompany Navratilova along with U.S. teammates Pam Shriver and Zina Garrison. All of them wanted to support Navratilova, knowing her return would be an emotional, unforgettable scene.

Evert had only been behind the iron curtain once before, cross-ing over to East Berlin in 1985 with her sister and brother-in-law while in West Berlin to play the German Open. The experience had made Evert think about Navratilova. At the border, two brusque East German guards rifled through Evert's car and bags. "One of us had a newspaper," Evert remembers, "and they ripped it up. You're not allowed to bring in any newspapers, and we didn't think of that." Evert took note of the bullet holes in the Berlin Wall, the armed guards in their sentry towers, and the expressions of the people in the streets. "There was not one smile on anybody's face," Evert says. "Not one. It was just grim, and it felt like misery because they had accepted that was their way of life. Their eyes were dull. Their eyes were dead. No glint . . . nothing."

When Navratilova arrived in Prague for the Fed Cup, she and her family had an emotional reunion at the airport. Cyril Suk, the husband of Navratilova's old coach Vera Sukova, was still the president of the Czech Tennis Federation. He had been widowed for four years by now. He met Navratilova at the airport and politely offered her his umbrella to shield her from the light drizzle. Navratilova was nervous about what to expect. As she and her family pushed through throngs of newsmen and photographers and fans who came to greet them, some of them lifted young children atop their shoulders to get a glimpse of Martina. Iva Drapalova, a Prague-based Associated Press reporter who was there, says, "It was interesting to see how many people came to the airport to see her. People surrounded her immediately, and they were shouting things like 'Martina, welcome home!' and 'You are ours! You are ours!' "

During her weeklong stay for the thirty-three-team Fed Cup competition, fans lined up five deep at Navratilova's old club to watch her practice. Spectators shoehorned their way into every seat and aisle at Prague's Stvanice Stadium for her matches, roaring their appreciation for Navratilova in open defiance of the Communist Party officials who sat in their private boxes, stone-faced.

Party officials had ordered that Navratilova's name not be spoken on the public address system during the opening or closing ceremonies. Helena Sukova, Cyril Suk's daughter, played for the Czechoslovakian team. She says that to this day she and her father have copies of the original Fed Cup program, which was never distributed. Seeing that some photographs of Navratilova had been included, party officials ordered new programs without her picture printed on the eve of the tournament.

"They said that it is not possible to promote Navratilova," says Sukova. "She was a symbol of freedom."

Navratilova always believed—correctly—that government agents tailed her during her stay. (A 2004 request to the Czech Republic's State Central Archive for a look at Navratilova's secret police file brought a reply that one was compiled during her Fed Cup visit but was destroyed when Communist rule in Czechoslovakia ended after the Velvet Revolution of 1989.) Mike Estep says that he and Martina were almost certain they were followed during the tournament when they drove around Prague. Judy Nelson remembers going for walks with Navratilova in the woods near Revnice where Martina used to go mushroom picking and berry hunting with their father, and hearing twigs snap from the footfalls someone else made. "We never saw anyone," Nelson says, "but it felt odd. It was spooky."

At the Fed Cup opening ceremonies, Hana Mandlikova, the captain of the Czech team, took the microphone to address the crowd. Ignoring the fact that she might be inviting trouble, Mandlikova brazenly welcomed Navratilova home by name, the stadium rocked with chants of "Nav-ROT-e-lo-va! Nav-ROT-e-lo-va!" When the band began to play the Czech national anthem "Where Is My Home," Evert bowed her head to listen and soon saw a tear of Navratilova's fall on her sneaker. So she slung an arm around Navratilova and kept it there.

On the U.S. team's first day of play, Zina Garrison remembers watching in wonder as a commuter train passing by on an elevated rail just beyond the tennis grounds came to a complete stop, then slowly began backing up so the passengers who had crowded up against the windows could steal a look at Navratilova as she played her first match against a woman from China. Navratilova finished the competition undefeated.

The United States won the Fed Cup title and Navratilova, as the team's number one player, stepped forward to formally accept the trophy at the closing ceremony. When she began to speak to the crowd in English, her countrymen and -women shouted, "In Czech, in Czech!" And she complied.

In a steady voice, Navratilova thanked her Czech hosts and her U.S. teammates and the fans. By now the stadium had fallen silent, and she said: "I don't have to tell you how special it has been for me to come back this week, to be here again. I only hope it's not another eleven years before I come back." Her words brought down the house again. The spectators clapped and screamed and stomped their feet, but this time they wouldn't stop. Navratilova finally let herself cry, burying her head on Pam Shriver's shoulder. When it was time to leave the stadium, Navratilova turned and waved one last time, surveying the scene as she left. When Evert and Shriver tried to talk about the awards ceremony later, they began crying too.

"It was so nice," Evert says, "to finally see Martina get her due."

Navratilova played singles until 1994, several years after young Steffi Graf, then Monica Seles, began to overtake her. But Navratilova's encounters with them never inspired the same interest and never became the can't-miss occasions that her steel-cage matches against Evert did.

By the gloaming of Navratilova's twenty-one-year, 1,650-match singles career, fellow players responded to Navratilova with the same intensity as fans.

When Navratilova lost in the 1993 Wimbledon semifinals, Graf was so disappointed about the lost chance to meet Navratilova in one last final, she sent word to Navratilova through a friend: how about the two of them meet secretly on the hallowed old grass courts one last time and play one more match with no linesmen, no crowds, no coaches—just the two of them?

By the time she retired from full-time singles at age thirty-eight, Navratilova had played so long that Conchita Martinez, the woman who defeated her in her swan-song run to the 1994 Wimbledon final, had grown up in Spain idolizing her and hitting practice balls against a wall she nicknamed "Martina." A former opponent of Navratilova's in Czechoslovakia, Melanie Molitor Hingis, named her only daughter Martina. The younger Hingis turned pro the same year Navratilova said farewell in 1994.

When Navratilova arrived in Oakland for the next-to-last stop on her retirement tour, she faced a young Czech-born woman named Marketa Kochta, a fifth-year pro who entered the event's qualifying tournament expressly because she had never played Navratilova before. Playing her way into the main draw in Oakland was Kochta's last chance.

Kochta's family had defected from Czechoslovakia when she was seven, and Navratilova's career and example had always been her faraway inspiration.

Navratilova—knowing none of that—beat Kochta in three sets all the same. At the net Kochta shook Navratilova's hand and bashfully told her, "You are my hero." Then Kochta fell into a friend's embrace once off-court and sobbed, explaining, "I could never tell Martina how I felt before today."

Asked later what Navratilova had meant to tennis, Kochta's eyes grew wide and she said, "Why, she is history. She made things *possible*, you see?"

SECOND ACTS

It is a perfect July afternoon, and Chris Evert is seated on a grass bank overlooking a skateboard park in Aspen, Colorado, where she and her family spend the summer. She is watching her three sons, Alex, Nicholas, and Colton, whip around the sunken cement track, through the steeply banked curves, then back down to the floor of the skateboard run again. Before long, Evert's husband, Andy Mill, drops by in his white pickup truck to check on everyone and then hurries off again.

Sixteen years have passed since the last ball of Evert's last match against Martina Navratilova bounded forever out of reach. As Evert sits here and talks, Navratilova is in Slovenia, playing in a 2004 Federation Cup match for the United States and winning yet another doubles contest in a career that she decided to continue into 2005.

"God love her," Evert says with a smile.

In another month, Navratilova would make her Olympic debut at age forty-seven at the Summer Games in Athens. A few months after that—on December 21, 2004, to be exact—Evert would celebrate her fiftieth birthday. Not that you can tell their ages by looking at either of them. Evert's hair is still sun-streaked blond, and she's whippet-thin and finely muscled, like a dancer. She looks as if she could still play on tour, if not perhaps contend for the major doubles titles that Martina won as late as 2003, her fourth decade as a professional.

Navratilova said that when she started her doubles comeback in May of 2000 in Spain, she had a dream the night before her first match. There stood Evert, droll as ever, squinting at her and saying, "Why are you doing this?"

"She *did*?" Evert squeals. Her mouth drops open and she slaps her thigh and laughs. "Well, you tell Martina I never dream about her," she needles.

Neither haunts the other anymore.

In the first few years after Evert retired, many of the conversations between her and Navratilova were dotted with now-it-can-be-told stories they could never have shared when they were still competing against each other. Navratilova was amazed, for example, to learn that Chris read her "like a book" before matches: "She told me she could tell if I was good-nervous or bad-nervous." During one of their Legends Tour trips, Navratilova wondered during a *New York Times* interview that she and Evert conducted together if Evert's famous calm had ever been helped by psychotherapy. Evert smiled.

"I never went to therapy except for three times when I was going through my divorce," she said, referring to the end of her seven-year marriage to John Lloyd. "On that third visit, the doctor told me to pretend to speak to my father in baby talk, like I was two years old, and I looked at my watch and said, 'Okay, that's it, I'm out of here.' "

As Evert and Navratilova glide into middle age, some of their differences have faded. But still others remain as vivid as ever. Former president George H. W. Bush is a regular at Evert's pro-celebrity tennis classic; Navratilova recorded a campaign message during the November 2004 elections for Democratic presidential candidate John Kerry.

One night when Navratilova and Evert were catching up over dinner in Aspen a handful of years ago, Evert ordered lamb, only to have Navratilova launch into a long, heartfelt explanation about the awful things that happen to baby sheep on their way to market. Evert listened intently and said, "Martina, I am *so* sorry."

Then, turning back to the waiter, Evert said, "Medium rare, please."

Evert segued smoothly from tennis into the life of being a wife and mother that she always craved. She has found it even more rewarding than she imagined. Shortly after her third son, Colton, was born, Evert said that one of the wonderful things about having children is, "all the layers—the fame, the celebrity, my own vanity, the image—are just stripped away, day by day. It's like I'm finally allowing myself to be uninhibited. I was so controlled."

To say Evert is retired is not quite right. Evert and her younger brother, John, run the Evert Tennis Academy, a junior camp and boarding school in Boca Raton, Florida. Since 1989, Evert's celebrity-pro tennis classic has raised more than $12 million for charity. She sits on numerous nonprofit boards and works for a long list of charities that help at-risk children and their mothers and fight drug abuse and the spread of HIV and AIDS.

Apart from that, Evert is a devoted mother. She and Andy Mill happily attend parent-teacher meetings and shuttle the boys to sleepovers with their friends. Evert spends great portions of her free time with her sons, whether they're at the skateboard park in Aspen or with Andy at the dirt bike track near their year-round home in Florida, where the boys compete. She plops down a lawn chair she keeps in her car and waits for the action to begin. She knows her boys' friends and catches up with their parents. The buttoned-up champion has been replaced by a down-to-earth woman who unselfconsciously shows all the feelings she once kept tamped down inside.

"Here's a picture of Alex on his motorcycle," Evert says proudly, pulling a dog-eared photograph from her purse that shows her oldest son, dressed in full motocross gear, standing on the pedals of his dirt bike after taking off from a hill. He is flying fifteen feet off the ground. "I know," Evert marvels, shaking her head. She seems thrilled at her son's precociousness and the daredevil streak that all three of her boys seem to have inherited from Andy, who rued the premature end of his Olympic ski racing career even though he broke his neck, back, and leg in violent falls.

Mill seems to have the perfect blend of machismo and tenderness, unpretentiousness and irreverence, that Evert needs in a partner. Family is extremely important to him as well. Mill's Olympic event was the downhill, the toughest, most kamikaze event of them all. Yet he is also the sort of man who cried at their wedding, cries at sappy movies. More than a decade after the 1991 birth of their first son, Mill still gets choked up in midsentence as he talks about Chris's difficult pregnancy and delivery—a day that Evert also calls the happiest of her life.

After Mill and Evert were married, he insisted on continuing his work as a television commentator and adventure series producer, and he continued to compete in world championship fishing tournaments, both avocations that required him to travel extensively. (Mill has become something of the Lance Armstrong of tournament fishing, having won the world bonefishing title five of the last six years through 2004. "We've got that competition wired," he says with pride.) After their second and third sons arrived, Evert wanted Mill home more when the boys were very young. They eventually found a way to compromise, Mill says. "One of the things I said to Chrissie was, 'Chrissie, I will love you and give you all of me for the rest of my life. But you have to allow me to be *me*.' "

Mill, who gave up his television work in 2003, jokes, "Our idea of a big night now is calling Domino's and ordering out for a pizza."

Evert laughs and says, "It's true."

Evert knew herself well enough to know that she didn't want to completely recede into the mists when she stopped playing. She may share her father's dislike for pretense, but she is not allergic to fame. A few years into her retirement, Evert laughed and confessed to feeling a pang when a flock of fans at the U.S. Open came running right at her—and then ran right by her, because just around the corner Andre Agassi was arriving with actress Brooke Shields. "I've been famous since I was sixteen years old," Evert pointed out. "It would be sort of shattering if, in two years, I went into a restaurant and said, 'Chris Evert would like a table' and they said, 'Who?' "

Evert loved the excitement and competition of the tennis tour, the unmatched thrill of putting herself on the line. But she doesn't miss the vagabond life or grinding toll the game took on her. "For literally the first couple years after I quit, I still felt like I was on vacation," she says. "I'd wake up in the morning and go, 'You mean I can do anything I want? Anything?' " She also appreciates that her personal life is no longer as open to public purview. "I remember when I got divorced from John Lloyd and I saw it in the *New York Times:* 'Christine Evert and John Lloyd Divorce.' That was the headline, and I remember thinking, 'I'm not quite sure all this is worth it. I'm not sure all the money in the world is worth this.' Your private life and emotions, they're priceless. I didn't want everybody to know everything about me."

By the end of her career, Evert believed her journey wasn't just a quest to win matches. She says, "It became a process of trying to get to know myself as a human being, and to figure out what I believed in." She became convinced that although being a sports star can make you larger than life, in some ways you're smaller too.

"For the longest time," she once said, "I had no idea how the real world worked."

Evert believes she does now. "Having kids was the best thing ever for me," she says. "I was so ready to be giving and not have the emphasis be on me, me, me.

"I've had a great life—a *great* life. I have such a great life now. And it's funny. Andy and I have been married fifteen years, and I said to him just the other day that I feel closer to him now than ever. I mean, it's different. It's not the goose bumps-passion-fireworks kind of thing. It's more like knowing he's a keeper. And I just know that I'm going to grow old with him."

When Navratilova announced her retirement from full-time singles play in 1994, she said that she too was eager to get on with the rest of her life. She still owned a home she had bought in Aspen shortly after meeting Judy Nelson, and she took daring skiing trips down pristine mountains reachable only by helicopter. She snowboarded to her heart's content. She rode the back roads of Colorado on her Harley-Davidson motorcycle and played ice hockey for a state champion women's team. She signed up for woodworking classes and went on photo safaris in Kenya, where she also lived for parts of several years. She had begun taking lessons to get her pilot's license weeks before John F. Kennedy Jr. crashed his small plane into the sea off Martha's Vineyard. "I don't have the greatest timing, I know," Navratilova told a skittish friend. Then she kept on flying anyway.

But what Navratilova insisted in May of 2000 was just a four-tournament foray back into doubles play quickly grew into a year-round return to the tour. At her Hall of Fame induction ceremony two months later, Navratilova told the crowd, "I thought I didn't need tennis anymore. Well, I was wrong." Navratilova found she enjoyed the pure pleasure she gets from tennis now. She likes the novel, uncomplicated feeling of being able to treat the game as pure play and not some win-or-else profession. During her heyday there were times when Navratilova took off no more than two or three days a year. If she lost, she used to think the best remedy was to work out even harder.

"Now it's bigger news when I win than when I lose," she says, laughing. "Now middle-aged suburban housewives go crazy when they see me."

When people constantly express their astonishment at Navratilova's comeback, she keeps reminding them, "The ball doesn't know how old I am."

Neither, it seems, does Navratilova. She still looks as muscular and fit as she did in the early 1980s. She's still as sharp, exuberant, feisty, curious, opinionated, and funny as ever. A few years ago, when Navratilova mentioned that she was going to play a doubles match with Serena Williams in Tokyo, she was jokingly asked if she planned to wear one of the black form-fitting Lycra catsuits that Williams had just debuted at the U.S. Open. And Navratilova shot back: "I could, you know."

As good as Navratilova's tennis remains, it's her mind that makes her different. She still reads voraciously, still loves a good debate. She has that brain that works like a radar dish, pulling in tons of disparate information and spitting out the sort of comments that make people think, laugh, nod in agreement, or bolt forward in their chairs and say, "Now, wait a minute . . ."

Former pro Ivan Lendl, Navratilova's more emotionally shuttered Czech countryman, used to call Navratilova a "limousine liberal," which is another way of saying a dilettante. Yet if not for Navratilova, neither Lendl nor Hana Mandlikova would have enjoyed the freedom to travel as they pleased and live in the United States years before the 1989 Velvet Revolution and peaceful end of Communist rule in Czechoslovakia.

To Czechs and Slovaks alike (though not just them) Navratilova was—and remains—a heroic figure, a clenched fist of defiance back when dissident victories were rare. When Navratilova returned to Prague in 1990 for the six-month anniversary of the end of Communist rule, Vaclav Havel, the newly installed Czech president, asked her to speak from the balcony of his Liberation Party's headquarters to the tens of thousands who had gathered below in Wenceslas Square. In 1994, when the United Nations' fiftieth anniversary board selected its U.S. national committee to help spread principles of peace, human rights, and social justice, it invited names such as Henry Kissinger and Coretta Scott King, as well as Navratilova, the only athlete chosen.

Navratilova has always seemed constitutionally incapable of remaining apolitical, even if the circumstances of her life had not made such a stance near impossible. Her many rebellions or stands, which started simply as a quest for personal freedom, expanded over time.

She is just as liable now to speak out against Arctic oil well drilling as she is tennis parents from hell. Navratilova supports same-sex marriage, and yet she vociferously fought Judy Nelson's attempt to sue her for palimony in 1991 after Navratilova ended their seven-and-a-half-year relationship. (After much brinkmanship and ugly publicity, they settled out of court.)

During one of her 2003 Wimbledon press conferences, Navratilova got into a spirited debate with a reporter who asked her to elaborate on comments she had made to the *Times of London*, lamenting the harsh treatment the Dixie Chicks received for opposing the U.S. invasion of Iraq.

Told that the band's critics were merely expressing their own right to free speech, Navratilova said, no, no, no, it wasn't the same at all.

"Expressing their views [about the band] is one thing," Navratilova said. "When people burn their CDs, I guess they have a right to do that too. But when radio stations boycott someone's music because of what they say, that's censorship. There goes your freedom of speech. And when disc jockeys get fired because they defy the [station] owner's request not to play the music, there's something wrong.

"What I was saying was, it's as if freedom of speech only goes so far—it's only okay if everybody agrees with you. But if they don't agree with you, you get in trouble. That's not freedom of speech anymore."

That's Navratilova. Perhaps the nicest thing about the second act of her career is that it has lasted long enough for her to feel the appreciation. She encounters it everywhere.

Today, fans sprint across the grounds when it's announced that one of Navratilova's doubles matches has been moved from one court to another. She invariably takes the court into a headwind of wild applause and often leaves to standing ovations. Subaru featured her in a car commercial that said, "It's what's inside that counts." When the 2003 U.S. Open was delayed by rain for a third straight day, the main room of the players' lounge looked like an airport terminal where no flights were taking off. Equipment bags were strewn on the floor. Players dozed on every available couch and chair. But Navratilova couldn't walk ten feet without getting stopped. Heads jerked up. People sprang to their feet for an autograph. One mother shoved the shy little girl peeking around her right hip forward and asked Navratilova if she could please pose with the child for a picture.

Before long, a tournament official approached Navratilova as she was eating lunch and sheepishly said, "They're, uh . . . looking for an all-time tennis great to hit some balls to the fans that are waiting out the rain delay in the stadium. Could you?" "Sure," Navratilova said. She walked on court fifteen minutes later to a burst of delighted squeals.

On her way back inside, former men's pro Vijay Amritraj asked Navratilova if she had five minutes for a TV interview. "Sure," Navratilova said again. Her hair was wet from the rain now. Soon Amritraj was asking Navratilova on camera how she felt to be among the younger players in the locker room.

"Well," Navratilova said, "one player in the junior draw here, I played against her mother."

Then here it came—that famous Navratilova roll of the eyes.

"Her *mother*," Navratilova repeated, sounding forty-six at last.

Evert and Navratilova have often been asked to predict their legacy. They understand that they represent different things to different people. Each is a symbol whose meaning is ambiguous, free-floating, and rooted as deeply in myth as in reality.

Like Billie Jean King, Evert and Navratilova are originals. But to say just that is too benign. The impact they had was revolutionary. Among the many things their sixteen-year rivalry illuminated was how women's sports are not just spinoffs of the games that men have been playing forever. Women's sports are distinct provinces unto themselves, with an ethos and a culture all their own. Evert and Navratilova helped shape that culture at a time when women's roles and rights were being redefined. They inherited one world and helped mold a new one.

Evert exploded a lot of the negative stereotypes about women athletes and assuaged a lot of parents' fears about whether it was acceptable for girls to play sports. She remains the best female ambassador tennis ever had.

Early in her career, especially, Evert was often accused of being too calculating or image-conscious. People whispered about the "real" Evert, the iceberg beneath the debutante exterior. Over time, what became clearer was that Evert had a grace unique to her. Her diplomatic public comments were intended to protect people's feelings. Her steely attitude and detached way of dissecting even her most emotional matches hinted at her deep reservoir of strength. What people labeled her consummate professionalism was the residue of having the sort of rearing that demands that you never complain publicly, never do anything to disgrace yourself or your family, and never, ever let on how damn hard anything is.

Navratilova, of course, was different. Unlike Evert, who grew over time into the person she became, Navratilova created a dramatic sense of herself from the start. And then she stuck to it—no matter what.

A substantial part of the late-career affection she has enjoyed has nothing to do with the details of what she stood for. Even people who don't agree with Navratilova nonetheless admire the way she has *endured*.

"Sometimes I look at Martina and what she went through," Evert says, "and, my God, I can't imagine. She defected, and for a while, she didn't have a country until she got her U.S. citizenship. She didn't have a family or that sort of unconditional love from anyone here. She's in a competitive field. People are out to get you. She's gay. She's vulnerable. She had all of that to contend with at a young age."

Navratilova admits she has wondered at times " 'How did I ever do it?' "

Of her adversaries, Navratilova has joked, "I've outlasted them. Definitely.

"And America has definitely changed," she said. "It's more acceptable for women to be assertive, for them to be athletes, to speak their minds, to be politicians or heads of the household. Gays are treated differently. And people realized I was not as threatening as they thought I was, especially when I was beating Chris. She's the perfect image of a lady who also happens to be a great tennis player. Whereas I was an athlete who happens to be a woman. The contrast was pretty great."

For all the contrasts that remain between them, what should fade is the idea that only one of them was rebelling. Evert privately fought the idealized image of perfection that she was given as a teenager and believes she became a happier, more interesting woman in the process. A small bit of her inspiration and daring came from watching Navratilova. What Navratilova fought against was isolation—a leaden life behind the iron curtain, the closet that gays have been shoved into—and she won. She has said that Evert's example taught her self-reliance, perseverance.

After years of walking into tennis stadiums or banquet halls unsure of what the reaction to her would be, Navratilova took the podium at the 1993 gay and lesbian rights march on Washington, and the crowd on the mall—an estimated half million people—cut loose a sustained, full-throated roar. For her.

Among the things she said: "If we want others to give us respect, we must first be willing to give ourselves respect. We must be proud of who we are. And we cannot do that if we hide. We have to make ourselves palpable. Touchable. Real. Then we have the opportunity to show the world what we are all about: happy, intelligent, giving people. We can show our whole strength, our dignity and character. We can show our joy and sorrow, our heartaches and our pain."

And then?

"Then," she said, "we can just be."

In that same speech, Navratilova said, "My sexuality is an important part of my life. But it's not all that I am." When asked once if she ever identified with something Arthur Ashe said—that bigotry or racism requires so much wasted energy—Navratilova nodded and said, "It has been so much wasted energy. So much. It's so negative and counterproductive and useless, all this hate talk."

For all the turns their lives took, both Navratilova and Evert steadfastly tried to just be.

Navratilova has joked: "I went through all the stages that other people do, but at the wrong times." In a more serious moment, she could have been speaking for Evert too when she said: "I hope when I'm gone somebody will say that I mattered. That's important to me."

The poet William Dean Howells once wrote that it is always the small, still voice the soul listens to. In some ways, Evert and Navratilova's lives are a parable about that. They are proof that conviction counts, and that by telling the truth, you carve out room for more truth around you. Evert and Navratilova's shared odyssey underscored that if you live honorably, time can leaven the ups and downs, the heartbreaks and the thrills. Even the hate talk that Navratilova spoke about can die out, diminish. And decency will prevail.

And then? Then you really can just be. Difference will not be seen as a bad thing, but rather as something precious. Something proud. And you will become people worth celebrating, not just worth remembering, long after your last tennis ball bounds out of reach.

ACKNOWLEDGMENTS

Writing this book has been a keen reminder of how much writers depend upon the kindness and grace of others. Any work of journalism relies heavily on the cooperation of subjects who have no final approval over the text, who are not paid for interviews, and often agree to talk out of the goodness of their hearts. I am deeply indebted to all the principals in this story, who were uncommonly generous with their time and recollections.

I am most especially grateful to Chris Evert, who not only trusted me with her story, but invited me to her home, introduced me to her family, and gave me immeasurable help in reconstructing her rivalry with Martina with honesty and care. I will never forget her generosity, her acute intelligence and wit, and her willingness to linger until we had covered every last question and revisited every important match.

This project would never have been undertaken without the initial encouragement of Martina Navratilova, who, when I approached her with this idea, enthusiastically agreed that her rivalry with Chris was a part of sports history that deserved to be written. Before Martina went on to pursue projects of her own, it was she who first approached Chris about this book on my behalf. On both counts, I am grateful.

Special thanks to Billie Jean King, whose faraway example was an inspiration to me long before I met her as a young sports writer. Some of the most fascinating days of my career have been spent at Wimbledon, listening to Billie spin out her stories late into the night.

She is one of those rare people who throw off light, and unfailingly leave you with your mind on fire, your heart touched, and your sides sore from laughing.

Abundant thanks to Andy Mill for sharing his insights and memories with me, and for making me feel so welcome during my visit to Aspen. I am exceedingly grateful, too, to Jimmy and Colette Evert. I was constantly told during the research for this book that the Everts were the best parents a tennis player could ever have. My own conversations with Colette and Jimmy left me with the same conviction.

Steve Flink, the eminent tennis expert and one of the sport's true gentlemen, has my deepest gratitude for helping to make my meeting with Chris Evert possible, and for sharing his encyclopedic knowledge of tennis with me.

I am very grateful to Bud Collins, the brightest light in any press box he walks into, for his innumerable kindnesses over the years, only the last of which was his willingness to talk with me for this book.

My deepest gratitude is also due to Mary Carillo, who within these pages again reveals why she's the smartest commentator in television sports. No one else divines as much, frames things as accurately, or explains things as entertainingly.

Tennis magazine senior editor and writer Peter Bodo has authored some of the best, most comprehensive tennis coverage in the last twenty-five years. I'm especially thankful to him for going beyond the call of duty and generously offering to share with me transcripts of lengthy interviews he conducted with Chris and Martina in 2002.

I owe a great debt to Prague-based journalist Katerina Zachovalova, whose enterprising and conscientious reporting helped to illuminate Martina's life in Communist Czechoslovakia, and the circumstances that led to Martina's defection.

Grace Lichtenstein made Billie Jean's 1973 Battle of the Sexes match against Bobby Riggs and the social mores of the time come alive for me. Nancy Lieberman's remarkable memory and vivid ability to describe the story of how she helped Martina become a legendary champion were an invaluable contribution. Dr. Renee Richards graciously invited me to her home in upstate New York and regaled me with stories, fed me chicken soup and sandwiches, then—our interview done—took me on a scenic ride in her vintage Corvette convertible for good measure. Judy Nelson was kind enough to sit with me for hours and entrust me with her very personal memories of her years with Martina, between laughs and tears.

I am also grateful for interviews given to me by Neil Amdur, Tracy Austin, Fred Barman, Shari Barman, Ingrid Bentzer, Jeanie Brinkman Evans, Rosie Casals, Georgina Clark, Iva Drapalova, Joel Drucker, Barbara Estep, Mike Estep, Laurie Fleming Rowley, Zina Garrison, Steve Goldstein, Brian Gottfried, Robert Haas, Sandra Haynie, Julie Heldman Weiss, Lee Jackson, Sally Jenkins, Peachy Kellmeyer, Jan Kodes, Robert Lansdorp, Brendan Lemon, John Lloyd, Hana Mandlikova, Jim Martz, Betsy Nagelsen McCormack, Diana Nyad, Barbara Perry, Dennis Ralston, Pam Shriver, Harold Solomon, Cyril Suk, Helena Sukova, Wendy Turnbull, and the inestimable George Vecsey.

My continued gratitude to Ilana Kloss, who years ago volunteered to give me an insider's tour of Wimbledon on my first visit there—though she didn't know me from a racket cover—and has only heaped more kindnesses on me since. Many thanks to Anita Ruthling Klaussen for her generous assistance, especially with material from Martina's 2000 Hall of Fame induction ceremony.

Several books were an especially important help to understanding Navratilova and Evert. Foremost was *Martina*, Navratilova's exceptional autobiography with George Vecsey, which contains unique material on many facets of Martina's life. *Chrissie*, by Chris Evert Lloyd with Neil Amdur, and *Lloyd on Lloyd*, by Chris Evert Lloyd and John Lloyd with Carol Thatcher, were also helpful sources. *Billie Jean*, by Billie Jean King with Frank Deford, provided keen insight into King's personality and her experiences as she built the women's tennis tour.

Other books that were of particular help include Grace Lichtenstein's *A Long Way, Baby,* her terrific, lively account of the

1973 season on the fledgling women's tour; Peter Bodo's *The Courts of Babylon*; Nancy Lieberman's autobiography, *Lady Magic*, with Debby Jennings; Steve Flink's *The Greatest Tennis Matches of the Twentieth Century*; Dr. Renee Richards's *Second Serve*; Tim Adams's *Being John McEnroe*; Gordon Forbes's *A Handful of Summers*; John McPhee's *Levels of the Game*; Tracy Austin's *Beyond Center Court* with Christine Brennan; Pam Shriver's *Passing Shots* with Frank Deford and Susan B. Adams; John Feinstein's *Hard Courts*; Judy Nelson's two memoirs, *Choices* and *Love Match* (the latter cowritten with Sandra Faulkner); Susan Brownmiller's *In Our Time*; Mary Jo Festle's *Playing Nice*; Ted Tinling's *Sixty Years of Tennis*; Joel Drucker's *Jimmy Connors Saved My Life*; Michael Mewshaw's *Ladies of the Court*; Hana Mandlikova's autobiography *Hana* with Malcolm Foley, Billie Jean King's *We Have Come a Long Way*, with Cynthia Starr; and the anthology *The Right Set* (edited by Caryl Phillips). I also relied on Bud Collins's *Total Tennis: The Ultimate Tennis Encyclopedia*, which is an unsurpassed resource on the sport.

I am grateful to my network television colleagues who graciously provided me with videotapes of Martina and Chris's epic matches: Kevin Sullivan and Laura Klein at NBC Sports, Leslie Anne Wade at CBS Sports; Sue Friedmann and Willie Weinbaum at ESPN, Amy Pempel of the Sunshine Network, and Margaret Grossi and Lisa Bennett of HBO Sports.

Many thanks to Tami Starr of Chris Evert Charities for her constant willingness to help; to Darrell Fry and his media relations staff at the Women's Tennis Association; and to Randy Walker and his staff at the United States Tennis Association. Susan Kirkman's sleuthing through the photo archives of the *Akron Beacon Journal*, until she found the 1973 photograph of the first match Chris and Martina ever played, was also much appreciated.

Tony Lance and the editors at *Tennis* magazine were especially generous in allowing me the use of their library. Many thanks as well to Audrey Snell at the Wimbledon library and museum, Mark Young of the International Tennis Hall of Fame in Newport, Rhode Island,

and the wizards in the *Newsday* library, who were always helpful on those occasions when I couldn't locate information on my own.

My editors and colleagues at *Newsday* were extraordinarily accommodating throughout this project. Heartfelt thanks are especially in order to Steve Ruinsky, Anthony Mauro, Howard Schneider, Bill Eichenberger, and Sandy Keenan.

I was exceedingly fortunate that this book landed with two editors who buoyed me with their expert advice and unebbing enthusiasm for this story. They are Stacy Creamer at Doubleday Broadway Books in New York and Tristan Jones at Yellow Jersey Press in Britain.

I owe a special debt to my friend David Hirshey for giving me the encouragement to make what was a vague notion for this book into a reality; and to my agent, Mark Reiter, for shepherding me through the process. Robert Kirby's fine work on my behalf in Britain was also much appreciated. Special thanks for their care and concern during my writing of this book to Joe Mamounas, Judy Szepesi (my favorite Canadian), and my dear friends Mark McDonald, Diana Reed, Mary Adkins, and the girls of North Haven—Linda Santanello, Susan Isenberg, Sally Jenkins, and Nicole Bengiveno, who also took the author's photograph for this book. Ann D'Ercole, still nice talking to you.

I would never have graduated college as anything resembling an employable journalist without the patient care and feeding I received from Marino Parascenzo, still the best teacher and professional example I have ever had.

I would never have become a writer without the early and enduring encouragement of my parents, John and Connie Howard, and the cooperation (willing or otherwise) of my siblings Mark Howard, Lisa Mamounas, and Tori Maize, who were all fodder for my earliest stories.

As ever, I owe far too much to recount here to the incomparable Susan Reed, to whom this book is dedicated with gratitude and love.

APPENDIX

KEY FOR TABLES

Rk (world ranking), TP (tournaments played), TW (tournaments won), TF (tournament finals), GS (Grand Slams), Aus (Australian Open), Fre (French Open), Wim (Wimbledon), US (U.S. Open), TM (total matches), MW (matches won), ML (matches lost), Pct (winning percentage)

NAVRATILOVA, Martina

Female, Born: Oct. 18, 1956, Prague, Czech Republic. Height: 5'7". Weight: 140 lbs. Plays: left. Status: Turned Pro 1975. Earnings: $20,527,874. Highest Ranking: 1 (July 1978). HOF: 2000

Year	Rk	TP	TW	TF	GS	Aus	Fre	Wim	US	MW	ML	Pct
1973	....	16	0	0	5–3	....	QF	3rd	1rd	23	16	.590
1974	....	19	1	0	5–3	....	QF	1rd	3rd	32	18	.640
1975	4	24	4	9	17–4	F	F	QF	SF	88	20	.815
1976	4	17	2	1	5–2	....	....	SF	1rd	41	15	.732
1977	3	22	6	4	9–2	....	....	QF	SF	68	16	.810
1978	1	20	11	0	11–1	....	....	W	SF	80	9	.899
1979	1	23	10	0	11–1	....	....	W	SF	89	13	.873
1980	3	24	11	0	11–3	SF	....	SF	4rd	87	13	.870
1981	3	23	10	0	19–3	W	QF	SF	F	89	13	.873
1982	1	18	15	0	20–2	F	W	W	QF	90	3	.968
1983	1	17	16	0	23–1	W	4rd	....	....	86	1	.989
1984	1	15	13	0	25–1	SF	W	W	W	78	2	.975
1985	1	17	12	0	25–2	W	F	W	F	84	5	.944
1986	1	17	14	0	20–1	....	F	W	W	89	3	.967
1987	2	12	4	0	25–2	F	F	W	W	56	8	.875
1988	2	16	9	0	18–4	SF	4rd	F	QF	70	7	.909
1989	2	15	8	0	16–3	QF	....	F	F	73	7	.913
1990	3	13	6	0	10–1	....	....	W	4rd	52	7	.881
1991	4	14	5	0	10–2	....	....	QF	F	53	9	.855
1992	5	12	4	0	6–2	....	....	SF	2rd	38	8	.826
1993	3	13	5	0	8–2	....	....	SF	4rd	46	8	.852

1994	8	15	1	0	8–2	....	1rd	F	....	33	14	.702
2002	....	1	0	0	0–0	....	....	....	....	1	1	.500
2004	....	5	0	0	0	0	0	0	7	2	5	.286

Held number-one tour ranking 9 times for a total of 331 weeks. Last ranked number one in 1987. (1982–1989). Doubles Titles: Aus (8), Fre (7), Wim (7), US (9).

Bud Collins, *Total Tennis: The Ultimate Tennis Encyclopedia*

EVERT, Chris

Female. Born: Dec. 21, 1954. Fort Lauderdale, FL, United States. Height: 5'6''. Weight: 125 lbs. Plays: right.

Status: Turned Pro 1973. Earnings: $8,896,195. Highest Ranking: 1 (Nov. 1975). HOF: 1995

Year	Rk	TP	TW	TF	GS	Aus	Fre	Wim	US	MW	ML	Pct
1971	10	5	4	0	4–1	....	....	....	SF	4	1	.800
1972	3	8	4	3	9–2	....	....	SF	SF	10	2	.833
1973	3	16	12	4	15–3	....	F	F	SF	18	3	.857
1974	3	20	16	4	20–2	F	W	W	SF	23	3	.885
1975	1	20	16	2	17–1	....	W	SF	W	24	3	.889
1976	1	15	12	3	13–0	....	....	W	W	15	2	.882
1977	1	15	11	3	12–1	....	....	SF	W	62	3	.954
1978	1	11	7	3	11–1	....	....	F	W	53	4	.930
1979	2	21	8	5	18–2	....	W	F	F	84	13	.866
1980	1	15	8	3	18–1	....	W	F	W	68	7	.907
1981	1	15	9	4	21–3	F	SF	W	SF	68	6	.919
1982	2	16	10	3	21–2	W	SF	F	W	69	6	.920
1983	2	15	6	7	15–2	....	W	3rd	F	56	9	.862
1984	2	14	6	7	24–3	W	F	F	F	67	8	.893
1985	2	18	10	7	23–3	F	W	F	SF	79	8	.908
1986	2	13	6	3	17–2	....	W	SF	SF	59	7	.894
1987	3	18	5	4	14–3	....	SF	SF	QF	72	13	.847
1988	3	15	4	4	18–3	F	3rd	SF	SF	61	11	.847
1989	....	9	0	3	9–2	....	....	SF	QF	32	9	.780

Held number-one tour ranking 8 times for a total of 262 weeks. Last ranked number one in 1985. Competed as Chris Evert Lloyd 1979–1986. Doubles Titles: Fre (2), Wim (1).

Bud Collins, *Total Tennis: The Ultimate Tennis Encyclopedia*

THE 80-MATCH RECORD OF THE NAVRATILOVA-EVERT RIVALRY

YEAR	WINNER	TOURNAMENT	ROUND	SCORE	SURFACE
1973	Evert	Akron	1	7–6 6–3	Carpet
	Evert	St. Petersburg	SF	7–5 6–3	Clay
1974	Evert	San Francisco	1	6–7 6–3 6–1	Carpet
	Evert	Italian Open	F	6–3 6–3	Clay
1975	Evert	San Francisco	SF	6–4 6–3	Carpet
	Navratilova	Washington	Q	3–6 6–4 7–6 (4)	Carpet

	Evert	Akron	Q	6–3 6–1	Carpet
	Navratilova	Chicago	SF	6–4 6–0	Carpet
	Evert	Philadelphia	SF	7–6 6–4	Carpet
	Evert	Los Angeles	F	6–4 6–2	Carpet
	Evert	Amelia Island	F	7–5 6–4	Clay
	Evert	Italian Open	F	6–1 6–0	Clay
	Evert	**French Open**	F	2–6 6–2 6–1	Clay
	Evert	US Open	SF	6–4 6–4	Clay
	Evert	Atlanta	F	2–6 6–2 6–0	Hard
1976	Evert	Austin	SF	6–0 6–3	Hard
	Navratilova	Houston	F	6–3 6–4	Carpet
	Evert	**Wimbledon**	SF	4–6 6–3 6–4	Grass
1977	Navratilova	Washington	F	6–2 6–3	Carpet
	Evert	Seattle	F	6–2 6–4	Carpet
	Evert	Los Angeles	F	6–2 2–6 6–1	Carpet
	Evert	Philadelphia	F	6–4 4–6 6–3	Carpet
	Evert	Tucson	F	6–3 7–6	Hard
	Evert	Palm Springs	R2	6–4 6–1	Hard
1978	Navratilova	Eastbourne	F	6–4 4–6 9–7	Grass
	Navratilova	**Wimbledon**	F	2–6 6–4 7–5	Grass
	Evert	Atlanta	F	7–6 0–6 6–3	Carpet
	Evert	Palm Springs	F	6–3 6–3	Hard
	Evert	Tokyo	F	7–5 6–2	Carpet
1979	Navratilova	Oakland	F	7–5 7–5	Carpet
	Evert	Los Angeles	F	6–3 6–4	Carpet
	Navratilova	Dallas	F	6–4 6–4	Carpet
	Evert	Eastbourne	F	7–5 5–7 13–11	Grass
	Navratilova	**Wimbledon**	F	6–4 6–4	Grass
	Navratilova	Phoenix	F	6–1 6–3	Hard
	Navratilova	Brighton	F	6–3 6–3	Carpet
1980	Navratilova	Chicago	F	6–4 6–4	Carpet
	Evert	**Wimbledon**	SF	4–6 6–4 6–2	Grass
	Evert	Brighton	F	6–4 5–7 6–3	Carpet
	Navratilova	Tokyo	SF	7–6 6–2	Carpet
1981	Evert	Amelia Island	F	6–0 6–0	Clay
	Navratilova	US Open	SF	7–5 4–6 6–4	Hard
	Navratilova	Tokyo	F	6–3 6–2	Carpet
	Evert	Sydney	F	6–4 2–6 6–1	Grass
	Navratilova	**Australian Open**	F	6–7 6–4 7–5	Grass
1982	Navratilova	**Wimbledon**	F	6–1 3–6 6–2	Grass
	Navratilova	Brighton	F	6–1 6–4	Carpet
	Evert	**Australian Open**	F	6–3 2–6 6–3	Grass
	Navratilova	East Rutherford, NJ	F	4–6 6–1 6–2	Carpet
1983	Navratilova	Dallas	F	6–4 6–0	Carpet
	Navratilova	New York	F	6–2 6–0	Carpet

	Navratilova	Los Angeles	F	6–1 6–3	Hard
	Navratilova	Toronto	F	6–4 4–6 6–1	Hard
	Navratilova	**US Open**	F	6–1 6–3	Hard
	Navratilova	Tokyo	F	6–2 6–2	Carpet
1984	Navratilova	Livingston	F	6–2 7–6	Carpet
	Navratilova	New York	F	6–3 7–5 6–1	Carpet
	Navratilova	Amelia Island	F	6–2 6–0	Clay
	Navratilova	**French Open**	F	6–3 6–1	Clay
	Navratilova	**Wimbledon**	F	7–6(5) 6–2	Grass
	Navratilova	**US Open**	F	4–6 6–4 6–4	Hard
1985	Evert	Key Biscayne	F	6–2 6–4	Hard
	Navratilova	Delray Beach	F	6–2 6–4	Hard
	Navratilova	Dallas	F	6–3 6–4	Carpet
	Evert	**French Open**	F	6–3 6–7(4) 7–5	Clay
	Navratilova	**Wimbledon**	F	4–6 6–3 6–2	Grass
	Navratilova	**Australian Open**	F	6–2 4–6 6–2	Grass
1986	Navratilova	Dallas	F	6–2 6–1	Carpet
	Evert	**French Open**	F	2–6 6–3 6–3	Clay
	Navratilova	Los Angeles	F	7–6(5) 6–3	Hard
1987	Evert	Houston	F	3–6 6–1 7–6(4)	Clay
	Navratilova	**French Open**	SF	6–2 6–2	Clay
	Navratilova	**Wimbledon**	SF	6–2 5–7 6–4	Grass
	Evert	Los Angeles	SF	6–2 6–1	Hard
	Navratilova	Filderstadt	F	7–5 6–1	Carpet
1988	Evert	**Australian Open**	SF	6–2 7–5	Hard
	Evert	Houston	F	6–0 6–4	Clay
	Navratilova	**Wimbledon**	SF	6–1 4–6 7–5	Grass
	Navratilova	Filderstadt	F	6–2 6–3	Carpet
	Navratilova	Chicago	F	6–2 6–2	Carpet

NAVRATILOVA LEADS, 43–37

Surface breakdown:
CEMENT: Navratilova 9–7
CLAY: Evert 11–3
GRASS: Navratilova 10–5
INDOORS: Navratilova 21–14

NOTES

PROLOGUE: **Remember My Name**

page 2: "Chris was like a perfect blond goddess": Martina Navratilova with George Vecsey, *Martina* (New York: Alfred A. Knopf, 1985), p. 96.

page 5: Evert admitted a career-long discomfort with her squeaky-clean image . . . I've lived a normal life": Sally Jenkins, "I've Lived a Charmed Life," *Sports Illustrated,* May 25, 1992, p. 60.

CHAPTER 1: **The Making of the Ice Princess**

page 13: "There are a lot of great people associated with tennis . . . healthy": Chris Evert Lloyd with Neil Amdur, *Chrissie, My Own Story* (New York: Simon and Schuster, 1982), p. 16.

page 14: "Maybe I'm old-fashioned . . . what else does he need?": Hubert Mizell, "Jim Evert: Tennis Father," *Tennis,* December 1971, p. 58.

page 16: When university researchers in England measured Court: Grace Lichtenstein, *A Long Way, Baby: Behind the Scenes in Women's Pro Tennis* (New York: William Morrow & Company, 1974), p. 45.

page 22: "It was a great way to grow up . . . at home and at the courts": Chris Evert cable television interview, October 8, 2000, *Florida Sports Profiles,* The Sunshine Network, Orlando, Fla.

page 28: "When I look at that grim little fixed expression . . . frustrated' ": Sally Jenkins, "I've Lived a Charmed Life," *Sports Illustrated,* May 25, 1992, p. 60.

CHAPTER 2: **Madame Superstar**

page 37: "He said it just like that . . . you have a nice backhand, Billie Jean' ": Billie Jean King with Frank Deford, *Billie Jean* (New York: The Viking Press, 1982), p. 191.

page 38: "Men are playing tennis for a living now . . . our money with them?": "Women's Lob," *Time,* December 7, 1970, p. 78.

page 38: "I'm just as happy never to see the girls . . . playing on the tour": Pete Axthelm, "Tennis: A Triumph for Women's Lob," *Newsweek,* June 26, 1972, pp. 56–63.

page 39: "The only prejudice practiced in tennis . . . when the women come on": Jack Kramer with Frank Deford, *The Game: My Forty Years in Tennis*, pp. 79–80.

page 41: "Billie Jean groomed me and she groomed Martina . . . I needed to be out front": Diane Pucin, "No Excuse for No-Shows," *Los Angeles Times,* Nov 10, 2003; p. D 7.

page 42: Her ex-husband Larry King says Billie Jean was constantly plagued by allergies: Larry King television interview, ESPN Classic: Billie Jean King, August 24, 2001.

page 43: "Joe Smith's wife . . . but who are *you?*": King and Deford, *Billie Jean,* p. 79.

page 48: "It was about *social change* . . . he said he loved me": Billie Jean King television interview, ESPN Classic: Billie Jean King, August 24, 2001.

CHAPTER 3: **One Dream You Were Allowed to Have**

page 53: "They couldn't say or write . . . under the table for decent meat": Pete Axthelm with Pamela Abramson and Stephanie Russell, "Martina: A Style All Her Own," *Newsweek,* September 6, 1982, p. 44.

page 56: "Give me a ride": Martina Navratilova with George Vecsey, *Martina* (New York: Alfred A. Knopf, 1985) p. 12.

page 60: "There was a lot of talk that the Russians would come in," Navratilova said. "But we never believed it would come to that": Martina Navratilova with George Vecsey, *Martina* (New York: Alfred A. Knopf, 1985), p. 69.

page 60: "Nobody was shooting . . . could start any minute": Ibid., p. 69.

page 61: "It was just depressing . . . what can you do?": Martina Navratilova television interview, ESPN Classic: Martina Navratilova, June 25, 2001.

page 61: Even as president, Havel used to carry: David Remnick, "Exit Havel: The King Leaves the Castle," *The New Yorker,* February 17 and 24, 2003, p. 90.

page 62: "Wimbledon was one dream": Kenny Moore, "Eight Is Not Enough," *Sports Illustrated,* June 12, 1989, p. 41.

page 68: "We used to discuss everything . . . got to know and care about each other": Richard Evans, "The Rivalry that Melted the Ice," *The Times* (London), March 19, 1986.

page 69: "I used to turn to Chris a lot for help . . . always so understanding": Richard Evans, "Celestial Twins of the Centre Court": *The Times* (London), March 18, 1986.

page 73: Mirek added, "Don't say a word . . . Someone could be listening . . . come back": Navratilova with Vecsey, p. 126; Navratilova television interview, ESPN Classic: Martina Navratilova, June 25, 2001.

CHAPTER 4: **Chris America**

page 75: "I carried it to the hilt. I probably overcompensated . . . the stereotyped jock": Frank Deford, "Love and Love," *Sports Illustrated*, April 27, 1981, pp. 68–84.

page 76: "If some people say we're unfeminine": Pete Axthelm, "Tennis: A Triumph for Women's Lob," *Newsweek,* June 26, 1972, pp. 56–63.

page 84: "I taught him he had to be a tiger . . . his court behavior": Caryl Phillips, anthology editor, *The Right Set* (New York: Vintage Books, 1999), p. 259. Excerpted from Rich Koster, *The Tennis Bubble* (New York: Quadrangle/Times Books, 1976).

page 95: "Her long fingernails were polished . . . perspiration": Dave Anderson, "The Chris and Jimmy Romance Revival," *New York Times,* September 6, 1975, p. 13.

CHAPTER 5: **Coming to America, Coming Out**

page 105: "Navratilova was on the run. We wanted to make sure the Czechs wouldn't somehow try to snatch me": Navratilova interview with Peter Bodo, March 2002.

page 107: "You have never seen such a cacophony": Jack Whitaker television interview, ESPN Classic: Martina Navratilova, June 25, 2001.

page 107: "I had no idea what a splash it would be": Navratilova interview with Peter Bodo, March 2002.

page 111: "I was more afraid": Martina Navratilova with George Vecsey, *Martina* (New York: Alfred A. Knopf, 1985) p. 134.

page 116: "Whenever I'm in America": Frank Deford, "A Head to Head," *Sports Illustrated*, July 9, 1984, p. 72.

page 116: "It's a delayed reaction . . . wear off": Peter Bodo, "Martina Navratilova Wins the Battle Against Herself," *Tennis*, June 1977, p. 54.

page 118: Not long after her September 1975 defection, Navratilova had . . . "It seemed so natural . . . everything felt great": Navratilova with Vecsey, p. 138.

page 120: "It all kicked in: 'It's been a year . . . world was against me'": John Feinstein, "Homecoming for a Champion," *Washington Post*, July 20, 1986, p. C1.

CHAPTER 6: **Birth of a Rivalry**

page 123: "The house was the first thing . . . roots and security": Richard O'Connor, "The Smashing Ms. Navratilova," *Sport,* September 1978; Bud Collins, ed., *Total Tennis: The Ultimate Tennis Encyclopedia* (Toronto: Sport Media Publishing, 2003), p. 427.

page 134: "How about number thirty-two? . . . Let's not get ridiculous": Peter Bodo, *The Courts of Babylon* (New York: Scribner, 1995) p. 215.

page 137: "All my life I pictured myself . . . other idealized little image": Peter Bodo, "Chris Evert Lloyd: How She's Changed," *Tennis*, March 1981, p. 33.

CHAPTER 7: **The Perfect Storm**

page 141: "When I was a kid . . . I wanted to be more like Chris . . . as well as I could have . . . what I was up against": Martina Navratilova interview with Peter Bodo, March 2002.

page 144: After that, Lloyd hung his head. "Oh, it's no good . . . Stuff it . . . I can't play": Chris and John Lloyd with Carol Thatcher, *Lloyd on Lloyd* (London: Willow Books, 1985), p. 90.

page 144: "It doesn't matter to me . . . heart into it": Ibid., p. 90.

page 149: John gently told Chris . . . *That's* the whole point": Chris Evert Lloyd with Neil Amdur, *Chrissie, My Own Story* (New York: Simon and Schuster, 1982), p.173.

page 151: Each night he set the air conditioner . . . each match": Tim Adams, *Being John McEnroe* (London: Yellow Jersey Press, 2003), pp. 13–15.

page 154: "I didn't want to lie to him . . . he was right": Martina Navratilova with George Vecsey, *Martina* (New York: Alfred A. Knopf, 1985) pp. 182–83.

page 159: "I virtually just started slamming balls . . . she was in tears": Lloyd and Lloyd with Thatcher, p. 119.

page 159: World Tennis magazine published an article: Ibid., p. 120.

page 160: "In our little speeches . . . the biggest reason": Martina Navratilova television interview, ESPN Classic: Martina Navratilova, June 25, 2001.

page 160: "I really felt America was": Ibid.

page 160: "In her wildest imaginings . . . un-American in her mind": Rita Mae Brown television interview, ESPN Classic: Martina Navratilova, June 25, 2001.

CHAPTER 8: **"Kill Chris"**

page 164: "Let's just say that that [night before] . . . ready for a match": Martina Navratilova interview with Peter Bodo, March 2002.

page 166: When Navratilova got to a nearby friend's house . . . "Nancy, Rita Mae shot me! Rita Mae shot me!": Nancy Lieberman with Debby Jennings, *Lady Magic: The Autobiography of Nancy Lieberman-Cline* (Champaign, Illinois: Sagamore Publishing, Inc., 1992) pp. 120–21.

page 170: "I was discovering true pain . . . I did not like pain": Ibid., p. x.

CHAPTER 9: **The Truth Comes Out**

page 175: The agent never glanced up . . . Navratilova felt enormously relieved: Martina Navratilova with George Vecsey, *Martina* (New York: Alfred A. Knopf, 1985), p. 207.

page 175: "I felt like cheering and clapping . . . filing quietly out of the room": Ibid., p. 208.

page 176: On May 5, 1981, King had returned: Billie Jean King with Frank Deford, *Billie Jean* (New York: The Viking Press, 1982) p. 3.

page 178: "If that isn't attempted extortion": Ibid., p. 213.

page 180: "a low point . . . closet in a big way": Martina Navratilova interview, ESPN Classic: Martina Navratilova, June 25, 2001.

page 180: Writing much later about those histrionic-filled days: Sandra Faulkner with Judy Nelson, *Love Match* (New York: Birch Lane Press, 1993), foreword by Rita Mae Brown, p. 14.

page 181: "The reason that Martina today has been transformed": Ibid., p. 15.

page 187: "They weren't cheering Martina the Complainer . . . maybe even love": Navratilova with Vecsey, p. 220.

CHAPTER 10: **Team Navratilova**

page 202: "I left one country because . . . it's pretty frightening": Martina Navratilova television interview, ESPN Classic: Martina Navratilova, June 25, 2001.

page 205: Lieberman's mother, Renee . . . "You should like it if I went to the door without a stitch?": Nancy Lieberman with Debby Jennings, *Lady Magic: The Autobiography of Nancy Lieberman-Cline* (Champaign, Illinois: Sagamore Publishing, Inc., 1992), p.130.

CHAPTER ELEVEN: **The Invincible Years**

page 211: "You have to have an arrogance . . . That's true arrogance": Sally Jenkins, "I've Lived a Charmed Life," *Sports Illustrated,* May 25, 1992, p. 60.

page 213: "I don't have to play my best to win . . . I beat myself": Pete Axthelm with Pamela Abramson and Stephanie Russell, "Martina: A Style All Her Own," *Newsweek*, September 6, 1982, p. 44.

page 216: "We were like strangers": Chris and John Lloyd with Carol Thatcher, *Lloyd on Lloyd* (London: Willow Books, 1985), p. 153.

page 220: "That's what Chris and Martina do to the rest of us . . . doesn't have a serious chance": Pam Shriver with Frank Deford and Susan B. Adams, *Passing Shots* (New York: McGraw-Hill Book Company, 1987), p. 129.

page 226: "If I lost, I was a choker . . . 'unfair' to women's tennis": Martina Navratilova with George Vecsey, *Martina* (New York: Alfred A. Knopf, 1985), p. 268.

CHAPTER TWELVE: **Climbing Back**

page 229: "Martina is so head and shoulders above everybody . . . kind of late for her to do that": Jaime Diaz, "New Format, Same Result," *Sports Illustrated,* March 12, 1984, p. 50.

page 230: "Everybody would go . . . I am still winning": Chris Evert interview with Peter Bodo, March 2002.

page 239: "How?" . . . "I'll ask Chris Evert how she did it three years ago": Barry McDermott, "Now It's Domination on Dirt," *Sports Illustrated,* April 30, 1984, p. 22.

page 239: "I started getting a lump in my throat": Ibid., p. 22.

page 239: "I couldn't find any weaknesses . . . how much better she can get": E. J. Dionne, "Miss Navratilova Makes It a Slam," *Washington Post*, June 10, 1984, sec. 5, p. 1.

page 240: "I know what people are saying . . . myself on the line": Curry Kirkpatrick, "Worthy of Really High Fives," *Sports Illustrated*, June 18, 1984, p. 14.

CHAPTER 13: **Full Circle**

page 254: "No matter how catty we get . . . on and off the court": Nick Pitt, "Meltdown on Centre Court," *The Times* (London), June 20, 1999.

page 254: "Maybe the most revealing thing of all": Frank Deford, "Pair Beyond Compare," *Sports Illustrated*, May 26, 1986, p. 70.

page 258: Her words brought down the house again . . . they began crying too: John Feinstein, "At Her Best, Navratilova Leads U.S. in Federation; Title Culminates Emotional Homecoming," *Washington Post*, July 28, 1986, p. B1.

EPILOGUE: **Second Acts**

page 262: "all the layers—the fame, the celebrity": Sally Jenkins, "Chris Evert Lets Loose," *Conde Nast Sports for Women*, p. 104.

INDEX